"Knickerbocker is a very valuable work, particularly as one of the few contemporary histories to explore how fictional texts and reading practices can have material effects on a particular place. Bradley's analysis of Knickerbocker's significance will be of great interest to literary scholars and historians of the American nineteenth century, and her counternarrative of New York's development will reward the professional and general reader alike."

—*Clio*

"Knickerbocker is a storied name steeped in tradition—one that I am proud to have been a part of. Bradley's *Knickerbocker: The Myth behind New York* offers a unique examination of how a name familiarized by Washington Irving two hundred years ago grew to become a cultural symbol of New York."

—Former U.S. Senator, BILL BRADLEY

"Those who puzzle at the incessant branding and rebranding of New York City would do well to read this fascinating, sophisticated, and witty social history of a myth. Bradley knows her facts and shrewdly and convincingly interprets them. A delightful contribution to urban studies."

—PHILLIP LOPATE, author of *Waterfront: A Journey Around Manhattan*

"Is New York different from other cities, or does it just have different myths? Focusing on a tale first spun by Washington Irving two centuries ago, *Knickerbocker* answers this question with grace and skill. It is a delight to read."

—KENNETH T. JACKSON, editor-in-chief, *The Encyclopedia of New York*

KNICKERBOCKER

KNICKERBOCKER

The Myth Behind New York

ELIZABETH L. BRADLEY

RUTGERS UNIVERSITY PRESS

NEW BRUNSWICK, CAMDEN, AND NEWARK, NEW JERSEY, AND LONDON

First paperback edition 2018
ISBN 978-0-8135-9425-5

Publication of this book was supported, in part, by a grant from
Furthermore: a program of the J. M. Kaplan Fund.

The Library of Congress has cataloged the hardcover edition as follows:
Library of Congress Cataloging-in-Publication Data
Bradley, Elizabeth L., 1973–
    Knickerbocker : the myth behind New York / Elizabeth L. Bradley.
      p. cm.
    Includes bibliographical references and index.
    ISBN 978-0-8135-4516-5 (alk. paper)
    1. Irving, Washington, 1783–1859. History of New York. 2. Irving,
Washington, 1783–1859—Characters—Diedrich Knickerbocker.
3. Irving, Washington, 1783–1859—Influence. 4. Group identity—
New York (State)—New York. 5. City and town life—New York (State)—
New York. 6. Manhattan (New York, N.Y.)—Social life and customs.
7. New York (N.Y.)—Social life and customs. 8. New York (N.Y.)—
In literature. 9. New York (N.Y.)—History—Chronology. 10. Dutch—
New York (State)—New York—History. I. Title.
    F122.1.I88B73 2009
    974.7 103—dc22
                 2008035428

A British Cataloging-in-Publication record for this book is available
from the British Library.

Visit our Web site: http://rutgerspress.rutgers.edu

Manufactured in the United States of America

FRONTISPIECE: Portrait of Diedrich Knickerbocker, engraving by
Childs & Jocelyn, from Washington Irving's *A History of New York from
the Beginning of the World to the End of the Dutch Dynasty . . . by Diedrich
Knickerbocker . . . With illustrations by Felix O. C. Darley, engraved by
eminent artists.* New York: G. P. Putnam, 1850. General Research Division,
The New York Public Library, Astor, Lenox and Tilden Foundations.

For
MLB and *JDB*

CONTENTS

CONTENTS

ACKNOWLEDGMENTS

This book, like its namesake, would not exist without the history collections of New York. It has been my supreme good fortune to research and write *Knickerbocker* while in the employ of the New York Public Library, and I have had access to that institution's unparalleled treasures, both in the form of books, manuscripts, and images and in the form of the library's exceptional staff. I am truly indebted to President Paul LeClerc for his unstinting encouragement and support; to Jean Strouse, the director of the Dorothy and Lewis B. Cullman Center for Scholars and Writers, for a thousand kindnesses great and small, and for the gift of a platform from which to try out all things Knickerbocker; to David Ferriero, the Andrew W. Mellon Director of the Research and Branch Libraries, for his infectious enthusiasm; and to my colleagues Pamela Leo and Adriana Nova, who graciously cheered on my efforts to do two things simultaneously.

The keepers of the New York Public Library's collections have been incomparably generous with their expertise, time, and patience, and I would especially like to thank Alice Hudson, Matthew Knutzen, and Nancy Kandoian of the Lionel Pincus and Princess Firyal Map Division; Ruth Carr and Maira Liriano of the Milstein Local History and Genealogy Division; William Stingone, Rebecca Federman, and Donald Menninger of the Manuscripts and Archives Division; Madeleine Cohen of the Science, Business, and Industry Library; and Tom Lisanti and Stephen Saks of Photographic Services. Edward Kasinec kept me in mind of Irving's NYPL connections when my energies flagged.

Beyond the New York Public Library, this book particularly draws on the splendid New York collections of the Bobst Library at New

York University, the Houghton Library at Harvard University, the Library of Congress, the collections of the Museum of the City of New York, and the New-York Historical Society Library. I am particularly grateful to Nancy McKeon of New York University and Mary Beth Clack of Harvard for helping me gain access to the riches of their respective institutions after I had graduated from each.

One of the delights of writing about two centuries of New York history, literature, and culture has been the opportunity to learn from people who know infinitely more. I will always be indebted to Cyrus Patell for his willingness to gamble on Knickerbocker and for the benefit of his friendship and assistance thereafter. Louis Auchincloss and Philip Lopate inspire by their inimitable example. I am pleased to have this opportunity to thank Elda Rotor, the first cheerleader and selfless shepherd of this project; Jane McNamara, who taught me the value of the New York Story; and Michael Miscione, without whose generosity "Father Knickerbocker" would be a shadow of his former self. I am grateful to Senator William Bradley for his enthusiastic interest in the first muse of his championship team, to Louise Brockett for her limitless energy, and to Susan Latos, Sandra Packard, and Jacob Ruppert for their kind and swift assistance. Various parts of this book were originally presented as lectures, and I am particularly grateful to the 2006–2007 and 2007–2008 classes of fellows from the Dorothy and Lewis B. Cullman Center for Scholars and Writers and to Sam Swope for their valuable suggestions, as well as to Charles Gehring, Edward Knoblauch, and Field Horne for gracious invitations to speak before the New Netherlands Institute and the New York State Historical Association.

Carol Mann saw the potential in Irving's historian, and it has been my excellent fortune to have her as one of this project's chief stewards. Marlie Wasserman is the other steward, and I am very grateful to her, and to Kendra Boileau, Christina Brianik, Marilyn Campbell, and India Cooper, for their sound judgment, scrupulous care, and patient guidance throughout.

I cannot hope to do justice here to the friends and family who have supported this enterprise with their affection and encouragement, including Eric Banks, Andrea Bielenstein, Randle and Suzanne Carpenter, Randy Cohen, David Cronin, Elaine Cunningham, Jenny,

Howard, and Lorna Elkus, David Feige, Mark Foggin, Ginna Foster, Alison Fraser, Doris Friedland, Jonathan Funke, Sarah Funke, Vickie Guarnowski, Reuven Har-Even, Philip Hollander, Greg Kasper, Mitchell Kelling, Claudia Kingsley, Geoff Kloske, Nina Leeds, Maura McDermott, Caitlin Macy, Jacob Nadal, Jean-Gabriel Neukomm, Sara Ogger, Juliet Page, Mary Peck, Gracelyn Pilgrim, Michael Pollak, Christopher Rickerd, Marc Rosenthal, Andrew Shore, Peter Steinberg, Kimberly Sushon, Catherine Tice, Alexandra Von Knorring, Jamie Wacks, David Wang, and Carrie Weber.

I am particularly happy for the chance to thank Eric Lai, whose kindness, compassion, and unflagging faith in my singular quest for "the Dutchness of things" both sustain and amaze me.

This book is dedicated to my parents, who taught me by example that there were all kinds of native New Yorkers, but there was only one kind of good writing. Their love, support, and sanctuary make all things possible.

ABBREVIATIONS

Quotations from Washington Irving's works are cited in the text using the following abbreviations:

BH   *Bracebridge Hall.* From *Washington Irving: Bracebridge Hall, Tales of a Traveller, The Alhambra.* Ed. Andrew B. Myers. New York: Library of America, 1991.

HNY   *A History of New York.* From *Washington Irving: History, Tales, and Sketches.* Ed. James W. Tuttleton. New York: Library of America, 1983.

RHNY *A History of New York.* Ed. Edwin T. Bowden. Albany: Twayne Publishers, 1964. This is the revised 1848 version, containing the "Author's Apology."

S   *Salmagundi.* From *Washington Irving: History, Tales, and Sketches.* Ed. James W. Tuttleton. New York: Library of America, 1983.

SKB   *The Sketch Book.* From *Washington Irving: History, Tales, and Sketches.* Ed. James W. Tuttleton. New York: Library of America, 1983.

TT   *Tales of a Traveller.* From *Washington Irving: Bracebridge Hall, Tales of a Traveller, The Alhambra.* Ed. Andrew B. Myers. New York: Library of America, 1991.

KNICKERBOCKER

INTRODUCTION

"DISTRESSING," began the notice in the October 26, 1809, issue of the *New York Evening Post*:

> Left his lodgings some time since, and has not since been heard of, a small elderly gentleman, dressed in an old black coat and cocked hat, by the name of KNICKERBOCKER. As there are some reasons for believing he is not entirely in his right mind, and as great anxiety is entertained about him, any information concerning him left either at the Columbian Hotel, Mulberry street, or at the office of this paper will be thankfully received.
>
> P.S. Printers of Newspapers would be aiding the cause of humanity, in giving an insertion to the above.

The "cause of humanity" was indeed aided, over the course of several days, as newspapers in the metropolitan area reprinted the notice, as well as the subsequent announcements that followed from the increasingly anxious landlord of the "Columbian Hotel." In one of these bulletins, the conscientious proprietor announced that he would be forced to sell a "*very curious kind of a written book*" that had been found in Knickerbocker's rooms if he did not receive the rent owed to him by the missing man.[1] No rent was forthcoming, because the ads were a hoax, the landlord a fiction, and the hotel nonexistent—but the book was quite real. On December 6, 1809, it was made available for sale in New York City with the title

A History of New-York, from the Beginning of the World to the End of the Dutch Dynasty; Containing, among Many Surprising and Curious

1

Matters, the Unutterable Ponderings of Walter the Doubter, the Disastrous Projects of William the Testy, and the Chivalric Achievements of Peter the Headstrong—The Three Dutch Governors of New Amsterdam: Being the Only Authentic History of the Times that Ever Hath Been or Ever Will Be Published.

The narrator of this daunting tome was given as "Diedrich Knickerbocker," he of the cocked hat and unpaid bills. The real author is much more familiar to posterity; it was a lawyer named Washington Irving, then just twenty-six years old.

A History of New York was a near-instant success, and brought its young author fame on both sides of the Atlantic. American reviewers noted that the "humorous *History of New York* by Knickerbocker" was the country's only homegrown satire thus far to warrant "public support" and "much applause by all classes of men."[2] English readers compared the book favorably to Laurence Sterne's *Tristram Shandy.* And yet at first look the book was an unlikely favorite: baggy, dense, and larded with editorial asides and footnotes, it was as "surprising and curious" as its title suggested. It was also a strange, protean creature, all the more captivating because it was so impossible to categorize. The *History* wasn't the firsthand report of a colonist, like William Bradford's *Of Plymouth Plantation;* Irving didn't claim that his narrator had been present at the creation. Nor was it a satirical record of a voyage to imaginary lands, like Jonathan Swift's *Gulliver's Travels;* New York was a real city, and the Dutch, even if long-vanquished by the British, had indeed ruled it from 1626 to 1664. The book wasn't even an actual "history," as that genre was classically understood—it did, after all, have a fictional narrator—but a rollicking, outlandish, embellished account of the discovery, colonization, cultivation, and ultimate loss of the New Amsterdam settlement, as told from the perspective of a very sore loser. The *History* was irreverent when it should have been pious, anarchic when it should have been orderly, and sentimental when it should have been academic and dry. New Yorkers had never encountered anything like it before, and they were enchanted.

From the beginning of Irving's book it is clear that the *History* exists to provide a platform for its narrator, Knickerbocker, who presents himself to the reader as a proud descendant of the Dutch settlers of New York, those burghers and members of the Dutch West India Company who make up the "Dynasty" of his title. The book's title strongly hints at the Dutch historian's unabashed agenda: to reclaim New York City and all New Yorkers for Holland. This repatriation takes place not through any outright subversion of historical fact, however—in Irving's book the English do still conquer the colony of New Netherlands and rename it New York—but by Knickerbocker's success at mapping the forgotten colony for contemporary New Yorkers. He does so through a constant litany of familiar, enduring city names and landmarks, reminiscences, and pointed anecdotes, all calculated to reveal the Dutch origins of a variety of "authentic" New York features. With charming and partisan persuasion, the historian insists that everything from the introduction of the doughnut to the invention of Wall Street can be credited to the city's Dutch founders. Whether humble or exalted, these examples of lingering Dutch influence bolster the implicit argument of the *History*: that the New York sensibility is unique and inimitable, and that its particularity derives from the traditions and institutions of New Amsterdam. This sense of New York's difference, Knickerbocker's satire shows us, has its roots not in the English colony that named it but in the far more idiosyncratic, bourgeois, and tolerant rituals and morals of New Amsterdam. It is there, he suggests, that readers should look for the solid foundation on which to anchor their own infinitely mutable and expanding city. The fictional historian gave Manhattan back to his readers as a mythic place: a small island traced with cow paths and stone bridges, inhabited by peaceable, phlegmatic burghers and their many-petticoated wives, undisturbed for so long by aggression from without or within. To New Yorkers (and to Americans) staring down the start of their nation's first, hectic century of independence, it must have sounded like a kind of paradise.

From a twenty-first-century vantage point, the celebration of New York as a place without peer is universally familiar, even clichéd: the city has been "sung" by everyone from Walt Whitman to Grandmaster Flash. Countless books, paintings, poems, songs, movies, and television shows have tried to capture the matchless qualities and breathless energy of the "Empire City," as it forever builds up and tears down monuments to its ineffable self. But contemplating New York's particular urban identity, whether through history or through satire, was a relatively new impulse in Irving's time and not yet the professional occupation that it would become in the decades (and centuries) that followed. In the aftermath of the Revolutionary War, Elihu Hubbard Smith had dismissed the "history of the City of New York," as "the history of the eager cultivation and rapid increase of the arts of gain . . . Commerce, News, and Pleasure," and his less-than-holy trinity did seem to dominate the wallets, hearts, and minds of those who lived or visited there at the beginning of the nineteenth century.[3] "Commerce" could be witnessed everywhere, from the seaport, unsurpassed in the new United States, to the bustling elegance of the Broadway shops to the nascent financial district at Wall Street. The reading public was offered "News" in the form of fifteen different newspapers. And "Pleasure" was available in entertainments high and low, from the American premiere of *The Comedy of Errors* to a display of "dromedaries from Arabia" on Chatham Street, "the first of the species ever imported into this country."[4] "In point of sociability and hospitality," Noah Webster wrote in 1788, "New York is hardly exceeded by any town in the U.S."[5] And yet the city was diminished. It was no longer the seat of the federal government, as it had been after George Washington's victory march from the Bronx to the Battery: that honor went to Philadelphia, New York's chief rival for population, trade, and refinement and still—for just a few years longer—considered the "London" to New York's "Liverpool."[6] Nor could it safely ignore the other major hubs of the eastern seaboard; in addition to its famous educational institutions, Boston was still a maritime stronghold, and the graceful southern ports of Richmond and Charleston dominated the new nation's trade in sugar, rice, cotton, and slaves. With competitors like these, what was it that set New York apart? Why had Abigail Adams complained, when the congressional move to Philadelphia was announced, "And, when all is done, it will not be Broadway"?[7]

Before the *History* was published, few American or European writers had attempted to address New York's identity crisis with any serious effort, possibly because all human exertion in New York, as its few chroniclers noted, was going into the expansion of the city itself. Visitors, bearing witness to the postwar rebuilding, marveled at the city's seemingly ceaseless activity and wondered at how New York fed on its own energy, "excited by the perpetual motion of the busy."[8] New roads and street signs were barely in place in one Manhattan ward before additional housing and commercial developments, creeping ever northward over the island's farms, pastures, and filled-in marshlands, necessitated more of the same. There wasn't time to pause and wonder who had trod the street that was now being paved by order of the Common Council, or even to question why that same street was called Cliff or Dey, Beaver or Pearl. Irving's book put a figurative halt to this expansion. His historian, Knickerbocker, instead invites New Yorkers to embark on an archaeological dig into the city's past, where the artifacts they turn up show how the genesis of their purposeful planning may be found in the domestic arrangements of the Dutch, whose "gradual advances, from the rude log hut to the stately dutch mansion," set in motion the rapid expansion they witnessed every day (*HNY* 476). The result of this exploration and education is a city with stories, mysteries, and depth; a New York that defies Elihu Hubbard Smith's flippant formula. It is also, as the *History* and its fictional scribe argue, a city with a distinct historical consciousness, a claim that no previous account of New York had ever advanced. The *History* looks forward as well as backward; Knickerbocker's account may be nostalgic, but it is also written for posterity—to enlighten, as the historian insists with some urgency, "the understanding and curiosity of some half a score of centuries yet to come" (*HNY* 437). In part, the book delivers this "understanding" to future generations by renewing New Yorkers' acquaintance with their predecessors, the Dutch settlers themselves. While this portrait gallery includes the two names most familiar both to Irving's contemporaries and our own, chiefly, Henry Hudson and Peter Stuyvesant, it also, crucially, introduces a more intriguing, if less famous, set of "patriarchs" to readers. With an ethnographer's pride, Knickerbocker sketches the complicated (and sometimes apocryphal) family trees of his "good grandmothers" and provides rose-tinted descriptions of the genteel hospitality, low-key politics, occasional battles, and shrewd business dealings of the Dutch (*HNY* 484). The book suggests that these early citizens should be reconsidered as an alternative set of ancestors for nineteenth-century, republican New Yorkers, who have all but forgotten their New Amsterdam inheritance, not to mention its iconography. To Irving's surprise, Knickerbocker's suggestion, made by the young author in jest, took immediate hold. Less than a year after the *History* was published, New Yorkers had already adopted Knickerbocker's faux forebears as their very own. They delighted in his portrait of the colorful, easygoing, off-kilter Dutch colony, whose inhabitants, they felt, resembled themselves much more closely than the hidebound, aristocratic English ever had. Readers across the United States and in Europe seized upon Knickerbocker's narrative voice, finding in his peculiar combination of wonder and weariness the ideal register in which to write and talk about his native city. And those who borrowed his "patriarchs" or adopted his style quickly began to call themselves—or to be called—"Knickerbockers," despite the fact that Irving had invented the loquacious Diedrich and borrowed his comical surname from a Dutch family living upstate. The reason for this new moniker's popularity was simple: Irving's mock-epic saga of New Amsterdam was the first to awaken New Yorkers to a consciousness of their trademark exceptionalism. Knickerbocker, claiming Herodotus as his inspiration, situated Manhattan at the center of the known universe, and the "New York Story" was born.[9]

In the chapters that follow, *Knickerbocker: The Myth Behind New York* will trace the creation, evolution, and prevalence of the "Knickerbocker" identity in New York literature and history, from Irving's satire to the present day. To the author's great amazement, Knickerbocker outlasted the *History*'s first print run, and its numerous reprintings after that as well. In fact, the ornery, insular Dutch bard became an instant icon for New Yorkers, who used him by their own means but always, finally, to the same end: to signal the city's myopic sense of destiny and difference. In his emotional, lofty, and revisionist telling of New Amsterdam's story, Knickerbocker originated that paradoxical combination of self-invention and nostalgia that has since become the New York note, and his readers adopted him as a symbol of the city's own ahistorical history and a seal of approval on their own urban ambitions. It is in part because Irving's fictional narrator outgrew his creator so quickly that the assembling of Knickerbocker "evidence" in this book has been primarily directed by a chronology of New York City history, the better to illuminate the ways in which

Knickerbocker usages have informed each other, or, in some cases, presented wildly divergent perspectives, in the two hundred years since *A History of New York* was published. I hope that a linear approach to this (sometimes dizzying) accumulation of "Knickerbockers" over time will allow the reader to see how the multiplying (and sometimes competing) invocations of Irving's historian themselves offer a surprising and rewarding counter-narrative of the changing city. Knickerbocker's presence in myriad situations and disparate media makes the character a bellwether for New York culture over time and at every echelon, from the city's infant literary efforts in the early nineteenth century to its advertising heyday in the twentieth. When did Knickerbocker keep pace with New York's endless activity? Why did he sometimes, spectacularly, fail? The answers to these questions provide fresh perspectives on a city prone to overdosing on self-examination. As New York's first biographer, Knickerbocker doesn't make his own biography easy; his story must be mapped across, under, and around genres, historical events, and cultural phenomena. The sheer variety of these examples is evidence not only of his enduring popularity but also of the way in which his "faithful portrait" gave rise to a genre of its own, the "Knickerbocker" customs, traditions, landmarks, and products that all use Irving's narrator as a way of announcing the New York pedigree, the "Authentic History," to borrow from the *History*'s title, of their subject, their party, their item for sale. As *Knickerbocker* will show, this was a process in which Irving himself was a (mostly) enthusiastic participant; throughout his life he would expand and refine the salient characteristics of Dutch New York (in both New York City and the Hudson River Valley) in additional Knickerbocker-narrated "sketches," as well as through numerous revised editions of the original work.

But Knickerbocker's story is not Irving's. While some American writers who took Irving as their mentor also appropriated his narrator as their muse, the fictional historian soon escaped his legendary creator. It was Knickerbocker, not Irving, who was repurposed throughout the nineteenth century for a host of political, commercial, and social agendas, and it was Knickerbocker's name that was soon in near-continuous use as shorthand for all things New York. Knickerbocker was the common link between a strange, sometimes

unholy assemblage of New Yorkers, one that came to include nativists, patriots, and pulp fiction writers; hatmakers, spice merchants,
and hoteliers; gossip columnists, society matrons, and sports fans. It
is a list that proves Knickerbocker could be as changeable as the city
that claimed him—and that the city's first icon was equally disposed
to self-aggrandizement: as New York grew both in size and international stature, so did the idea of "the Knickerbocker." By the Gilded
Age, Irving's mock-aristocratic Dutch customs and family trees had
been transformed by hopeful "descendants" of his "patriarchs" into
totems of class segregation and genealogical jingoism, and "Knickerbocker New York" became synonymous with "old-money New York,"
a slang term used alternately with reverence or disdain. But for some,
the "Knickerbocker" worldview was instructive, rather than exclusive,
and the *History* was seized upon as an inspiring manual of city stewardship and civic pride. These New Yorkers invoked the historian's
vocal longing for "days gone by" in the service of projects to document and preserve some of Manhattan's oldest and most endangered
buildings from what Edith Wharton would call the "Atlantis-fate of
Old New York"—historical oblivion.[10] A more forward-thinking activism was associated with Knickerbocker's role as the city's first symbolic mascot, a position he was given in 1898 during the negotiations
to consolidate the five boroughs of New York City. This new, two-
dimensional role (represented in turn-of-the-century newspaper cartoons and illustrations) gave the historian civic gravitas and a national
platform, from which, without an iota of his former bookishness and
reluctance, he brokered the consolidation of Greater New York, suppressed Tammany thugs, and fought in Albany for the interests and
needs of the newly expanded city.

New Yorkers also exported Knickerbocker, pitching their icon to
the nation, along with the other recognizable symbols of the city's
inimitable, cosmopolitan allure. Throughout the twentieth century,
Knickerbocker's image (variously imagined and rendered) and name
proliferated in diverse and sometimes astonishing ways; once asked to
guard the most venerable families of the "Four Hundred," the modern Knickerbocker championed a liberal social agenda, sold beer,
and even, in one of his most durable incarnations to date, dribbled
a basketball. He also continued in his role as midwife to the New

York Story, those insider accounts whose revelations about the hidden history and workings of the city were so often built on Irving's founding tales. Regardless of the arena, the invocation of "Knickerbocker" presence always signified an authentic connection to the city's past, and one that honored the invoker, by association, as belonging to the city's mythic future. It mattered little whether the historian was appropriated to sell "Knickerbocker"-style toilets, Knickerbocker Beer, or the New York Knicks; his name and image had become synonymous with a "real" New Yorker—sometimes more, but never less. It might not necessarily be a person who is Dutch-descended, or even one who is native-born, but it is always one whose claim to be both a survivor and a champion of the Empire City is above question or reproach.

How did the word "Knickerbocker" become shorthand for the New York experience? Why did such an odd little name, cribbed from an even odder book, develop such a compelling and complicated meaning over time? What links those who claimed Knickerbocker for their own New York agendas? Does this half-remembered, made-up moniker have a future? By tracing Knickerbocker's two centuries of use, I hope to answer these questions, and to show not only how Irving's improvisational creation set the New York Story in motion but how the Dutch historian, once loosed from his inventor, inspired New Yorkers to assert their own idiosyncratic relationship to the city, and to its history, which he was the first to celebrate. Before there was a "Big Apple," there was Knickerbocker.

CHAPTER 1

THE PICTURE OF KNICKERBOCKER

THE HISTORICAL SOCIETY AND THE HISTORIAN

It was, the *New-York Evening Post* reported, an "elegant dinner" in every respect. The bill of fare included "a variety of shell and other fish with which our waters abound" as well as "wild pigeon . . . the favorite dish of the season," and "the different meats introduced into this country by the European settlers."[1] But if the menu was elaborate, the ceremonial toasts were even more so. It could hardly have been otherwise: the company that had assembled at Manhattan's stylish City Hotel on the evening of September 4, 1809, had more to raise their glasses to than just the delicacies they found on their plates. It was the two hundredth anniversary of Henry Hudson's discovery of the island of Manhattan, and the New-York Historical Society, the host of the banquet, did not mean to let the occasion pass without a thorough commemoration. The festivities began before the feast, with a rather substantial, scholarly aperitif: a "Discourse, designed to commemorate the Discovery of New-York by Henry Hudson," given by the Reverend Dr. Samuel Miller, a member of the society and a pastor of the First Presbyterian Church. Dr. Miller's address pointedly kept to "well authenticated facts," giving the highlights of Hudson's famous journey and the botched shortcut to the Far East that brought him to New York in the first place. "To trace the gradual advances of the colony," Miller proudly concluded, "from small beginnings, to wealth, power, and universal improvement . . . to mark the growth of our CITY, from a few miserable trading huts, which, for a number of years after the discovery, formed but a single street, of small extent, until it has become the *fourth*, if not the *third*, trading town in the world . . . —these are the splendid subjects which lie before our future annual orators."[2]

After this optimistic finale, the diners were at last free to lift their forks, and their cups. First to be toasted were the explorers who helped to discover the Americas, and New York, from Christopher Columbus and Giovanni da Verrazano to Hudson himself, although the orators glossed over his grisly demise: "though disastrous his end, yet fortunate is his renown." Next, the society hailed those who first colonized their beloved island metropolis, including the last governor of New Amsterdam, Peter Stuyvesant ("an intrepid soldier and faithful officer") and the first governor of the English colony of New York, Richard Nicholls. The assembled company also drank the health of the city's current mayor, DeWitt Clinton; saluted the memory of George Washington, recently deceased; hailed their posterity, "a century hence"; and gave gallant thanks for the ladies of New York: "the *American fair*." With all this cheer, it must have been a merry evening, at least until the eminent physician and founding society member Dr. David Hosack stood up to give his "volunteer toast." "To the memory of St. Nicholas," Hosack declared, adding that he hoped "the virtues and simple manners of our Dutch ancestors be not lost, in the luxuries and refinements of the present time." While this remark seems innocuous to a contemporary reader, it would surely have deflated his audience at the City Hotel, brimming as they were with self-satisfaction, as well as with the "luxurious and refined" repast that they had just enjoyed. To the membership of the Historical Society, Hosack's plea to remember the "virtues and simple manners" of the Dutch was more than just a criticism of their multicourse banquet; it was also a pointed reminder that pigeon wasn't the only featured dish on this bicentennial menu: they were also eating humble pie.

The truth was that the Historical Society was in desperate need of history. It had been five years since Mayor DeWitt Clinton, City Inspector John Pintard, and a high-profile assortment of New York's best-known scholars, politicians, and civic leaders had organized the society to serve as the city's preeminent storehouse of records, relics, and information about "whatever may relate to the natural, civic, or ecclesiastical History of the United States in general, and of this State in particular," but aside from the Hudson bicentennial dinner, they had little to show for their efforts.[3] How much of a challenge could the gathering of history be for New York? Already, the city was the nation's foremost destination for refinement and for spectacle, from the newly expanded Park Theater, whose domed interior was touted as resembling "the Temple of Jupiter at Athens," to the Corlear's Hook Circus, where "the Royal Tiger Nero" could be seen in contest with a "large Wild Bull, and immediately after, a large Wild Bear."[4] Surely such a cosmopolitan place, "the first city in the United States for wealth, commerce, and population," could compile an account of its own past?[5] New York's rivals seemed to have little trouble with the same assignment: the Massachusetts Historical Society, toasted at the City Hotel dinner for setting an "honorable example," had been amassing founding documents and artifacts since 1791, and the 185th anniversary of the Plymouth landing of the Pilgrims had recently been celebrated in New York by the New England Society, a benevolent group for expatriate "Yankees," as New Englanders in New York were often called.[6] The southern states weren't far behind: new histories of Virginia and Delaware were readily available from American publishers. And yet, to the New-York Historical Society's great mortification, their city had almost nothing to show. The society's offices in the Picture Room of City Hall were largely empty; no trove of letters or annotated family Bibles had as yet emerged from the cobwebbed attics of New York's first families, nor had any metropolitan church, meetinghouse, or Masonic lodge unearthed ancient ledgers, charters, or other evidence of the founding past. Even the Dutch law books moldering in the state government's archives at Albany remained inscrutable, because the Dutch-speaking New Yorker commissioned to translate them had made off with his fee in advance. It had been two hundred years since Henry Hudson discovered Manhattan, but those who lived there now knew nearly as little about the history of their city as had that doomed explorer. What could be done?

The Revolutionary War was largely to blame for these gaps in New York's historical memory. The war had split the state: while George Washington's regiment fought landmark battles in the pastoral countryside, New York City endured a very different kind of strife. Manhattan had belonged to the English for seven long years of occupation.

It is not hard to see why England would have chosen to make New York City its wartime headquarters; although small compared to London, the pre-Revolutionary city was sophisticated all out of proportion to its size. Those billeted there during the war reported that the city was "one of the prettiest, pleasantest harbor towns [to be] seen . . . [with] houses . . . built fine and regular in English style."[7] But the war obliterated much of what had made the city so charming to visitors—and did so with appalling speed. Four days after General William Howe's arrival in Manhattan, the Great Fire of 1776 destroyed five hundred buildings at the southern end of the island, leaving a devastating scar that ran up the west side of the city, from Whitehall Slip to Barclay Street. The fire also leveled some of the colony's most venerable and significant buildings, including the first Trinity Church at Broadway and Wall Street, which had been completed in 1698 under royal charter from King William III; parts of King's College (given its royal charter in 1754), including the library; the new City Hospital; and the holdings of the New-York Society Library, the first subscription library in the American colonies. If Manhattan Island was scorched, the East River was left with a different kind of disfigurement: the corpses of thousands of captured American soldiers were dumped into the river from the British prison ships moored in Brooklyn's Wallabout Bay, in sight of the occupied city. Their bones would wash ashore in lower Manhattan for decades to follow. Rather than bear witness to these atrocious sights or endure the British lockdown, thousands of New Yorkers fled the city during the occupation, including Tory sympathizers (such as the Delanceys, who forfeited their farm on the Lower East Side when they headed for England) and patriots alike. Those who stayed, or who returned after Washington's triumphant Bronx-to-Battery march in 1783, found their metropolis almost unrecognizable and devoid of the genteel, urbane tone that had defined the colony. Not only had the city's most elegant edifices been charred or disfigured by the barbaric interlude of occupation, but the war had also ensured the obliteration of countless records, manuscripts, letters, and books pertaining to New York's colonization and development. The city's collective memory seemed to have vanished with the occupying troops.

The New-York Historical Society set itself the task of restoring that memory, hoping, at the same time, to renew the city's reputation and establish Manhattan as the new nation's cosmopolitan hub. The lack of founding documents made this an exceptionally challenging assignment. How could the society hope to assemble a coherent narrative for the city without any original texts? And how could it, as Miller's "Discourse" had so hopefully suggested, make New York an internationally renowned "trading town" without the emotional and moral grounding provided by a communal understanding of its past? The growing city itself inadvertently thwarted the society's project as well: liberated from the English, it had become a moving target. While the plan of New York after the Revolution still looked like something seen through the wrong end of a telescope—Manhattan in miniature—the city was, in fact, a place very much engaged in reconstruction and on the brink of tremendous change. As the contemporary English journalist John Lambert pointed out in wonder, New York's population had "more than tripled itself" in the twenty years since the war, and in 1807 John Pintard reported to the Common Council that New York had 83,530 inhabitants, "both free and slave, male and female."[8] For many of these New Yorkers, the island's contours did not yet reflect this rapid growth: the nucleus of "New-York" seemed the same as it had when the city was evacuated in 1783. The most desirable district of the city was still bounded by the Battery, Bowling Green, and lower Broadway, a short walk from the venerable Tontine Coffee House, unofficial hub of New York's stock exchange. To the north was the diminutive Saint Paul's Chapel, whose elegant Anglican appointments had survived the Great Fire and the war; it had served as Washington's place of worship during his brief presidential tenure in New York. Close by was Trinity Church, the venerable Episcopalian parish whose stone steeple was already a local landmark. A close-knit merchant elite (including many founders of the New-York Historical Society) worshipped at Trinity or the Dutch Reformed Church and presided over this microcosmic Manhattan from their Georgian brick or gable-fronted houses, whose classic Dutch "stoops" protected the doors (and feet) of their residents from some of the hazards to be found on Manhattan's unpaved streets. As late as the year of Hudson's bicentennial, 1809, a city ordinance had been passed to forbid "the running at large of hogs, pigs, etc. without rings in their noses," a ruling that suggests that New York's agrarian past was not as distant as some of its more cultivated residents liked to pretend, nor as far from their homes as they might desire.[9]

Not all who lived in this urban nucleus were elevated from the city's effluvia by stoops: then, as now, wealthy and poor New Yorkers lived side by side, albeit in very different accommodations. As Elizabeth Blackmar has noted, housing for all classes could be found close to the waterfront "slips," but the dwellings of the growing community of journeymen workers, Irish immigrants, and freed African Americans were more likely to be highly combustible wooden frame houses, whose basements (where entire indigent families could be found living) were routinely swamped by runoff from the tanneries and slaughterhouses that dumped into the once-potable waters of the Collect Pond, north of City Hall.[10] Least desirable of all was the Five Points neighborhood, named for the intersection of what were then Mulberry, Anthony, Cross, Orange, and Little Water streets. Although this nexus of poverty and shanty housing was only beginning to acquire its international reputation as the city's headquarters for vice and violent crime, it already assaulted unwary pedestrians with the pungent odors of nearby markets and left them stranded ankle-deep in the waste of unpenned livestock and the omnipresent mud. The mud was a needless reminder to Manhattan residents that their city was an island, latticed with streams, creeks, and ponds, and its oldest streets were close to sea level. The Common Council was just starting to grade many of the residential streets of what is now called lower Manhattan, to create sidewalks for major thoroughfares, paved with brick (or, in the case of Broadway, with flagstone), and to remove or bury the small bridges around the city—visible remnants of the Dutch settlement—that forded the waterways they planned to fill in.[11] Working-class New Yorkers also worshipped within the colonial city limits at this time: the oldest Roman Catholic parish in the city was Saint Peter's, built on the corner of Barclay and Church streets in 1786. The cornerstone of Saint Patrick's, the first Roman Catholic cathedral in New York, had been laid on Mott Street, between Bowery and Broadway, but the location was so far north of the urban center at this time that it would have seemed like another country.[12]

North of the narrow colonial city, with its gilded theaters, venerable thoroughfares, and hectic slips, the rest of Manhattan Island was indeed another country, and the opportunities for development appeared limitless. At the top of the Old Commons, freshly landscaped with "poplar-lined footwalks," a City Hall made of gleaming Berkshire marble was being constructed at a total cost to the city of $500,000.[13] Like New York itself, the new government seat could be seen as cosmopolitan or confused, depending on one's perspective. While the façade was to be done in a "French Renaissance" style and topped with a grand dome, a cupola topped with a wooden statue of Justice, sans blindfold, and a dazzling copper roof, the interior of the building, in keeping with its republican purpose, would be decorated along more austere, Federalist lines. The extravagance of the architects of this temple to democracy ended at the north side of the building, however, for the Chambers Street front of City Hall was to be faced in economical brownstone. This decision had been made in the firm belief that few would see the grand building from that vantage, so far north of what was then "uptown." It was a reasonable assumption in 1809, when Chambers Street was all but suburban, and the Commons and City Hall had been purposefully situated far from the smells and sounds of the harborside markets and safe from the polluted runoff of Collect Pond. In fact, until very recently Chambers Street had served as a refuge from the city's multiple yellow fever epidemics. During the outbreak of 1805, more than fifty thousand New Yorkers had left the city proper, heading north and east to the lots that had once been Delancey Farm and west to a "tent city" that was set up in Greenwich Village, itself originally a Dutch community built on the banks of Minetta Creek.[14] Some of these evacuees stayed and began to build speculatively in this verdant region, betting their fortunes on future plague, urban sprawl, or both.[15] The indigent who did not survive the outbreaks also remained north of the city, to be buried at the potter's field, a mass grave that marked the future site of Washington Square Park, around whose leafy perimeter New York University would be built in thirty years' time.

Perhaps in order to regulate these large-scale population shifts and the residential and commercial development they required, the Common Council of New York voted in 1807 to authorize the surveying of the entire island of Manhattan above Houston Street. The city, the councilmen decreed, was to be laid out in "streets, roads, and public squares, of such width, extent, and direction, as to them shall seem most conducive to public good."[16] It was a mammoth assignment, fit for a soothsayer rather than a surveyor. How could anyone dream what New York City would become, or anticipate how many people it might contain? Most of Manhattan was a wilderness: actual sheep grazed on the future site of Sheep Meadow in Central Park, where the Metropolitan Museum of Art and the American Museum of Natural History would not disturb their pasture for another sixty years, while farms, shantytowns, and Seneca Village, a community of slaves freed by the Manumission Act of 1799, occupied the wooded northern reaches that would later be decorated by the limestone turrets of the Vanderbilt, Rhinelander, and Frick mansions on Fifth Avenue. Elm Park, formerly known as the Tory property Apthorp Farm, dominated the Upper West Side (where the Apthorp Apartment Building would be built a century later), and the Upper East Side was still called Bloomingdale, a collection of meadows and suburban mansions (including two that are still standing, part of the residence of Abigail Adams Smith, a daughter of President John Adams, and the country seat of Archibald Gracie, now known as Gracie Mansion, the mayor's residence, on present-day York Avenue). The daunting assignment of yoking these disparate communities together fell to the young engineer John Randel Jr., who was given a team of "Commissioners of Streets and Roads" and four years to complete the survey. "When the intended improvements are completed," John Lambert commented, "it will be a very elegant and commodious town, and worthy of becoming the capital of the United States. . . . [L]and which [twenty years ago] sold . . . for fifty dollars is now worth 1,500."[17] The numerical street grid that resulted from Randel's project is still the one that orients visitors to New York today.

But land speculation was not limited to the guesses of admiring visitors such as Lambert. By 1809, the council had discovered with dismay that numerous entrepreneurial New Yorkers had already beaten the commissioners to their task, and the councillors issued an official warning that "no other persons are authorized to give the lines of streets for the purposes of building . . . [and] no building can be erected fronting on any street in this city, unless the lot shall have been first surveyed."[18] Cowboy surveyors weren't the council's only problem: amateur geographers had drawn up their own proposed maps of the future city, plowing imaginary avenues of differing widths through private property, as only the commissioners had been given license to do. The resultant, often improbable, matrices of suggested New York streets, squares, and parks (and even, in one case, "crescents") created by these ambitious laypeople were then christened with new names of their own choosing. And why not? The city itself had already begun the process of renaming its crooked colonial roads with staunchly republican replacements: to this end, George Street had been given the apolitical name of Spruce Street, King Street was dubbed Pine Street, and Little Queen Street was changed to Cedar Street.[19] Wealthy New York residents had been naming streets for themselves for centuries, a practice that still forced the Common Council to occasionally adjudicate between angry landowners, such as Samuel Jones of "Great Jones Street" and Dr. Gardiner Jones of "Jones Street," both in the Greenwich Village area.[20] Dutch street names, however, were pointedly exempted from the wholesale rechristening of the city. These "grandfathered" New Amsterdam streets came to serve as a kind of roadside concordance to actual city fathers, and their names offered clues for contemporary New Yorkers to the people and events that had shaped the Dutch colony. The exempted streets included Courtland Street (named for settler Oloff Van Cortlandt, one of the richest men in New Amsterdam), Ten Eyck's Pier, and Coenties Slip (a name that combined the nickname of Conraet Ten Eyck, a cobbler and patriot who participated in the Riot of 1665 against the English, and the first name of his wife, Antje).[21]

In anticipation of the Commissioners' Plan, the Common Council also authorized the filling of Collect Pond and the creation of Canal Street, its name yet another nod to the original topography of New Amsterdam.[22] But once the numerical grid of the plan was finished and adopted in 1811, would any New Yorker give a thought to the illogical, troublesome streets of Governor Stuyvesant's time? Would their ancient routes be straightened, their names changed or lost forever, their meaning simply erased? Intriguingly, a would-be surveyor named William Bridges proposed to avoid that particular cultural amnesia with a "plan of the city" that would have transformed the old Stuyvesant farm, then still known as the Bouwerie, into a tidy graph of streets named in honor of their original Dutch inhabitants, including Rotterdam, Amsterdam, Rensselaer, Peter, Stuyvesant, Nicholas, and Verplanck. His suggestions were not adopted by the Common Council, which may well have questioned whether any New Yorker could be expected to recognize Bridges's nostalgic references to New Amsterdam in several decades' time. Would they not, along with "Coenties Slip" and "Cortlandt Street," just become the city's hieroglyphs, cryptic markers of a forgotten civilization?

The city's transformative sprawl galvanized the Historical Society with questions like these. The society had attempted to rally New Yorkers to its cause with a beseeching handbill entitled "An Address to the Public," which pleaded for donations of "Manuscripts, Records, Pamphlets and Books relative to the History of this Country," in the hopes that these artifacts might offer up information about the New Netherlands settlement, however bizarre, mundane, or unsavory. "Do you know anything respecting the first settlement of New-York by the Dutch," the handbill earnestly inquires:

> the number of the settlers; the time of their arrival, their general character; their condition with respect to property; the authority and encouragements under which they came; or any other circumstances attending the first attempt at colonization? . . . Can you give any information which will throw light on the state of *morals* in our country, at different periods, such as the comparative frequency of *drunkenness, gambling, duelling, suicide, conjugal infidelity, prostitution,* &c. &c.?[23]

This prurient-sounding public appeal is necessitated, the society admits, by the "paucity of materials" pertaining to New York's Dutch past and the "extreme difficulty of procuring such as relate to the first settlement and colonial transactions" of New York. Without these documents, how could New York possibly come to understand itself, and how would it measure its progress? To this question the society has only the gloomiest of replies: "without the aid of original records and authentic documents, history will be nothing more than a well-combined series of ingenious conjectures and amusing fables." In other words, not even the commissioners' orderly street plan could secure a city built on historical quicksand. New York's colonial identity had been erased from public memory, and its Dutch past was at grave risk of being completely made up.[24]

While waiting for New Yorkers to respond to their calls to arms, the society began to augment its meager library of primary documents with research conducted by the philosophers, scientists, and divines who made up its membership. This clubby group delivered papers about various aspects of the city at meetings held in the society's new quarters at Government House on Bowling Green, which they shared with the American Academy of the Arts. The previously mentioned bicentennial tribute by Dr. Miller, a "Discourse, designed to commemorate the Discovery of New-York by Henry Hudson," is a sterling example of their efforts. While, as we have seen, Miller was loud in the defense of his paper's "well authenticated facts," he has nothing new to say about what Hudson found, since, as he admits, only the previously published journal of Robert Juet, an English mate of Hudson's ship, the *Half Moon*, is available to keep him from "conjecture or fable" about the voyages, or even about Hudson's fate at the hands of his mutinous crew.[25] But while Miller's lecture may have delivered old news, it does show that New Yorkers were already developing the collective solipsism that would become the hallmark of their urban identity. This can be seen in Miller's comments on the explorers who preceded Hudson to America, in which he demonstrates astonishment that the Cabot brothers seem to have passed over New York City completely:

> They do not appear to have landed anywhere . . . nor to have made any observations worthy of being recorded. It is not certain that they even *saw* at a distance any part of the coast which is now *New-York*. They certainly, however, sailed by it, and probably saw it. But still intent on the long sought passage to *India*, and meeting with nothing but what they considered an obstacle to the attainment of their wishes, they returned to *England*.[26]

The idea that the Cabots could have physically not *seen* New York is evidently shocking to Miller, who, like his colleagues in the society, has worked so hard to make the city both literally and metaphorically visible.

The most significant scholarly contribution made by the Historical Society in these early years was another work of legitimate, "well authenticated facts": Dr. Samuel Latham Mitchill's *The Picture of New-York; or, The Traveller's Guide Through the Commercial Metropolis of the United States, By a Gentleman Residing in this City*, published in 1807. Mitchill's catalog of the natural landscape, colonial history, and contemporary civic institutions of the city was one of the first comprehensive New York guides to be written by a resident, and at first glance, Dr. Mitchill certainly seems like the New Yorker for the job. He was a polymath of dazzling range, renowned first as a surgeon and pioneer of anesthesia and later as a politician and lawmaker. Mitchill had helped to found the College of Physicians and Surgeons (now part of the University Hospitals of Columbia and Cornell), he served as the first president of the Lyceum of Natural History (later the New York Academy of Sciences), and his reputation as a talented amateur geologist and botanist was widespread. He was also, unfortunately, a terrible writer. *The Picture of New York* might have been a product of its author's lively and eclectic range of enthusiasms, but it is about as absorbing to read as the telephone book.

Whether out of deference for his scientific profession or respect for the serious purpose of his colleagues at the Historical Society, or to repair the damage done by earlier, inaccurate guidebooks, Mitchill opens the *Picture* with a long and anxious insistence on the documented truth of the facts he is about to present. "An apology for the present publication," he begins,

> may be derived from the scantiness and incorrectness of the information to be found in any collected and methodical form relative to New-York. . . . The only effectual method of preventing the misrepresentation of those who visit our city, is to write a full and true account of it ourselves. By taking this course, ample and genuine information will be given to all who seek it; and there will be no excuse afterwards for such authors and compilers as treat our city and its inhabitants with their accustomed neglectfulness or perversion.[27]

Among the "misrepresentations" that Mitchill may have had in mind was the colorful account of the Scotsman Patrick M'Robert, whose 1776 guidebook *A Tour Through Part of the North Provinces of America* described with frank delight the "500 ladies of pleasure" who live "in great cordiality" at the "Holy Ground" near Saint Paul's Chapel.[28] Or Mitchill may have been thinking of Henry Wansey, an Englishman who focused his 1794 account of newly independent Manhattan on a different kind of hospitality. After asserting that New York's "water was very bad to drink," Wansey instead quenches his thirst at the city's taverns, smugly noting that "almost all the beer drank at New York is brewed in London. They have one or two breweries here but they do not succeed very well."[29] For Mitchill, touristic editorializing of this kind is not at all the same as giving a "full and true account" of New York, and if not exactly "neglect," it definitely qualified as historical "perversion." To mitigate the slanderous effects of such accounts, Mitchill's *Picture* exhaustively records and footnotes every natural and artificial feature of the city and attempts to certify the accuracy and authenticity of its author's research at every turn. But from its precise beginning ("*Situation*—The City of New-York stands on the island of Manhattan") to its descriptions of the "primeval arrangement" of the city's mineral strata to the enumeration of New York's major municipal facilities, commercial outlets, and philanthropic organizations (everything from the Tammany Society to the "Ladies Society for the Relief of Widows with Small Children"), Miller's *Picture* succeeds mostly in giving the reader the portrait of a pedant.[30] Its digressions provide some relief, however, for they are unintentionally comic: for example, the author provides the stomach-turning requirements for "Cargo-Pork" (it "shall not contain in one barrel more than four shoulders without the legs, nor more than 2 heads with the ears and snouts cut off and brains and bloody grizzle taken out").[31] This, then, is Mitchill's idea of "ample and genuine information" about life in contemporary New York!

However Mitchill defines it, his New York bears few marks of Dutch civilization. He belittles the meaningful Dutch place names in the city, noting that while the name of the city's time-honored "Fly Market" comes from the Dutch *vlaie*, or wetland, since it was situated on a former salt meadow, "a better [name should be] adopted."

Mitchill's dismissal of the sale of "Hudson's River" to the Dutch is still more damning: in his opinion it is a minor transaction, done "without license from [Hudson's] sovereign." Finally, his account of the battles that led to the English conquest of New Amsterdam is so perfunctory it almost reads like parody, and he finishes off the colony with the terse statement: "After the surrender of the city, by the last Dutch governor, Stuyvesant, to the English commandant, colonel Nicoll [sic], in 1674, a new order of things took place."[32] Not a single aspect of the Dutch settlement—its government or society, industry, city planning, architecture, religious or secular culture—is explored in Mitchill's account: he devotes more space to a description of the "strata of granite" in New York's harbor than he does to the entire Dutch rule. Perhaps the vestiges of New Amsterdam still extant in New York City—such as the Fly Market—reminded Mitchill and his colleagues in the Historical Society of just how unsure their scholarly footing was in this half-remembered period. Certainly, the physical evidence of the Dutch settlement that remained in nineteenth-century New York disturbs his empirical data and complicates his claims to accurate "representation." But there is one unusual entry in the *Picture* that directly addresses the vulnerability of the remaining fragments of Dutch civilization in metropolitan New York and points to Mitchill's recognition of their endangerment. This is his description of the contemporary, Dutch-speaking neighborhood of Flatbush, Brooklyn:

> The principal inhabitants of this county are descendants of the Dutch settlers, who first encroached upon the natives, in these parts. They have Dutch preaching in some of the religious meeting-houses, and many families learn no other language, until they are old enough to go abroad. But there are no Dutch schools, and, consequently, the language is on the decline.[33]

There is a surprisingly custodial quality to this portrait of Flatbush, and Mitchill's poignant evocation of a vanishing culture and a soon-to-be unintelligible tongue is very much of a piece with the rallying cry of the Historical Society: to collect that which is "on the decline," before it disappears for all time. But Mitchill's brief lapse into anthropological curiosity may also have served as a provocation for the creator of a very different "picture" of New York, one without hogs' heads or Holy Grounds: Knickerbocker's *History of New York*. Mitchill's "faithful statistical portrait" does not seem calculated to fire the imagination of nineteenth-century New Yorkers, or to rouse their indignation. However, there proved to be space enough in the physician's plodding rhetoric and hasty gloss on New Amsterdam to construct an entire semifictional universe, complete with its own creation myth. That universe was unveiled on December 6, 1809, a day then still observed by Dutch-descended New Yorkers as Saint Nicholas Day, when Bradford and Inskeep published Irving's outlandish *History of New-York, from the Beginning of the World to the End of the Dutch Dynasty . . . Being the Only Authentic History of the Times that Ever Hath Been or Ever Will Be Published*. Two thousand copies were printed, and sold for three dollars apiece. The book was dedicated to the New-York Historical Society, as "an humble and unworthy testimony of the profound veneration and exalted esteem of the Society's sincere well wisher and devoted servant, Diedrich Knickerbocker."[34] But who was this mysterious "well wisher," Diedrich Knickerbocker, who began in such a grand manner? In later years, Irving admitted that the *History* had been intended to "burlesque the pedantic lore displayed in certain American works," such as Mitchill's "small handbook," which he referred to by name (*RHNY* 350). He also hastened to add that the book was originally to be nothing more than a "temporary *jeu d'esprit*," and not a statement of outright protest against Mitchill's erasure of Dutch colonial history, or that book's effort to reduce New York's story to a dreary litany of geological facts and mercantile statistics. Knickerbocker's winking dedication suggests otherwise: how could Irving's competing account of New York help but be interpreted by its readers as a direct reproach, a thrown gauntlet to those who would deny the city an eccentric, accessible, and memorable past? There was to be nothing "temporary" about this new historian, with his outsized ambitions and funny Dutch name.

THE DAYS OF THE PATRIARCHS

Like his pseudonymous narrator, Washington Irving was a native New Yorker. Born in 1783, the year the Revolutionary War ended, he was named in honor of General George Washington by his grateful and admiring parents, immigrants from Scotland and England who had made a home for themselves and their eight children on William Street in New York City. Unlike Knickerbocker, however, Irving was no historian: at the time the *History* was published, he was serving a halfhearted apprenticeship in the law offices of Judge Josiah Hoffman, and his primary interest seemed to be his sideline career as a writer. Before he was twenty, Irving had contributed chatty theater reviews to his brother Peter's paper, the *Morning Chronicle*, under the pseudonym Jonathan Oldstyle, and in 1807 he cemented his reputation as a local pundit with *Salmagundi*, a short-lived but influential magazine that recorded fashionable life and culture in New York in the manner of its celebrated contemporary, the English magazine *Vanity Fair*. Irving coedited *Salmagundi* with his brother William and William's brother-in-law, James Kirke Paulding, and their satirical commentary offered an early window on what Walt Whitman would later dub "Fifth Avenoodledom," the social activity of upwardly mobile New Yorkers in a rapidly expanding, highly self-conscious young city.[35] *Salmagundi* had engaged its readership in a delicate dialectic, one that was particular to New York: the gulf between the post-Revolutionary longing for markers of status and class, on the one hand, and the city's pride in its new republican traditions and collective, populist feeling, on the other.[36] For *Salmagundi*'s fictional correspondents, status took the form of nostalgia for eighteenth-century (i.e., pre-Revolutionary) customs, or what the editors referred to, only half-jokingly, as the "honest, unceremonious intercourse of those golden days" (*S* 347). Interestingly, "those golden days" invariably translated to "New Amsterdam," a subject that Irving, writing as Will Wizard or Launcelot Langstaff, loved to mine. Irving's own Scottish heritage notwithstanding, he and his colleagues credited the Dutch with the invention of many of the city's enduring rituals, such as sleigh rides to "Kissing Bridge" (on what is now the Upper East Side); paying calls on New Year's Day, when well-to-do New Yorkers could expect to be plied with "bumpers" of "cherry-bounce or raspberry-brandy" by their neighbors "until not one of them was capable of seeing"; and even the holiday customs associated with Saint Nicholas, or "Santaclaus," as *Salmagundi* was among the first to dub the saint (*S* 346). It was to the stolid

Dutch clans of the metropolitan region that the magazine turned in order to illustrate the genteel code of post-Revolutionary New York "Society," or to spoof, by contrast, the unbecoming "thirst for style [and] pedigree" displayed by families of a more recent vintage (S 166). Dutch culture gave the satirists a way to describe and digest the singularity of the New York experience, one that was at once safe—having no vestigial whiff of Loyalism or Continental title-worship—and also subversive, because it presumed to comment with authority on the customs of an era that the Historical Society had declared forever lost in obscurity. *Salmagundi* also gave Manhattan its first nickname, one that acknowledged the comic absurdities that must attend a twice-colonized city attempting to find its own, democratic way. That nickname was "Gotham," and Irving and his fellow editors hailed their own city as a modern incarnation of the medieval village of that name in Nottinghamshire, England, whose residents pretended to be fools in order to avoid paying taxes to the king.[37] The magazine was short-lived, but "Gotham," the first entry in New York's lexicon of self-description, has lasted to this day, and New Yorkers still pride themselves on being a town of gifted shape-shifters whose natives recognize one another by their ability to adopt a cultivated mien or a mad, mute stare, as the situation requires.

But it was Irving's next satire that gave the city of Gotham its first bard, Diedrich Knickerbocker, author of the "curious" *History of New York*. The Dutch historian seems to have been willed into being by the Historical Society's protestations, existing solely to provide what it could not: a meaningful sense of place to New Yorkers struggling to orient themselves in their new-old city, as it grew. No voice like his could be found in Mitchill's *Picture*, to give a human timbre to that book's mechanical recitation. And although Knickerbocker's snobberies about the nouveau riche "mushrooms of an hour" that are invading Manhattan echo the comic laments of *Salmagundi*, the *History* has a more ambitious and urgent point to make than did Irving's previous literary lark. Without his book, Knickerbocker declares at the outset, the "early history of this venerable and ancient city" will fall "piecemeal into the tomb," and "the origin of our city will be buried in eternal oblivion" (*HNY* 377). As we have seen, that threatened burial of history was not just the prevailing fear of the New-York

Historical Society but a process that a New York resident like Irving would have daily witnessed through the constructions and demolitions taking place all around him. The wants and ambitions of contemporary New York could not help but overrule the vague claims of the distant past. For Knickerbocker, this potential erasure is a gravely personal threat as well as a civic one; he is, as we have seen, a self-proclaimed member of the "Dutch Dynasty" of his book's title and "of very great connections, being related to the Knickerbockers of Schaghtikoke, and cousin-german to the Congressman of that name" (*HNY* 375). As I noted earlier, Irving took the Knickerbocker name from an actual Dutch New York family, who resided in the Rensselaer County town of Schaghtikoke (or Schaghticoke). These Knickerbockers were the lineal descendants of Herman Jansen Knickerbocker of Friesland, Holland, and at the time of Irving's writing, the clan included an ancestral namesake, Herman Knickerbocker, who was a U.S. congressman from New York.[38] This bona fide Knickerbocker had been elected to office just months before Irving's book was published, thus adding another layer of mock-authenticity to the claims of his narrator and to his improbable stories.[39] Despite its absurdity, the borrowed genealogical backbone gives credence to Diedrich Knickerbocker's assertion that his expertise is supported by inherited wisdom, and unlike Mitchill, he is not merely a scientist but a true blood relation to the "Dutch progenitors" of New Amsterdam (*HNY* 377).

As promised, the partisan historian pays "just tribute" in the *History* to the "many great and wonderful transactions" of the Dutch colony, including their border wars with Indian and "Yankee" neighbors, their settlements on and around Manhattan Island, and their various attempts at statecraft and self-fashioning. Irving's rendering of these events interleaves verifiable historical facts with outrageous falsehoods, a mischievous recipe that makes for addictive and unpredictable reading. At any given point in the narrative, Knickerbocker (or the author, sometimes in the guise of a printer's devil or an anonymous editor) is equally likely to cite credible primary sources relating to the colony's founding (such as the journal of Robert Juet, Henry Hudson's mate), declaim from Horace or quote the early English historian Holinshed, note helpfully that Block Island is "famous for its cheese," or insist that the first wall on Wall Street was no wall at all but a pine picket fence, "a very strong and curious piece of workmanship" ordered by Peter Stuyvesant and "the admiration of all the savages in the neighborhood" (*HNY* 589). The reader soon realizes that his guide through these milestones of Dutch rule is so caught up in his ancestral story that he seems to be experiencing it in real time; he even occasionally interrupts his own narration to offer a tearful plea to Saint Nicholas, patron saint of New Amsterdam, to protect the colony as it endures whatever crisis he is in the process of relating.[40] These descriptions are inevitably fantastical, poking fun at Dutch attributes while at the same time revealing a larger truth about the settlement of the city. To this end, he insists that the Indian population in one area was not exterminated but instead effected a kind of aesthetic voluntary surrender, having fled en masse upon hearing the "tremendous and uncouth sound of the low Dutch language" of the New Amsterdam settlers (*HNY* 436). Knickerbocker also uses the classic emblem of the Dutch pipe to contrast the management styles of New Amsterdam governors Wouter Van Twiller and Wilhelmus Kieft—whom he dubs "Walter the Doubter" and "William the Testy," respectively. He suggests that Van Twiller's "tranquil and benevolent" administration was due to his long pipe, contemplatively smoked, while the "positive, restless" Kieft (whom many early readers saw as a caricature of Thomas Jefferson) preferred the "little captious short pipes" that caused the governor to become "meddlesome and fractious" and to institute "a multitude of good-for-nothing laws" (*HNY* 466, 513, 544, 539). But Irving, not forgetting his first purpose, takes care that his narrator reassures his readers periodically that his outlandish assertions have legitimate sources; they were "gleaned . . . among the family chests and lumber garrets of our respectable dutch citizens," or from an "elaborate manuscript . . . found in the archives of the Stuyvesant family," or by consulting "sundry family traditions, handed down from my great great Grandfather," purported "cabin boy" to Henry Hudson (*HNY* 378, 427). Throughout the book, Knickerbocker's assertions of privileged information mock the efforts of the Historical Society, as he proposes an answer for every "Dutch" query posed in the society's pleading handbill, and even for some they never dreamed of including, rebuking

their stated efforts to maintain a distinction between fact and conjecture, between reason and emotion. The cumulative effect of Irving's
History is to suggest that an element of self-invention, of fable, is
essential to New York's story. "For after all, gentle reader," Knickerbocker ends his introductory address, "cities *of themselves* . . . are
nothing without an historian" (*HNY* 379).

But Knickerbocker is as interested in the domestic arrangements
of his "patriarchs" as he is in setting down their political gains and
losses, and it is his nostalgic stories of New Amsterdam life that
made a lasting impression on his readership. The historian's portrait
of the colonial city offer persuasive explanations for the vestigial customs, structures, and names that haunted nineteenth-century New
York. These explanations not only fill in the gaps in the narratives of
his nonsatirical predecessors but give the historian an opportunity to
rebut his rivals' dismissive or reductive accounts of the Dutch colony
with a version that is explicitly paradisical. "The busy hum of commerce," Knickerbocker sighs, "[was] unknown in the peaceful settlement of New Amsterdam. . . . The whole island, at least such parts
of it as were inhabited, bloomed like a second Eden" (*HNY* 473). He
credits the bucolic nature of the colony with giving rise, among
other things, to the contemporary city's crooked streets:

> The sage council, as has been mentioned in a preceding chapter, not
> being able to determine upon any plan for the building of their city—
> the cows, in a laudable fit of patriotism, took it under their particu-
> lar charge, and as they went to and from pasture, established paths
> through the bushes, on each side of which the good folks built their
> houses; which is one cause of the rambling and picturesque turns and
> labyrinths, which distinguish certain streets of New York, at this very
> day. (*HNY* 476)

The "patriotic" Dutch cows, in this interpretation, are the forerun-
ners to the city's current commissioners of streets and roads, and
despite their lack of training in the science of surveying or the philosophy of the urban grid, the perambulating cattle served as determined and effective shapers of the geography of lower Manhattan, a
geography that still confounds and charms visitors today.

Throughout the *History*, Knickerbocker's etymologies for the names of New York's landmarks and his explanations for its traditions are at once satisfyingly plausible and pleasingly silly. The Battery got its name because Peter Stuyvesant "fortified the water edge with a formidable mud breast work, solidly faced, after the manner of the dutch ovens common in those days, with clam shells"; Spuyten Duyvil was so named by the settlers because it was home to the devil himself, who appeared to the unlucky in a form much like the Loch Ness Monster; and Dutch houses always have their gable end to the street because "our ancestors, like their descendants, were very much given to outward shew, and were noted for putting the best leg foremost" (*HNY* 591, 477). The *History* was also the first American book to popularize the figure of Saint Nicholas as New York City's patron saint and to draw attention to the Dutch tradition of "hanging the stocking in the chimney" for Santa Claus on Christmas Eve—not yet a ritual familiar to most Americans.[41] But the most unlikely tradition that Knickerbocker lays to New Amsterdam's credit is a culinary one: the humble doughnut. Taking his cue from American poet Joel Barlow, whose 1793 ode to "Hasty Pudding" had glorified the New England origins of that cornmeal-based dish, Irving claimed the doughnut for New York. The now-classic fried cake was the centerpiece of a groaning Dutch tea table, Knickerbocker notes, with a keen anthropological appetite: "Our ancestors were fond of sturdier, more substantial fare. . . . Sometimes the table was graced with immense apple pies, or saucers full of preserved peaches and pears; but it was always sure to boast an enormous dish of balls of sweetened dough, fried in hog's fat, and called dough nuts, or oly koeks—a delicious kind of cake, at present, scarce known in this city, excepting in genuine dutch families; but which retains its pre-eminent station at the tea tables in Albany" (*HNY* 480). Not only did the doughnut belong to New York, but as the invention of "genuine dutch families," it was *older* than New York—it was part of the legacy of the New Amsterdam settlement, to be revered as a holy and delicious relic of the city's "golden age."[42] Like Barlow's poem to porridge, Irving's hymn to pastry suggests that Americans were already attuned to regional differences, and, as John T. Edge has pointed out, authentic, Dutch-descended cookery and local cuisine was one way for an emergent

New York to define itself against its rivals.[43] This conjunction would have delighted (but not surprised) Irving's New York readers, who had already adopted many of the culinary traditions for which the city is still known. Street food could be found in the form of oysters (raw or roasted) and "hot corn," among other pedestrian-friendly treats, while Samuel Fraunces had begun an early version of takeout service in the 1760s, offering meals to the captains and passengers aboard the ships that docked in the harbor, just a few blocks from his famous tavern.[44] At the same time, the "genuine dutch" doughnut also gives Knicker-bocker a convenient outlet for his genealogical snobbery, albeit one cloaked in a deep-fried layer of patriotism. What better way to dis-tinguish the decidedly "plain" Dutch colony from its aristocratic, English successor than through this humble, edible tradition?[45]

Dutch culinary history also gave Irving the opportunity to offer a strangely prescient comment on the internecine debates taking place among the membership of the Historical Society at the time the *His-tory* was published. "Thrice happy, and never to be forgotten age," Knickerbocker rhapsodizes about New Amsterdam under Governor Wouter Van Twiller, "when everything was better than it has ever been since or ever will be again—when Buttermilk Channel was quite dry at low water—when the shad in the Hudson were all salmon, and when the moon shone with a pure and resplendent whiteness instead of that melancholy yellow light which is the consequence of her sick-ening at the abominations she every night witnesses in this degener-ate city!"(*HNY* 487). With this offhand remark, Irving seems to have incited a scientific debate between Samuel Mitchill and the Reverend Samuel Miller, author of the aforementioned "Discourse" on Henry Hudson. In his anniversary speech, Miller had stated that salmon were once native to the Hudson River, a comment that appears to have gone publicly unchallenged until March 1810, when Mitchill, in the course of a lengthy open letter, contested Miller's sources and offered a point-by-point rejection of the suggestion that Hudson and his men found anything resembling a salmon in the river that now bears his name.[46] "Salmon love clear and limpid water," Mitchill wrote, "and I should question much whether the ooze and mud of [the Hudson] was so agreeable to them." Instead, the "Herring, the Shad, and the Sturgeon [are] the annual visitants to this stream," Mitchill declared, referring Miller to "the Dutch word 'salm' or 'salmpie,' commonly in use to signify *salmon*, [but which] means also, in ordinary and loose conversation and composition, *trout*." The author of the *Picture of New-York* concludes with a triumphant flourish: "It is, therefore, a fair presumption, that these fishes never found within its waters sufficient inducement to visit them in great numbers, or at regular times, and that those which have been taken are merely strays and wanderers. I beg you to accept my friendly salutations."[47]

It is impossible to say with certainty whether Irving's offhand remark is the result of his careful study of Miller's "Discourse," which had been published in the society's *Collections for the Year 1809*, or just a lucky guess. It is also impossible to ascertain whether Mitchill's response to his colleague's minor error would have been delivered with such asperity if the salmon-shad confusion had not been reiterated by the mocking faux history that had been published to such acclaim just four months earlier. Certainly, Mitchill must have become bitterly aware of Washington Irving and his popular satire by that point, if only because area booksellers had begun advertising the *Picture* as "*Not* by Mr. Knickerbocker" but by a "gentleman residing in this City," to avoid the anticipated confusion with that other—and best-selling—account of New York.[48] The possibility that the *Picture*, a book of "ample and genuine" facts, might be mistaken for a work of light humor written by an unscientific unknown would likely have been a blow to the eminent doctor's sense of propriety, as well as his pride. It also suggests that New Yorkers had already begun to embrace Knickerbocker's version of their city's story, however far it might be from the truth. Regardless of how Irving received, divined, or mistook the information that would spark a fish feud in the Historical Society, the controversy marked the first of countless instances in which Irving's revisionist *History* would be invoked or appropriated in the service of actual, historical fact.[49]

The *History* also addresses the reference the *Picture* makes to the slow death of Dutch culture and language in Flatbush, Brooklyn. Mitchill was not the only writer to comment on the idea of a self-imposed linguistic isolation at this time; Henry Wansey (one of the foreign visitors whose account Mitchill sought to debunk) had written that "if a stranger speaks to [an Albany man] in English, he will scarcely open the upper hatch of his door, but a single word uttered in German or High Dutch, will make the whole hatch fly open instantly, and the person, whoever he is, welcome to every thing in his house."[50] Irving's rendering of Peter Stuyvesant's retirement to the wilds of "his *Bouwery,* or country seat," after the surrender of New York, offers a touching fictional context for Wansey's Albany story: "No persuasions could ever induce [Stuyvesant] to revisit the city. . . . He railed continually at the degenerate innovations and improvements introduced by the conquerors—forbade a word of their detested language to be spoken in his family, a prohibition readily obeyed, since none of the household could speak anything but dutch" (*HNY* 723). The impending extinction of the Dutch language in New York is as moving here as it is in Mitchill's account, but it also serves as a useful screen for Knickerbocker's nostalgic message. To this day, New Yorkers find common ground in lamenting the passing of their city's "golden days"—regardless of when they believe that era to have been— and in fighting the prospect of any kind of change. And some New Yorkers still identify themselves and recognize their compatriots by their shared "Noo Yawk" patois, an inheritance available to native-born and proudly adoptive citizens alike.[51] Irving's book institutionalized this communal yearning for the symbols of "old New York," whether those symbols take the form of a forgotten street name or a dropped *r.*

In the effort to provide a balanced portrait of the Dutch colony, Knickerbocker also credits his ancestors with some of the contemporary blights on his beloved city. He suggests that the Dutch are responsible for the strange contours and "fragrant effluvia" of the island, explains how the New Amsterdam colonists installed "the acres of artificial ground, on which several of our streets, in the vicinity of the rivers are built," and built the swamplike streets (around the Five Points in particular) that were now the bane of the city's sanitation efforts. Taking the joke to its macabre limits, Knickerbocker notes that these marshy wards had proved, "if we may credit the assertions of several learned physicians of this city . . . very efficacious in producing the yellow fever," a disease with which his New York–area readers would be only too familiar, since the most recent epidemic in the city had taken place just four years before (*HNY* 477). Irving's choice of example and argument follows Mitchill's lead to the letter, by rebutting (albeit negatively) the comments of Englishman Charles William Janson, whose 1807 travelogue *The Stranger in America* asserted that while the "narrow, crooked and inconvenient" streets and gable-ended "old Dutch tenements" of the New Amsterdam settlement still "disgrace" the city, they "cannot give rise to those pestilential fevers which have raged there every summer, in some degree, since the year 1794."[52] Knickerbocker disagrees and patriotically reclaims all of Manhattan for the Dutch: the appealing and the appalling alike.

As self-appointed curator of the vanishing culture of Dutch New York, Knickerbocker undertakes not only to commemorate the recognizable innovations and characteristics bequeathed by New Amsterdam but also to memorialize the colony's founding families for posterity. In the narrator's estimation, the true glory of the colony lay in the "regular, well organized, antediluvian dutch families" by whom it was first settled and protected, whom he calls "the only local nobility [in New York], and the real lords of the soil" (*HNY* 500, 673).[53] Knickerbocker's "local nobility" is more or less a petite bourgeoisie, with organizing principles similar to those of the city in which Irving and his readers lived. At the same time, there is a perverse, meritocratic streak to the New Amsterdam class hierarchy; in the Knickerbockerian universe, it is genteel to be somewhat shabby. The "higher classes, or noblesse," the historian insists, were those who "kept their own cows, and drove their own wagons," and "neither drove in their curricles nor sported their tandems, for as yet those gaudy vehicles were not even dreamt of" by a population that tended cabbage-gardens and were all "in full snore before nine o'clock" each night (*HNY* 480, 485). In contrast to the contemporary genteel gatherings that Irving had lampooned as society editor of *Salmagundi*, the tea parties of New Amsterdam were characterized by neither "suffocating crowds, nor brilliant drawing rooms, nor towering feathers, nor sparkling diamonds, nor immeasurable trains ... [nor] choice anecdotes of scandal, for in those primitive times the simple folk were either too stupid, or too good natured to pull each other's characters to pieces" (*HNY* 479). These comments are at once a critique of the aristocratic trappings of New York's social life under the British and a sly commentary on the contemporary city's increasing fascination with class stratification, close on the heels of a republican revolution. Just a few years earlier, John Lambert had noted the importance New Yorkers attributed to the City Assembly balls, which admitted "none but the first class of society" as subscribers. According to Lambert, a rival group, the Juvenile Assembly, sprang up almost immediately to admit "the genteel part of the second class," thus soothing the wounded pride of would-be socialites who had not made the original cut.[54]

In contrast, the "noblesse" depicted by Irving are "good natured," unfashionable, and a little dull. Knickerbocker's rundown of the traits that characterized the various Dutch clans that accompanied Peter Stuyvesant into battle reiterates his message of "simple" gentility. While the families he lists are ostensibly the founders of New York City, there is little that is particularly sophisticated or urbane about their characterization, and many seem better suited to lead a game of touch football than a City Assembly waltz:

> First of all came the Van Bummels, who inhabit the pleasant borders of the Bronx—These were short fat men, wearing exceedingly large trunk breeches, and are renowned for feats of the trencher—they were the first inventors of Suppawn or Mush and milk. . . . Then the Van Nests of Kinderhook, valiant robbers of birds' nests, as their name denotes; to these, if report may be believed, we are indebted for the invention of slap jacks, or buck-wheat cakes. . . . Lastly came the KNICKERBOCKERS of the great town of Scaghtikoke, where the folk lay stones upon the houses in windy weather lest they should be blown away. These derive their name, as some say, from *Knicker*, to shake, and *Beker*, a goblet, indicating thereby that they were sturdy toss pots of yore; but in truth it was derived from *Knicker* to nod, and *Boeken* books; plainly meaning that they were great nodders or dozers over books—from them did descend the writer of this History. (*HNY* 630–631)

This motley genealogy offers the reader a founding aristocracy for New York, one composed solely of Knickerbocker's honored clans. It is a caste, however, that rejects the very idea of caste and mocks

American ancestor-worship with its irreverent eye for detail. Once again, the historian asserts Dutch cultural primacy through culinary inventions (this time, he credits his ancestral burghers with flapjacks and "suppawn," which Barlow had insisted was another name for New England's culinary invention, hasty pudding), while at the same time debunking his own genealogical authority with etymologies based on truly juvenile puns (the Van Bummels of the "large trunk breeches" get particularly unfair treatment in this respect). But these are affectionate characterizations: the "improving" Yankee interlopers of New York fare much worse with Knickerbocker. The narrator christens the New Englanders with a medley of tongue-twisting Quaker and biblical names, including "Preserved Fish, and Habbakuk Nutter, and Return Strong, and Zerubabbel Fisk" (*HNY* 529). The fact that some of these impossible handles—such as Preserved Fish—were the names of Irving's real-life New York contemporaries would have made their recitation that much more comic for his original readership in 1809.[55] The author's delight in odd and unmanageable American names (even his friend and admirer the publisher Evert Duyckinck did not escape Irving's punning) would reappear in his tales of the Hudson River Valley, where Knickerbocker would have the chance to introduce ever more impossible Dutch and "Yankee" monikers.

The historian's recitation of the names and peculiar attributes of his "lords of the soil" (and their chief enemies) holds a funhouse mirror to the genealogical litanies that genteel New Yorkers could read at that time in *The Correct Peerage of England, Scotland, and Ireland*, a genealogical reference guide that had been published annually in England since 1769 (and was familiarly referred to as *Debrett's Peerage*, after the name of its publisher). No such book had yet been published for American families, although Irving would likely have known about the closest stateside approximation: the Society of the Cincinnati, a patriotic and genealogical association founded in 1789 to honor men who had served at least three years in the Continental Army during the Revolutionary War, and whose membership was limited to these veterans and their direct (male) descendants. As Tom Lewis points out, New York's Revolutionary forces mingled the most esteemed Dutch and British names of both Manhattan and the Hudson River Valley, so Knickerbocker's list of Stuyvesant's warriors would have had an aristocratic resonance for his first generation of readers, too.[56] In this way, the historian's proud recounting of "the early planting of those mighty Dutch families which have taken such vigorous root and branched out so luxuriantly in our state" antici-pates both Mrs. Astor's famous "Four Hundred" society list and its more canonical counterpart, the cryptic phone book of high society known as the *Social Register*, two Gilded Age phenomena that will be discussed in chapter 3 (*HNY* 302). Even the laughable errors in Knickerbocker's translations (from the Dutch surnames to the English definitions) prefigure some of New York society's own translating efforts in the decades that followed, as the self-made robber barons who rose through its ranks began to purchase royal titles, commission castles, and design family crests to advertise their newfound noblesse. In all these ways, the *History* acknowledges the increasing social seg-regation between classes in the growing city, and predicts the corre-sponding geographical divide with uncanny foresight. In the years that followed, the historian's New Amsterdam genealogy would be borrowed by roots-seeking readers, many of whom would mistake Irving's tongue-in-cheek depictions for sober genealogical fact.

And yet the New Amsterdam settlers that Knickerbocker depicts do live by a code of manners that Irving's readers would recognize, even if they hoped for more patroons and fewer "toss-pots" on the colony's family tree. The quiet dignity of the historian's ancestors is manifested most poignantly at the end of the *History*, when Colonel Richard Nicholls and "a legion of British beef fed warriors" take pos-session of the colony for the Duke of York. "According to treaty," Knickerbocker notes with evident pride, "the [Dutch] inhabitants . . . were allowed to maintain quiet possession of their property, but so inveterately did they retain their abhorrence to the British nation, that in a private meeting of the leading citizens, it was unanimously determined never to ask any of their conquerors to dinner" (*HNY* 721). It is a final little joke by Irving on the swift and peaceable capit-ulation of the mild-mannered Dutch, but it is also a thoughtful comment on the evolutionary progress of New York society and the distinctions that New Yorkers had already begun to draw between newcomers and "first families." And it is a reminder of Knicker-bocker's own announcement, earlier in the *History*, when he decided to take his audience fully into his hospitable confidence: "My readers must doubtless perceive how completely I have altered my tone and deportment since we first set out together. This is just my way, I am always a little cold and reserved at first, particularly to people whom I neither know nor care for, and am only to be completely won by long intimacy" (*HNY* 634). This, then, is the Knickerbocker hauteur: like most New Yorkers, he is in no hurry to make friends with strangers. The point of the *History*, after all, is not to be "companionable" but to bear witness to the "chivalric achievements" of the Dutch colonists and to have his claims for the supremacy of New Amsterdam sanctioned by his readership.

Knickerbocker's trumpeting of New Amsterdam is the constant music of Irving's book, and the reason that the *History* captured the imagination of so many. New Amsterdam, "Manna-hatta," New York: whatever its name, it is the place that enabled the Dutch colony to thrive "like a luxuriant vine . . . [from] a munificent dung hill," in the words of the exuberant, scatological historian (*HNY* 450). The incomparable perfections of the city are at the base of all of Knickerbocker's bragging, a litany that is familiar today because he was the first to set it down. Whatever is pleasant, quaint, or charming about New York he credits to the planning of his hospitable and peculiar ancestors, just as he credits the Dutch cows with shaping New Amsterdam's meandering, narrow streets. Whenever the opportunity arises, Knickerbocker pauses his narrative to exult in some magnificent outlook or inimitable feature of the island he dubs "the fairest spot in the known world," and he does so with an unabashed wonderment that is out of character with his typical scholarly mien (*HNY* 449). He even confesses that despite the "melancholy progress of improvement" in the nineteenth-century city, he is as enamored with it as ever—a bittersweet sentiment that a twenty-first-century reader might share (*HNY* 489). Knickerbocker's euphoria is equally captivating today because some of the New Amsterdam vistas he describes still remain. We might still see the moonlight on the Battery "light up the white sail of some gliding bark," visit Peter Stuyvesant's family vault at Saint Mark's Church, wander down Wall Street toward the site of the old Dutch slips, or just observe the "constant bustle" that has defined New York since its founding (*HNY* 591, 635). To convey an "authentic" impression of one's romance with the city and to offer a true "picture of New York" did not require geological analysis or archival documentation, Irving's book suggests, only imagination and unabashed joy. "That I have not written a better history of the days of the patriarchs is not my fault," Knickerbocker protests, in closing; "had any other person written one as good I should not have attempted it at all" (*HNY* 728). While this final salvo is meant to slight the failed efforts of the Historical Society, it proved instead to be a challenge that his fellow New Yorkers would take up with alacrity. The "days of the patriarchs" had only just begun.

CHAPTER 2

INHERITING KNICKERBOCKER

GIVING IT THE HOME STAMP

"I find myself almost crowded off the legendary ground which I was the first to explore," Irving wrote with mock bitterness in 1848, looking back on the debut of his Dutch historian (*RHNY* 352). From a vantage of nearly forty years, Irving marveled, with a modesty he may not have felt, at how quickly his Knickerbocker landscape had been co-opted by readers who adored and identified with his quixotic portrait of the early city. More important, he wondered at how fast they had embraced his totemic narrator. Knickerbocker, he noted with amazement, was now used "to give the home stamp to everything recommended for popular acceptation, such as Knickerbocker societies; Knickerbocker insurance companies; Knickerbocker steamboats; Knickerbocker omnibuses; Knickerbocker bread, and Knickerbocker ice" (*RHNY* 352). In reality, New Yorkers did not wait for brand-name bread, ice, and omnibuses—or Irving's blessing—before embracing "Knickerbocker" as a "house-hold word," as he noted: they adopted Irving's imaginary historian as a mascot for the city almost immediately after the *History*'s publication. The earliest usage can be found in local newspapers, where critics and columnists began to reference Diedrich Knickerbocker in support of their political and civic positions. As early as 1810, Irving's satirical account of New York (and its citizens) was being reported by some as an accurate record of the Dutch colonial past, and his historian's aphorisms, quoted out of context, achieved a Solomonic gravity they had never had in the original.[1] "One might as well look for the city of Communipaw, which

41

makes such a figure in Knickerbocker's history, as to look for the city of Washington," the *National Intelligencer and Washington Advertiser* declared in 1810, poking fun at the mosquito-ridden backwater that had been chosen for the nation's new capital; "they are neither of them to be found—except on paper."[2] Few of Knickerbocker's borrowers explicitly acknowledged that the character was make-believe, the impromptu and impish offspring of a young lawyer's boredom, but they primarily used the historian in a satirical context. An 1810 editorial from an Albany paper scolded the state Council of Appointment for foolish actions that were "a proper subject for the pen of Diedrick"— Diedrich Knickerbocker—rather than "the pen of a profound historian," while a patriotic "Extract from Washington" published in the *New-York Commercial Advertiser* declared, "The people of this country, says the immortal historian Knickerbocker, are a talking people; and whoever should attempt to curtail his privilege would stand a chance to be himself silenced." New Yorkers were already dressing their daily realities in the whole cloth of Irving's creation, but the line between the fiction of Knickerbocker and the fact of urban life had not yet begun to blur.

That same year, however, the New York newspaper *The Columbian* published "The Knickerbockers," a pseudonymous letter to the editor that took Irving's nomenclature even further.[3] This missive was a mock rebuttal to the *Columbian*'s earlier report on the New-York Historical Society's first-ever Saint Nicholas Day dinner, and it describes those "descendants" of Dutch settlers who attended the society's dinner as "Knickerbockers" themselves. It was the first recorded instance of the historian's name being used to describe a group of people, and his new namesakes seem to be a certain kind of native New Yorker; they are citizens who strive to be civic leaders, improvers, and boosters, and they possess land, power, and (according to the *Columbian*) a certain degree of pomp.[4] The paper's facetious application of the Knickerbocker name took serious hold, and over the next decade it was used to sign op-eds about coastal security around Manhattan, as a seal of approval on advertisements for the circus, and to refer to political constituencies in Albany ("what an uproar and confusion there will be in this fair city . . . and among all the Knickerbockers," the *National Advocate* wrote in 1816, noting the federal government's nonpayment of a loan from "the *goodly* corporation of New-York").[5] A letter to the editor of the *New-York Gazette* even invoked the historically sensitive stance of the original: "an old Knickerbocker congratulates his younger brethren on the probable preservation of the great open walk of his ancestors . . . recently called the Battery."[6] Suddenly, Irving's Diedrich had a raft of self-proclaimed cousins—and Knickerbocker references in New York were everywhere.

The range of these references—from historical and political to commercial enterprises—is evidence of the versatility of Irving's creation and proof of the increasing interest that his readers took in the nostalgic landscape of the Dutch settlers about which they had previously known so little. It also suggests that New Yorkers were looking for their own, post-Revolutionary mythology and for the words that would relay this mythic sensibility to their neighbors and to the rest of the world. It was the salesmen, as befitted the city's mercantile heritage, who figured out the dollar value of Irving's little onomatopoetic word first. Less than five years after the *History* was published, urban residents could patronize the Knickerbocker Bakery, which advertised "loaf bread . . . in a superior style" for sale at its Mott Street store; buy a share in the *Knickerbocker* packet ship, which carried rum from Jamaica; visit the American Museum to see a rowboat built for speed and christened *Knickerbocker*; or enjoy "beef-steaks, oysters, and relishes of every description, at the shortest notice," at the Knickerbocker Hotel, a "spacious and airy" tavern on Little George Street.[7] By 1818, the historian's name had acquired such local cachet that yet another bakery, the Old Established Knickerbocker Bake-House (with a different proprietor, and on William Street), could advertise its talents for "Christmas and New-Year's Cake" made in the "true Knickerbocker style," without any need for further explanation.[8] Without ever being explicitly defined, "Knickerbocker" had become a New York word.

What exactly was a "true Knickerbocker"? It would be ten years before Irving returned to his Dutch themes or gave his proud little historian new tales to tell.[9] In the intervening decade, the community of readers who reveled in Irving's "old New York" became an international one. While Irving served as the editor of the Philadelphia magazine *Select Reviews*, and later as colonel of state militia and aide to Governor Daniel D. Tompkins of New York, the *History* was published—and enthusiastically received—in London. Charles Dickens and Samuel Taylor Coleridge took delight in Irving's burlesque, but it was Scotland's beloved bard of highland romance, the novelist and poet Sir Walter Scott, whose documented enthusiasm had the greatest impact on Irving's career: "I have been employed these few evenings in reading [the *History*] aloud to Mrs. S[cott] . . . [and] our sides have been absolutely sore with laughing," he wrote to Henry Brevoort.[10] An invitation from Scott prompted Irving's journey to England in 1815, a visit that would last more than fifteen years and result in three matching volumes of "sketches": *The Sketch-Book of Geoffrey Crayon, Gent.* (1819); *Bracebridge Hall; or, The Humorists, a Medley by Geoffrey Crayon, Gent.* (1822); and *Tales of a Traveller* (1824). Although these collections of "Old World" pastoral vignettes mostly lack the rapid pace and anarchic charms of the *History*, they were, for the most part, critical and commercial successes on both sides of the Atlantic and prompted the English literary magazine *Blackwood's* to assert that "Mr. Washington Irving is one of our first favourites among the English writers of this age—and he is not a bit the less so for having been born in America."[11] Thanks to Knickerbocker, Irving had become America's first literary celebrity, and his steadily increasing fame can be charted in the writing of his stateside peers, as well as in his international reviews. In "To a New England Poet," a bitter ode published in 1823, Philip Freneau scolded American writers with evident sarcasm, urging them to follow Irving's expatriate example:

> Why stay in such a tasteless land,
> Where all must on a level stand,
> (Excepting people, at their ease,
> Who choose the level where they please:)
> See Irving gone to Britain's court
> To people of another sort,
> He will return, with wealth and fame,
> While Yankees hardly know your name.
>   . . .

Dear bard, I pray you, take the hint,
In England what you write and print,
Republished here, in shop, or stall,
Will perfectly enchant us all.[12]

This remonstrance ignores a crucial fact: the Irving material "republished" in collections such as the *Sketch-Book* was not simply the hackneyed hymns to English aristocracy that Freneau deplored but also fresh stories from the first source of Irving's fame: Diedrich Knickerbocker. Beginning with the *Sketch-Book* in 1819, Irving resurrected his now-famous Dutch historian to narrate a series of tales set among the Dutch communities of the Hudson River Valley and Manhattan. The chronology of these stories roughly picks up where the *History* left off, tracing the fate of the Dutch during and after the English colonial period. The Knickerbocker stories include what today are arguably Irving's most famous works, "Rip Van Winkle" and "The Legend of Sleepy Hollow," as well as some that are all but forgotten: "The Haunted House: From the Mss. of the Late Diedrich Knickerbocker," "Dolph Heyliger," "The Storm Ship," "Wolfert Webber; or, Golden Dreams," and "The Money-Diggers." While "Rip" and "Sleepy Hollow" have become part of the American literary canon, the entire post-*History* Knickerbocker repertoire deserves fresh attention: taken collectively, the stories not only advocate for a new, distinctly American literary form but offer a comprehensive catalog and reference guide to the traits and behaviors that define the Knickerbocker persona Irving's readers had come to love.

It is hard to say when or how quickly the fashion for invoking Knickerbocker would have waned if Irving himself had not chosen to use these new stories as a platform from which (even in London) to observe and comment on the physical development of his native city and state. There was plenty to discuss: during his absence, the plans were approved for the 363-mile-long Erie Canal, to be the largest man-made waterway in the United States upon completion—stitching together the state's farms, forests, and mountains, from Buffalo to New York City. At the same time, the New York Commissioners' Plan continued its own sewing project, embroidering the Randel grid ever further "uptown," through stubborn cliffs of Manhattan schist and across old Dutch and English farms. The grid did not spare the ancient contours of New Amsterdam, either: by the time of Knickerbocker's return, the Common Council was busy sinking colonial piers, acquiring the deeds to private thoroughfares (such as from Anthony Bleecker, who ceded his street to the council in 1809), and opening, repaving, and widening the tangle of downtown streets that had comprised the original Dutch settlement and whose current population of poor, immigrant, and largely disenfranchised New Yorkers seemed to increase every day.[13] But it was not just the old neighborhoods that were growing: by 1820, just a year after Irving published "Rip Van Winkle," the population of Manhattan Island—only twenty-three square miles in total—outstripped Boston and Philadelphia, making New York the largest city in the United States, a distinction it still maintains. While New Yorkers were busy creating the infrastructure for a powerful "Empire State," Knickerbocker's increasingly elaborate mythologies provided a sentimental counterpoint, connecting this collective plan for the future to a satisfying vision of the past. Once again, the historian offers readers a primer on what he deems to be the "authentic" history of the city and the region, with the focus this time on the descendants of the "valiant" founding families whose praises he sang, to humorous effect, in the *History*.

"Rip Van Winkle," one of two Hudson River Valley stories that first appeared as part of *The Sketch-Book of Geoffrey Crayon, Gent.*, is the story of one of the most famous naps in literature, second only to that of Sleeping Beauty. It is also Irving's opening salvo in the battle to reclaim the Knickerbocker territory he had ceded in the ten years since the *History* was published. "Rip," like the *History*, is presented by a fictional compiler (whom Irving dubs "Geoffrey Crayon") as a primary document,

> found among the papers of the late Diedrich Knickerbocker, an old gentleman of New York, who was very curious in the Dutch history of the province, and the manners of the descendants from its primitive settlers. . . . Whenever, therefore, he happened upon a genuine Dutch family, snugly shut up in its low-roofed farm house, under a spreading sycamore, he looked upon it as a little clasped volume of black letter, and studied it with the zeal of a bookworm. (*SKB* 767)

The appeal of "Rip Van Winkle" to Irving's New York readership is not difficult to understand, even without its "genuine Dutch" pedigree. Who would not envy the sweet-tempered Dutch layabout whose twenty years' sleep in the Catskill Mountains allows him to miss the American Revolutionary War, outlive his shrewish wife, and assume the honorable (and pensioned) position of town father, all without having to do more than speak his name? How delightfully removed and quiet the hamlet of Tarry-town must have seemed to contemporary New Yorkers—and Americans in general—as they struggled to keep pace with the demands of a hectic, sprawling new democracy. But while Rip's amnesiac adventures may have seemed improbable to Irving's readers, the landscape of his hometown would have been comfortingly familiar to many:

> At the foot of these fairy mountains . . . is a little village of great antiquity, having been founded by some of the Dutch colonists in the early times of the province, just about the beginning of the government of the good Peter Stuyvesant (may he rest in peace!) and there were some of the houses of the original settlers standing within a few years, built of small yellow bricks brought from Holland, having latticed windows and gable fronts, surmounted with weathercocks. (*SKB* 769)

This scene of "great antiquity" has been recycled, almost verbatim, from the *History*, in particular from Knickerbocker's praise of New Amsterdam homes, with their "yellow Dutch bricks," "gable ends," and "fierce little weathercocks."[14] Irving's self-referencing is a calculated strategy: it gives the original work additional historical credence by virtue of being the accredited source material for this latest tale. At the same time, this repetition also reassures New York readers that their mercurial city *does* have a past and that the evidence of it may still be seen in the remaining Dutch-style homes of Manhattan, Brooklyn, and the Hudson River Valley.

Architecture lessons aside, Knickerbocker's chief preoccupation remains the fate of his endangered kinsmen. As one of the narrator's "genuine" Dutchmen, Rip is a worthy curator of New Amsterdam's past, which appears to him, before his epochal sleep, in the form of Henry Hudson and the crew of the *Half Moon*. Unlike the New-York

Historical Society, Irving's story implies, Rip is able to recognize these ghostly figures because he has been steeped in the history of his ancestors and their colony. Rip's heritage also makes his own recognition possible when he awakes, twenty years later, to find his "little village" utterly transformed. It was common practice, as Thomas Wermuth has shown, for mid–Hudson Valley towns to ban "outsiders with no visible means of supporting themselves" from taking up residency in a community, making Irving's depiction of Rip's harassment at the hands of Tarry-town's obstreperous, newly republican townspeople more true to life than the author may have known.[15] It is only when Rip thinks to speak his (decidedly Dutch) name out loud that the threat of banishment from his hometown is averted: "finding himself thus alone in the world—every answer puzzled him too by treating of such enormous lapses of time and of matters which he could not understand—war—Congress, Stoney Point—he had no courage to ask after any more friends, but cried out in despair, 'Does nobody here know Rip Van Winkle?'" (SKB 781). Consequently he is not only certified as a legitimate resident of the town but established, by virtue of his advanced age, at the top of its hierarchy. From that point on in Irving's story, Rip functions as a living landmark: through no action of his own, he has become "one of the patriarchs of the village," to be seated on a bench at the town center like a tribal elder or cigar-store Indian and celebrated for being a survivor—not of the Revolutionary War but of Anglo-American attempts to erase the Dutch past (SKB 783). His long-dead contemporaries' "wooden tombstone[s] in the churchyard" have "rotted and gone," leaving no legible record of their existence, but Rip's story can still be read in his living person (SKB 780). Canny contemporaries of Irving might also have noted that the name of Irving's triumphant hero is the same as that of the author's new American publisher, C. S. Van Winkle. Rip's Dutch patrimony ensures his survival in Tarry-town, and on the printed page as well.[16]

    The second Hudson River Valley story in the Sketch-Book requires Knickerbocker to act as his own Rip Van Winkle. Lacking a genial native to serve as his narrative stand-in, the historian himself provides the "precise and authentic" account of "The Legend of Sleepy Hollow," a semi-supernatural tale of warring suitors, a headless horseman, and a way of life on the verge of extinction. "I mention this spot with all possible laud," Knickerbocker says of the Hudson River Valley town of Sleepy Hollow, "for it is in such little retired Dutch valleys, found here and there, embosomed in the great state of New York, that population, manners, and customs remain fixed, while the great torrent of migration and improvement, which is making such incessant changes in other parts of this restless country, sweeps by them unobserved" (*SKB* 1060). The archaeological instincts that were brought to bear on New Amsterdam in the *History* are intensified in Irving's microcosmic depiction of Sleepy Hollow. Borrowing a technique from contemporary popular attractions such as the Grand Panorama, a miniature tableau on view in Manhattan that promised "a view of the city of New York and the adjacent country . . . twenty-five feet high and 136 feet in circumference," Irving lays the little town out before the reader in full.[17] But the "enbosomed calm" of Knickerbocker's panorama is menaced by outsiders, just as his Dutch colony was. The threat, in this case, comes in the form of Ichabod Crane, a Yankee schoolmaster with the "dilating powers of an Anaconda" who has been imported from Puritan Connecticut to instruct the children of Sleepy Hollow (*SKB* 1062). Ichabod was likely modeled on the teachers who first taught English in the upstate towns, many of whose residents clung to the Dutch language in their schools and churches well into the early nineteenth century.[18] The post of schoolteacher in the staunchly noncerebral society of the New Netherlands was a famously humble one: in his 1891 book *Historic Towns: New York*, Theodore Roosevelt notes that the first schoolteacher in the Dutch colony "failed ingloriously in his vocation, and then tried to eke out his scanty salary by taking in *washing*."[19] Similarly, Irving describes Ichabod Crane as having "various ways of rendering himself both useful and agreeable," including daycare; "he would sit with a child on one knee, and rock a cradle with his foot, for whole hours together" (*SKB* 1062). Nevertheless, Irving's—and Roosevelt's—schoolmasters are still strangers to the communities they teach, and when Ichabod dares to woo the local Dutch heiress, he is literally run out of town as punishment for his audacity.

Sleepy Hollow contains, at a glance, all the elements of Dutch New York that Knickerbocker celebrated in the *History*. Irving's cultural catalog begins at the home of the object of Ichabod's affections, a wealthy farmer's daughter named Katrina Van Tassel who lives in "one of those spacious farmhouses with high ridged, but lowly sloping roofs, built in the style handed down from the first Dutch settlers" (*SKB* 1066). Irving most likely modeled the little fiefdom of the Van Tassel family on the home of Luykas Van Alen, a Dutch farmhouse built in Kinderhook, New York, in 1737. The Van Alen House was not far from Kleinrood, the Peter Van Ness estate, which Irving had visited in early 1809 while he was writing the *History*.[20] Kleinrood itself would soon be better known to Americans as Lindenwald, the country home of the Dutch-descended U.S. president Martin Van Buren, who will be discussed at greater length later in this chapter. But Knickerbocker had expounded on the virtues of the cozy Dutch homestead elsewhere, and in "Legend" he focuses his energies instead on the Van Tassels' lavish hospitality, taking pains to accurately represent "the ample charms of a genuine Dutch country tea-table" to his readers:

> Such heaped up platters of cakes of various and almost indescribable kinds, known only to experienced Dutch housewives! There was the doughty doughnut, the tenderer oly koek, and the crisp ginger cakes and honey cakes, and the whole family of cakes. And then there were apple pies and peach pies and pumpkin pies; besides slices of ham and smoked beef; and moreover delectable dishes of preserved plums, and peaches, and pears, and quinces; not to mention broiled shad and roasted chickens, together with bowls of milk and cream, all mingled higgledy-piggledy, pretty much as I have enumerated them . . . I want breath and time to discuss this banquet as it deserves, and am too eager to get on with my story. (*SKB* 1076)

In this story, Knickerbocker's genealogical preoccupation enters the kitchen, and the reader is offered nothing less than a family tree of authentic Dutch cookery. The description is meant to provoke a nostalgic response from readers acquainted with the handiwork of "experienced Dutch housewives," or perhaps with Irving's first book and the Dutch dishes he swooned over therein. Interestingly, while the doughnut still has pride of place at Knickerbocker's ancestral table, the historian no longer claims that salmon could be found in the Hudson River. The Van Tassel menu, perhaps as a result of Mitchill's open letter of 1810, offers only "broiled shad."

It is little wonder, then, that the agent of upheaval in Sleepy Hollow is introduced to the narrative in the language of food: Ichabod Crane, "with his clothes bagging and fluttering about him," is first described as resembling "the genius of famine descending upon the earth" (*SKB* 1061). Though his name is less outlandish than those of the Yankee villains of Knickerbocker's *History*, such as Preserved Fish and Habbakuk Nutter, the skinny schoolmaster's Connecticut pedigree, rapacious appetite, and disregard for Dutch mores pose the same threats to the long-standing hierarchies and traditions of the region. Ichabod's hunger is absolutely at odds with the static life of Sleepy Hollow: he hopes not only to consume the "dainties"—be they cakes or Dutch heiresses—that he sees in Sleepy Hollow but also to liquidate them for future profit:

> As . . . he rolled his great green eyes over the fat meadow lands, the rich fields of wheat, of rye, of buckwheat, and Indian corn, and the orchards burdened with ruddy fruit, which surrounded the warm tenement of Van Tassel, his heart yearned after the damsel who was to inherit these domains, and his imagination expanded with the idea, how they might be readily turned into cash, and the money invested in immense tracts of wild land and shingle palaces in . . . Kentucky, Tennessee, or the Lord knows where. (*SKB* 1067)

It is a dream that would put an end to the "fixed" calm of the community and to the bountiful generosity of his hosts. Irving's enterprising schoolmaster is suggestive of the pioneers who settled the Western Reserve—those New Englanders with a similar lust for real estate who followed Moses Cleaveland to territory in northeast Ohio after the Revolutionary War. The fantasy of "cashing in" that Irving depicts here also anticipated the impact of the construction of the Erie, Delaware, and Hudson canals on the topography and economy of New York state. These new waterways would not only open up the Hudson River to commerce from the Great Lakes region, cutting through centuries of Dutch patroon-held property, but would also

connect the Hudson River to northern Pennsylvania. It was an inno-
vation that would irrevocably alter the Sleepy Hollow–like demography and traditions of New York towns such as Utica, Port Jervis,
and Monticello.[21]

But none of this land and none of these heirlooms are destined
to be Ichabod's. Spooked by a supposed encounter with the town's
resident ghost, a headless Hessian mercenary haunting the battle-
grounds of the Revolutionary War, he flees, leaving the Van Tassel
bounty behind. And yet expulsion from the "green, fertile nook" of
Sleepy Hollow proves to be the making of the Yankee teacher. After
leaving the community, Knickerbocker reports, he had subsequently
been "admitted to the bar, turned politician, electioneered, written
for the newspapers, and finally been made a justice of the Ten Pound
Court. . . . [F]or a country schoolmaster to be refused the hand of a
Dutch heiress, is a certain step to high preferment in the state" (*SKB*
1086–1088). What logic informs this ironic moral? If Ichabod must
quite literally be cast out in order to achieve what is commonly considered the American dream of economic advancement, what dream
does Sleepy Hollow represent? "High preferment in the state" does
not, by the historian's lights, confer the same glory as high birth in
the Dutch community, nor is the small claims court (what Irving calls
the "Ten Pound Court") and the petty, litigious society it represents
a particularly desirable fate. Sleepy Hollow epitomizes Knickerbocker's
affable, bourgeois values, and Ichabod's fate, finally, corroborates the
Dutchman's wondering refrain: why would anyone choose to leave
New York, of his own free will, for "Tennessee, or the Lord knows
where"? Many New Yorkers still ask this question, and their native
insularity can be traced back to Irving and to his xenophobic narrator, back on home turf once more.

"Knickerbocker is himself again," the *Ladies' Literary Cabinet*
cheered, reviewing "Rip Van Winkle" and greeting the historian's
return with palpable delight and relief.[22] Irving responded to this
welcome by offering more of the same: *Bracebridge Hall* and *Tales of
a Traveller* include several additional "found" Knickerbocker tales.
Like their predecessors, these accounts either double back to the New
Amsterdam settlement of the *History* or mine the drowsy, bewitched
hills of the Hudson River Valley for lore and local color. But these later

stories—of which "Dolph Heyliger" from *Bracebridge Hall* and "Wolfert Webber; or, Golden Dreams" from *Tales of a Traveller* most reward the reader—are, finally, less interesting as freestanding narratives than as linked opportunities for Knickerbocker to continue advancing the historian's argument for the central influence of Dutch culture on the development of the region. The stories also, of course, allowed Irving to maintain some control over his now-famous property and refine the salient, salable features of his popular portrait of Dutch—or "old"—New York.

The Knickerbocker stories in the *Sketch-Book* had spurred still more unabashed appropriation of Irving's narrator. A three-year-old racehorse named Knickerbocker ran a one-mile heat at the racetrack in Jamaica, Queens, and the Tammany Society drank the health of the Knickerbocker Yacht Club, "thrice triumphant over foreign competitors." Anonymous writers signed the historian's name to editorials castigating the city council for financial mismanagement ("For the Evening Post, $399,326 20/100, Lost or Mislaid"), as well as to penetrating reviews of the New York theater scene. His kinsmen were praised by writers pining for the "quiet Knickerbocker fashions" now "superseded by frivolity, noise and extravagance," and at the same time, the present-day "descendants of the Knickerbockers, the Stuyvesants, the Vad Schlaks and the Hoggenbottoms" were singled out for "sadly departing from the Dutch economy of their progenitors" in their "culinary competition and abdominal luxury." "How," one editorial admonished, "would the old square-sided, leather-pocketed Hollanders stare" at the accounts of New York feasts beginning with "green turtle soup" and ending with "plum-puddings . . . mince pies, tarts, puffs, jellies, blancmange, syllabubs, ice creams, custards, trifles, fruit, &c."?[23] That Irving's most recent depictions of the laden dinner tables of those same "Hollanders" showed little concern for "Dutch economy" did not seem to disturb the editorial writer's vision of colonial simplicity. This immunity from criticism may also have been a Knickerbocker side effect: although the ancestral "Stuyvesants" and "Hoggenbottoms" might have been misconstrued, they were rarely, at this time, ever maligned.

Irving's later stories respond to the backward-looking sentiment in contemporary Knickerbocker invocations—a sentiment that was increasingly prevalent in American literature and culture. The city's immensely prosperous economy was partly responsible: the further well-to-do New Yorkers moved from their burgher origins and the farther north they migrated, away from the storied streets of lower Manhattan, the more wistful they became for the symbols of the past. There was suddenly a market for nostalgia, and Irving's historian was poised to control it. However, unlike Rip Van Winkle or the "vegetating" Van Tassels, the next generation of Knickerbocker heroes cannot triumph over outsiders or stave off the new; they succeed in spite of change, and their financial and social positions are only truly secure after they have learned to adapt to the dominant status quo. In both "Dolph Heyliger" and "Wolfert Webber," that status quo is driven by the emerging rhythms and hierarchies of the English colony, when the founding families of Knickerbocker's "jolly, little old city of the Manhattoes" had been replaced by a new social order and a new city plan, one that was analogous to the metropolitan transformation Irving witnessed during his childhood in postwar New York. Self-preservation is the prevailing philosophy in "Dolph Heyliger," the story of an impoverished but optimistic Dutch New Yorker living in a colony that "groaned under the tyranny of the English governor, Lord Cornbury," who forbade the Dutch to preach or teach "in their language without his special license" (*BH* 304). Dolph, the story's hero, naturally defies this ban on Dutchness in his very person. He is part of Knickerbocker's stalwart, vanishing elite, "descended from the Vanderspiegels, of Amsterdam," and he has the "family arms painted and framed" to prove it (*BH* 304, 362). With this casual information, the blatantly partisan historian shows his hand: Dolph's heroism is predetermined by his pedigree, as much as by the courage he will later be called upon to show.

The plot of "Dolph Heyliger" allows Irving to revisit and amplify the themes that made Knickerbocker popular in the first place. On a quest for his fortune, the hero visits Albany, which Irving depicts as a wide-awake version of Sleepy Hollow—a utopian dream of Knickerbocker power, ruled by powerful but affable Dutch families who operate as if the English had never arrived. "In those days," Knickerbocker crows, "Albany was in all its glory, and inhabited almost exclusively by the descendants of the original Dutch settlers, for it has not as yet been discovered and colonized by the restless people of New England. Every thing was quiet and orderly; every thing was conducted calmly and leisurely; no hurry, no bustle, no struggling and scrambling for existence" (*BH* 349). Our hero is welcomed to this peaceable kingdom by Anthony Vander Heyden, a patroon whose home is the Van Tassel farm writ large: "Good old mahogany . . . embossed silver, and painted china," and, "as usual, the family coat of arms, painted and framed" are all in evidence, the recognizable litany of any Knickerbocker tour (*BH* 350). Dolph notes the evidence of Dutch hospitality as well ("the variety and abundance of good household luxuries bore testimony to . . . open-handed liberality") and succumbs, like his literary predecessors, to the charms of his host's blooming daughter, a "little Dutch divinity" who could be the twin of Katrina Van Tassel (*BH* 351). For Dolph, the Vander Heyden home is full of familiar signs; like Rip Van Winkle, he was born into the material culture and mythology that Knickerbocker is attempting to preserve. But for his narrator, this pristine society functions as a teaching tool: it is a living museum of the aesthetics and virtues of Dutch New York.

The Albany of the Vander Heydens may seem today like an irresistible dream of aristocratic privilege, but to Irving's nineteenth-century readers it would have been a reality, albeit a fading one. The Dutch families (such as the Van Rensselaers, whose manorial lands once covered almost all of present-day Albany and Rensselaer counties and even stretched into what is now Vermont) who descended from the original patroons of the New Netherlands had only had their jurisdiction over their patroonships abolished by the English in 1775, and many of them remained large landowners in the Hudson River Valley. The patroons of "Dolph Heyliger" are described respectfully, without the bawdy comedy of the *History*: instead of the "Van Wycks and the Van Dycks and the Ten Eycks . . . the Ten Breecheses and the Tough Breecheses" with their flapjacks and birds' nests, Knickerbocker hymns "the worthies of the place, the Van Rensselaers, the Gansevoorts, and the Rosebooms," and uses Albany, their protected milieu, to refine the concept of a "Knickerbocker" code of conduct for his readers and as a launch pad for his hero, an exemplar of that code (*HNY* 649–650; *BH* 351–352). After discovering, at the story's climax, a "great silver porringer . . . [marked] with armorial bearings" and filled with gold,

Dolph sets about to give this windfall the appearance of a trust fund. Like a clever speculator or canny social climber, he "gradually manage[s] to bring his property into use without exciting surprise and inquiry," and, trading on his old name and even older gold, he immediately assumes the role of New York City "patriarch," much as Rip Van Winkle became the oracle of Tarry-town (*BH* 361). Dolph becomes a "distinguished citizen . . . and a member . . . of the corporation" and ensures his complete integration into "public esteem" and high society by becoming a minor philanthropist and "great promoter of public institutions, such as beefsteak societies and catch-clubs":

> He presided at all public dinners, and was the first that introduced turtle from the West Indies. He improved the breed of race-horses and game-cocks, and was so great a patron of modest merit, that anyone who could sing a good song, or tell a good story, was sure to find a place at his table. . . . He was a member, too, of the corporation, made several laws for the protection of game and oysters, and bequeathed to the board a large silver punch-bowl, made out of the identical porringer before-mentioned, and which is in the possession of the corporation to this very day. (*BH* 362)

With this description of Dolph's middlebrow munificence, Irving puts his hero in the pantheon of New York's compulsive "founders" such as DeWitt Clinton or John Pintard, who helped to organized so many of the city's earliest benevolent and cultural institutions, including the Society for the Relief of Distressed Debtors (which would be renamed the Humane Society), the Society for the Promotion of Agriculture, Arts, and Manufactures, and the New York Free School Society, as well as the New-York Historical Society and the New York Academy of the Fine Arts. He also uncannily predicts the "beefsteak societies" and genealogical groups that would soon spring up in honor of the actual Dutch founders whom Knickerbocker claims, although these groups were more likely to serve canvasback duck and charlotte russe at their "public dinners" than they were to offer West Indian turtle or quantities of beef.[24] But this satirical prescription for City Fatherhood also contains a calculated wisdom: Dolph may not be particularly lofty, but he is shrewd and civic-minded, and his patronage "of modest merit" and proto-environmentalist "protection of game and oysters" may render him more valuable to the city than some of the planners and improvers whom Irving took as his youthful target.[25] Knickerbocker's fantasy of the triumphant Dutchman, one who finds wealth without sacrificing his virtue, and who returns to New York as a restorer of Dutch traditions, is also a subversion of the idea of "new money" in that growing city. Who knows how many heirloom silver punch bowls on display at the New-York Historical Society have similarly questionable provenance?

The marginalization of Dutch culture that was predicted in "Dolph Heyliger" has become a fact of life by "Wolfert Webber; or, Golden Dreams," a story that takes urban sprawl as the starting point for its cautionary message: "The city gradually spread its suburbs round their domain. Houses sprang up to interrupt their prospects. The rural lanes in the vicinity began to grow into the bustle and populousness of streets; in short, with all the habits of rustic life they began to find themselves inhabitants of cities" (*TT* 669). Contained within the "Money Diggers" section of *Tales of a Traveller*, Irving's third anthology of sketches, "Wolfert Webber" is Irving's most poignant real estate saga, a digressive, two-part account of the fortunes of a failed Dutch cabbage farmer in English New York. Much like the patriarch of Sleepy Hollow, Wolfert is a "worthy burgher" with a blooming, marriageable daughter. But Wolfert Webber's urban farm is failing, and despite his honorable descent from an original New Amsterdam settler "famous for introducing the cultivation of cabbages," he is sinking into poverty and obscurity (*TT* 669). There is no room, Knickerbocker reports with touching understatement, for a "rural potentate in the midst of a metropolis." The cost of living in New York "doubled and trebled; but he could not double and treble the magnitude of his cabbages" (*TT* 669–670). It was an economic threat that Irving's New York audience, familiar with their city's sprawl, could well understand. Nor is there room for the quiet Dutch culture of agrarian families such as the Webbers, Knickerbocker insists; those whose ancestors "reigned and vegetated over . . . paternal acres" in New York are now "hemmed in by streets and houses, which intercepted air and sunshine," making "vegetating" and vegetation equally impossible (*TT* 670). Total extinction, the narrative implies, is imminent: despite their "paternal acres" and dynastic rights, the Webber family has no clout in English New York, and no place in its hierarchy.

Once again, Irving exploits the popularity of his own narrator. In a meta-fictional twist, Wolfert Webber is inspired by Knickerbockerian success stories like that of "Dolph Heyliger" to seek his fortune in the form of buried treasure, the kind that "had never been found but by some descendant of the good old Dutch families" (*TT* 676). But Knickerbocker's genealogical mandate does not turn up a pot of gold for Wolfert, who is finally saved by his own clueless obsolescence. Sick with longing (and digging) for a hidden fortune, nearly dead with hopelessness and worry, the penurious farmer is thought to have breathed his last when he learns that his land is to be bought by the city at a high price to be "laid out in streets . . . [and] cut up into snug building lots" (*TT* 716). Far from being outraged at the prospect of losing his land, the farmer is instead instantly and satisfactorily restored to health: "Wolfert Webber was one of those many worthy Dutch burghers of the Manhattoes whose fortunes have been made, in a manner, in spite of themselves. Who have tenaciously held on to their hereditary acres, raising turnips and cabbages about the skirts of the city, hardly able to make both ends meet, until the corporation has cruelly driven streets through their abodes, and they have suddenly awakened out of a lethargy, and to their astonishment, found themselves rich men" (*TT* 716). Wolfert's surrender of his hereditary property and its transformation into "building lots . . . rented out to safe tenants" returns him to the old-money status that his ancestors enjoyed, even as it obliterates his ancestral profession—and one of the last Dutch farms within the New York city limits. At the time of Irving's writing, a similar negotiation had only recently taken place between New York's street surveyors and the descendants of Peter Stuyvesant. The gracious "bouwerie" of the last governor of New Amsterdam, with its famous gardens and fruit trees, had become one of the casualties of Randel's all-encompassing grid in 1806, when the heirs to the family estate ceded their land to the city, free of charge. Third Avenue would ultimately be driven through the property, sparing only the diagonal driveway to the estate, which is now known as Stuyvesant Street.[26] Wolfert, however, does not give his land away for free, and as a wealthy rentier he can now enact the Knickerbockerian fantasy of revenge and repatriation in the city of his birth: he enlarges (but does not tear down) the "ancient mansion of his forefathers," fills it with his daughter's "chubby progeny," and buys a "great gingerbread coloured carriage drawn by a pair of black Flanders mares," which he emblazons with a brand-new family crest: "a full blown cabbage . . . with the pithy motto ALLES KOPF: that is to say, ALL HEAD; meaning thereby that he had risen by sheer head work" (*TT* 717). Like Dolph's porringer–punch bowl, the carriage both prefigures and charmingly subverts the coming American mania for patrician symbols and "baronial" family crests. Both heroes are at once arriviste and "first family," a self-negating combination that only New York, the story implies, could possibly sustain.

Given the bias of their narrator, it is no surprise that the unwitting Dutch protagonists of Knickerbocker's stories invariably end up embodying the virtues and enjoying the privileges that the historian ascribed to his ancestors in the *History*. The same virtues and privileges, as we have begun to see, were starting to accrue to Knickerbocker himself as well, and to his creator. Irving's mock-historical repetitions of his own accounts significantly strengthened the market for all things Knickerbocker, which he had been first to instigate. The post–New Amsterdam stories that followed the *History* reinforced Irving's portrait of the cosmopolitan, tolerant, idiosyncratic landscape that was his vision of Knickerbocker New York. But the mischievous little Gotham of 1809 had grown apace into something more like Bedlam, and Irving soon left Knickerbocker in the care of a new generation of New Yorkers, who found him still nostalgic, still persuasive, and still very much in the urban fray.

NOSTALGIA AND NATIVISM

"In some thirty years every noble cliff will be a pier, and the whole island will be densely desecrated by buildings of brick, with portentous *facades* of brown-stone, or brown-*stonn*, as the Gothamites have it."[27] While a similarly gloomy forecast for New York sprawl could easily be made today (with the substitution of "glass and steel" for "brown-stone"), it was delivered in 1844 by a new visitor to the land of the Gothamites, the young writer Edgar Allan Poe. Poe, who had recently had his first critical success with *Tales of the Grotesque and Arabesque*, had been commissioned to write a series of dispatches from New York entitled "Doings of Gotham" for a Pennsylvanian paper called the *Columbia Spy*. It is impossible to say for certain that the *Spy*'s choice of correspondent was meant as a mordant comment on the physical transformation of the Empire City, but the author of "Murders in the Rue Morgue" certainly found fertile ground for his dark musings in New York. The fretful letters that Poe sent from Manhattan did not flatter the city or its inhabitants: he found the streets "insufferably dirty" and dismissed the architecture as a collection of "monstrosities" representing "taste in its dying agonies." With barely concealed envy he laments the collective "infatuation" of New York's reading public with Charles Dickens, who had made a triumphant lecture tour of the United States just two years earlier.[28] Poe, who was born the year that Washington Irving first published the *History*, does not see fit to mention that Irving had been sent as the American ambassador of letters to greet Dickens when he arrived in Baltimore in 1842 (whereupon the two literary giants had shared an "enormous mint julep" sent by an admirer, a cocktail so big that they had to sip at it, each with his own straw).[29] When Poe is not sulking, however, his critical distance on Manhattan as it approached midcentury enables him to see, as if from one of those "noble cliffs," the island in full and to contrast the breakneck pace of its "dense" development with the pastoral northern regions that had yet to become casualties of the Randel street grid: "Some portions of [New York's] interior have an air of rocky sterility which may impress some imaginations as simply *dreary*—to me it conveys the sublime. Trees are few; but some of the shrubbery is exceedingly picturesque. Not less so are the prevalent shanties of the Irish squatters."[30] Poe's depiction of the city's wild reaches is today among the remaining evidence New Yorkers have that such prairie-like tracts ever existed on their island, before the onslaught of those predicted "portentous *facades*."

What *was* happening to New York? Perhaps a better question is: what wasn't? By the advent of the Civil War, New York had again been scorched (the Great Fire of 1835 destroyed 674 buildings in lower

Manhattan, and a smaller fire in 1845 incinerated 300 properties) and bankrupted (by the financial panics of 1837 and 1857, which depressed both the local and national economies) and had suffered several epidemics of cholera and yellow fever. At the same time these disasters were taking place, the city was also distinguished by a number of major municipal innovations that further cemented New York's reputation as America's most technologically advanced urban center, regardless of Poe's detractions. These advancements included gas for Manhattan's streetlamps (beginning in 1823), clean water from the Croton Aqueduct (from 1842), and the beginnings of a citywide sewer system. But the real transformation was taking place at street level, not below: the number of people living in the city was growing at an astonishing rate. From the 1830s through the 1870s, New York was quite literally overtaken by the political, social, and geographical ramifications of immigration. The population of New York County more than tripled between 1800 and 1830 (from 60,515 to 202,589), and in 1855 the state census would report that nearly half of the city's 629,904 residents were foreign-born.[31] This boom strained New York's municipal resources and revealed the prejudices of many of the city's self-proclaimed "natives." The potato famine of 1845 would bring nearly one million Irish to New York's shores, and by 1855 more than a quarter of all New Yorkers would list Ireland as their country of birth on the census.[32] Even before this influx, the steady arrival of white European immigrants and of freed and runaway slaves had already had an impact on living conditions, as Poe had noticed in his letter to the *Spy*.[33] As early as 1833, the impoverished, racially diverse Five Points and Lispenard Meadows neighborhoods, plagued by overcrowding, flooding, and disease, had already been the targets of several institutional "slum clearance" campaigns, but with little success, and by the time of the famine, New York's tenements were international tourist attractions, "exposed" and bewailed in countless sermons, pamphlets, sentimental novels, and penny dreadfuls.[34] The fact that so many of the poorer immigrants were also Roman Catholics only compounded the horror and the fascination of their wealthier, Protestant neighbors.

The seismic shifts in New York's demography coincided with a number of significant nationwide movements, including the Second

Great Awakening, a revival of evangelical Protestantism that emphasized civic reform and social accountability; the abolitionist movement
and the Underground Railroad; and the beginnings of anti-immigrant,
or "nativist," and anti-Catholic feeling and legislation, particularly in
the arena of American public schools.[35] The combination set the melt-
ing pot aboil. From the attacks on abolitionists and African Americans
that spanned four days in July of 1834 to the Astor Place Riot of 1849
to the 1857 Police Riots, Bowery Boys, Dead Rabbits, and Kleindeutschland brawls to the three-day-long Draft Riots of 1863, an alarming
continuum of public violence can be mapped across antebellum New
York. These clashes primarily involved the poorest and the newest
New Yorkers, but they revealed religious and ethnic fissures that de-
stabilized the entire city. Irish and African American workers, native
and foreign-born populations, Protestants and Catholics, the wealthy
and the destitute—all fought their battles in the streets, in the newspapers, and at City Hall. These encounters—and the casualties they
engendered—gave new and painful meaning to Poe's prophecy of the
city's "dense desecration."

Regardless of whether New Yorkers described their city's upheav-
als as "desecration" or as progress, though, one thing was certain:
they claimed Diedrich Knickerbocker for their mascot and muse, as
never before. Faced with unprecedented numbers of newcomers and
"outsiders," Anglo-Saxon city dwellers created collective identities:
they could be abolitionist Brooklynites or Copperhead Catholics, but
they were increasingly also Knickerbockers. These new readers were
antebellum New Yorkers who may not have had any significant connection to the Dutch settlement and perhaps, like Poe, had no memory of the *History*'s first publication. Nevertheless, many now turned
to the navigable contours of Knickerbocker's "ancient city of the
Manhattoes" for reassurance that their own mercurial Manhattan was
built on something more lasting than rent and credit: by the 1840s,
the city was richer than ever before. Irving was not the only writer
in that era to romanticize the "ancient city" of the Dutch. A cottage
industry of New York histories emerged at this time, including the
serial publication of David Valentine's *Manuals of the Corporation of
the City of New York*, first published in 1841 to "trace the progress of
the city of New York . . . from a wilderness condition" to the present

day with salvaged founding documents, maps, and lithographs in each edition, as well as Edmund O'Callaghan's two-volume *History of New Netherland; or, New York Under the Dutch*, published from 1846 to 1848.[36] As Edward Widmer has noted, nineteenth-century Americans in general looked to seventeenth-century Holland as a model, finding in that country's struggle for political independence and commercial dominance a "miniature simulacrum" of the newly booming United States.[37] But Irving's breezy fictions—less an imitation than a delightful, impossible ideal—were the ones New Yorkers revived as sacred texts, to be consulted when they grew alarmed, exhilarated, or just confused by the pace and politics of Manhattan. And it was his Knickerbocker (rather than James Fenimore Cooper's Natty Bumppo, for example) whom they chose to serve as the city's prophetic bard.

The second wave of popularity for Irving's stories installed his narrator in the American imagination, seemingly for all time. As Irving himself had noted in 1848, one proof of this permanency was that "Knickerbocker" had become that most ephemeral and insidious of entities: a brand. The diverse packaging of Knickerbocker affords an unusual perspective on the rise of mass production and marketing in the United States. In addition to the New York–area ice, steamboat, and horsecar companies that Irving mentioned in his *Apology*, the historian lent his name to still further Knickerbocker Bakeries (this time on Ann Street in lower Manhattan), the Knickerbocker Mills (a spice company incorporated in New York in 1842), and the Knickerbocker style of men's hat, sold as far away as Macon, Georgia (where it was advertised by Belden and Company's Wholesale and Retail Hat and Cap Emporium as a "Pearl Sporting Hat"). Bartenders also took Knickerbocker as their inspiration and, building on the historian's suggestion that his family name could be parsed as "*Knicker*, to shake, and *Beker*, a goblet, indicating thereby that they were sturdy toss pots of yore," created several potent Knickerbocker cocktails (including the nineteenth-century ancestor of Trader Vic's signature drink, the mai tai).[38] Although few of the merchants who sold "Knickerbocker" made an explicit connection to Irving's book, his narrator's name was clearly intended to lend an aura of Empire City sophistication to their products.

Manhattan's growing creative class also adopted Knickerbocker, invoking not only the historian's name but also his narrative voice, and occasionally even his person, to give symbolic resonance and hoped-for instant credibility to literary productions of varying quality. It is not difficult to understand why white middle- and upper-class New Yorkers seized upon Knickerbocker and the Dutch colony as a marketable source of inspiration and solace during these complicated decades. In Irving's version, Broadway is not the tidal "human ocean" that the delighted writer Lydia Maria Child saw in 1844 but a peaceable country road.[39] Knickerbocker's idealized New Amsterdammers never seemed to contend with increasing populations of émigrés, or witness the horrors of epidemics and overcrowding, or observe the obliterating march of progress through colonial homesteads and eighteenth-century neighborhoods. How tempting, then, for New Yorkers to invoke those unruffled, pipe-smoking forebears, and their safe, monolithic city, rather than come to terms with their own heterogeneous and harried urban reality. Unfortunately, most of these literary homages to Knickerbocker and his genre fall quite wide of the mark. The self-proclaimed inheritors to Irving's outspoken historian rarely do justice to his clear-eyed, satirical engagement with the dangers that attend progress: the swindling and extermination of the native population, for example, or the many instances of greed and mismanagement among the Dutch. Instead, they conjure up a rose-tinted colonial confection, swapping Knickerbocker's blunt candor in favor of gentle sentiment.

The most widely known appropriation of Knickerbocker in Irving's lifetime was one that took the historian as logo, brand, and muse, with the explicit goal of capturing both the author's cultural capital and his loyal audience, now that Irving himself had moved from "sketches" to weightier subjects, such as the American West (about which he wrote *A Tour on the Prairies*, *The Adventures of Captain Bonneville*, and, most famously, *Astoria*, an account of his travels with John Jacob Astor). The author's temporary departure from his own Dutch genre created an opportunity for other writers, and in 1833, nine years after "Wolfert Webber," Irving's friend Charles Fenno Hoffman founded the *Knickerbacker Magazine*, a New York–based literary monthly. The first issue of the *Knickerbacker* wasted no time in asserting its literary pedigree: against a Hudson River backdrop, the editor conjures the ghost of Diedrich Knickerbocker out of a cloud of pipe smoke and explains to him (and to the presumed readership) why his name has been taken in vain—and misspelled, at that:

> After stating to the sage that he had misconceived our design, in thinking we meditated anything so presumptuous as supplying his place, as the quondam guardian of his favorite city, and that we had only assumed his name as good catholics when they take the cowl sometimes adopt that of their tutelar saint . . . [he] readily [forgave] us the liberty taken with his name, in consideration of our having restored it to its ancient spelling, a little matter, but which in fact tickled him mightily.[40]

In fact, the *Knickerbacker Magazine* meant not to supplant its eponymous "guardian" but to link his image and the Knickerbocker iconography to an incipient literary patriotism. The editorial mission statement asserts that the magazine plans to harness the "unsuspected powers" of America's "cultivated classes," the better to overcome the national infatuation with "all the absurd trash of driveling sentimentality and pseudo-fashion . . . from the London press."[41] With Diedrich Knickerbocker as its straw "patriarch," the magazine hoped to share in Irving's literary popularity, thereby guaranteeing itself a place in the parlors of the "cultivated classes" (both in America and abroad) that already adored the Dutch historian. This anticipation of commercial success by proxy was the likely motivation behind the decision of the second editor, Lewis Gaylord Clark, to change the spelling of the journal's name to *Knickerbocker* six months later, for a more explicit—if less "authentic"—association with Irving and his scribe.[42]

Although the *Knickerbocker Magazine* was popular during the years of its publication (it was discontinued in 1859), it is remembered today—if at all—only as the midwife to more celebrated magazines of midcentury New York such as the *United States Magazine and Democratic Review*. These opinionated, experimental publications were the incubator for literary nationalism, or what Walt Whitman would dub "home literature."[43] In contrast, under the conservative direction of Clark, a staunch Whig, the *Knickerbocker* did not, in fact, "harness

the unsuspecting powers" of new American voices but instead became a kind of Irving factory, churning out hackneyed homages to
his vivid Hudson River Valley tales. The *Knickerbocker*'s pieces inevitably shied away from the gritty realities of metropolitan living
and were purposefully blind to the changes that technology and population growth had made to the region that was universally understood to be Knickerbocker turf. In plagiarizing pastiches such as "The
Legend of Whooping Hollow," "A Dutchman 'Done,'" and "Reminiscences in the Little Church at Lake George," no New Yorker has
to learn to cope with the demands of the city of the perpetually busy
or struggles, as the suburbs overtake the colonial pastures, to maintain a meaningful connection to the ancestral past. Instead, every 1830s
farmer is still euphemized as a "jovial old blade of the true Dutch
school," while every contemporary housewife is a "goede vrouw."[44]
Even the highly modern and innovative railroad, its tracks newly laid
along the shores of the Hudson River, becomes a "snorting steam-
horse" in the hands of the *Knickerbocker*, as it chugs "past golden
'Sunnyside,' disturbing not, let us hope, the inmates of that nest of
genius and refinement."[45] The magazine's trademark (and, for a time,
highly lucrative) adherence to the blandest and most "refined" aspects
of Irving's oeuvre would result in some of its more prominent contributors being grouped together, post facto, as the "Knickerbocker
School" of literature. The nickname is something of a misnomer,
for it links the writers to the magazine and not to the exceptionalist
Dutch historian for whom the magazine was named. Furthermore,
the most celebrated writers in the group, which included poets William Cullen Bryant and Fitz-Greene Halleck and essayist Nathaniel
Parker Willis, are best known today, if at all, for their independent
work, such as Bryant's "Thanatopsis."[46] And yet, as mediocre as the
Knickerbocker Magazine may have proved to be, it is a useful early
measure of the extent to which Irving's Dutch stories had become,
and would continue to be, a source of valuable social and civic identification in the antebellum city. The beginnings of a genre of "old
New York" stories, poems and sketches, like those to be found in the
Knickerbocker, is further evidence of a reading public hungry for
palliative fictions and escapes from a troubling reality. Sometimes
the exigencies of this reality warranted outright flight, as in the poem

"Sunrise at New-York, in 1673," published by the magazine in the aftermath of the cholera outbreak of 1832, which killed more than 3,500 of the city's poorest residents. The poet, known as Mrs. Sigourney, has no truck with the tragedies of present-day Manhattan, preferring to offer readers a rapturous remembrance of wealthier, healthier ancestors:

> Oh, had those ancient dames of high renown
> The Knickerbockers and the Rapaeljes
> With high-heel'd shoe, and ample, tenfold-gown,
> Green worsted hose, with clocks of crimson rays,
> Had they, through time's dim vista stretch'd their gaze,
> Spying their daughters fair in these degenerate days . . . [47]

This ode to the modest, uncomplicated "dames" of the "Knickerbockers and the Rapaeljes" rejects the "degenerate" modern metropolis, with its heterogeneous population and undiscriminating epidemics, in favor of a safe, vague vision of a bygone New York, where the "ancient" names mattered. It was an attempt at literary time travel that would be tried with greater success by a number of other writers throughout the nineteenth century, as the American appetite for nostalgia grew and grew. And while credit must be given to the *Knickerbocker* for being the first to formally connect the Dutch historian to the genre he helped create, in the attempt to imitate what Michael Warner calls Irving's "language of the sublime," the magazine proved to be a poor ventriloquist.[48]

Irving himself was on the *Knickerbocker*'s payroll, but his contributions did surprisingly little to improve its quality. It wasn't for lack of opportunities: the magazine gave the author several platforms from which to speak. Sometimes he wrote as "Washington Irving," the universally revered elder statesman enshrined at Sunnyside, on serious matters such as the pitfalls of international copyright law, under which he had been one of the first American writers to suffer. As Geoffrey Crayon and under a number of other (often Dutch) pseudonyms, he contributed arch and repetitive vignettes to the magazine, sketches that trod the same ground as his early work but blunted their characteristic satire. These offerings strike the reader as flat and inconsequential, and for good reason: Irving was less interested in the quality of these pieces than he was in being paid for them, and he reportedly allowed his nephew and amanuensis, Pierre M. Irving, to make final revisions to these submissions as he saw fit.[49] Among the Dutch noms de plume that Irving tried on for the *Knickerbocker* was Roloff Van Ripper, the narrator of a story entitled "Conspiracy of the Cocked Hats." The message of the "Conspiracy" suggests that Irving may have understood the anti-immigrant uses to which his Knickerbocker material could—and soon would—easily be put, as Van Ripper reveals the supposed existence of "a confederacy among the Dutch families [of New York], by dint of diligent and exclusive intermarriage, to keep the race pure, and to multiply." Van Ripper finds evidence for this conspiracy in "the establishment . . . of secret, or rather mysterious associations" such as the Society of Saint Nicholas, "composed of the genuine sons of the Nederlanders, with the ostensible object of keeping up the memory of old ties and customs, but with the real object of promoting the views of this dark and mighty plot and extending its ramifications throughout the land." After dropping this bombshell, the narrator concludes:

> I have, thus, I trust, . . . opened your eyes to some of the grand moral, poetical, and political phenomena with which you are surrounded. You will now be able to read the signs of the times. You will now understand what is meant by those "Knickerbocker Halls" and "Knickerbocker Hotels," and "Knickerbocker Lunches" that are daily springing up in our city. . . . You will see in them so many clouds before a storm; so many mysterious but sublime intimations of the gathering vengeance of a great though oppressed people.[50]

What *is* meant by "those 'Knickerbocker Halls' and 'Knickerbocker Hotels'"? It is possible that Irving had the newly instituted Knickerbocker Masonic Lodge in mind when he described the Dutch "conspiracy": the Manhattan branch had formed just seven months prior to the publication of his piece. But ultimately, for Irving, the answer was neither "moral, poetical," nor "political" but frankly commercial. Van Ripper's dark forebodings were nothing more than advance publicity for Irving's own Knickerbocker works, soon to be newly available for sale as part of a complete set of revised editions that he was in the process of preparing for George P. Putnam & Sons.

Putnam's revised editions would bring the *History of New-York* back into print after a six-year hiatus, and therefore Irving took this opportunity to reinforce his primal connection to the Dutch founding myths that had so quickly escaped their creator in 1809. This included appending the "Author's Apology" that has previously been discussed, diluting the political satire of his original (which had become less topical post-Jefferson), and cutting some of his bawdier humor in favor of those details of quaint Dutch tradition that had since become the hallmarks of the Knickerbocker "brand." Knickerbocker's treatment of Saint Nicholas is the most obvious example of these canny editorial changes, which few today would call improvements, although the 1848 public clearly disagreed: Putnam's had to issue a second printing of the revised *History* after only six weeks.[51] In the 1809 edition, he is simply New Amsterdam's "tutelar saint," guiding the colonists to choose Manhattan, a site "with all the singular inconveniences and aquatic obstacles necessary for the foundation of a great Dutch city"; by 1848, Saint Nicholas has acquired more of the recognizable trappings of the "jolly elf" that would be familiar to his second generation of readers from Clement Clarke Moore's famous poem, *A Visit from Saint Nicholas* (first published anonymously in 1823). Now Irving's saint, like Moore's, "[lays] a finger beside his nose" and smokes a meditative pipe before riding "over the tops of the trees in that selfsame wagon wherein he brings his yearly presents to children" (*HNY* 454, 436; *RHNY* 109).[52] Why did Irving modify the book that made him famous? Perhaps he was paying homage to the recent work of his friend and former collaborator James Kirke Paulding, who had published a book of stories entitled *The Book of Saint Nicholas* in 1836. Or it may have been that in his late-in-life role as the "father" of American literature, the author wished to extend an olive branch to those prominent Dutch New Yorkers (such as the writer Giulian Crommelin Verplanck) who had taken offense at his youthful attempt to restore their jolly ancestors to the public eye. After all, Irving was now a founding member of the Saint Nicholas Society, and perhaps he felt obliged to present a dignified Dutch patron saint and a less scatological Dutch narrator. Irving had been among those who signed the constitution of this private, Anglo-Saxon, by-invitation-only association of men in 1835, a group whose membership was drawn exclusively from New Yorkers whose families had resided in the city prior to 1785 (the year New York became the capital of the new republic). Irving, the son of Scottish and English immigrants, barely qualified, but the society had already furnished sufficient proof of its mandate "to preserve knowledge of the history and customs of New York City's Dutch forebears" by electing a direct descendant of Peter Stuyvesant as its first president, and it was not going to relinquish its muse over a technicality.[53] The Saint Nicholas Society, which quickly spawned a sibling society for the Dutch-descended families of Brooklyn, walked the same line between homage and parody as Irving's *History*: it became famous for its elaborate Astor House dinners, held each year on December 6, Saint Nicholas Day. The menus from these feasts read today like the fever dream of a culinary historian, featuring everything from authentically Dutch dishes rendered with Dutch orthography, such as "Kole Slau," "Oly Kooks," and "Kookies," to nineteenth-century riffs on colonial fare, including "Squirrel Pie, Knickerbocker style" and "East River Oysters, Baked in the Shell."[54] This was the historian's mouth-watering New Amsterdam tea table all over again—proof that no matter how much Irving tried to control and sanitize his founding narrative, aspects of it would continue to be gleefully reinterpreted by latter-day "Hollanders" trying to find their own place at the Knickerbocker feast.

At the same time Irving was returning to the Dutch themes that had made him a celebrity, the country's first native-born New Yorker entered the White House: the "Flying Dutchman," President Martin Van Buren. Raised a Dutch speaker in Kinderhook, New York, Van Buren could have been a stock character in the Irving repertoire, and, in fact, he was a friend of the author and a frequent visitor to Sunnyside. But the "Flying Dutchman" wasn't a success in Washington: he occupied the White House for one term only—from 1837 to 1841—before returning to Lindenwald, his country estate (formerly the Peter Van Ness house) in Kinderhook.[55] Although it is generally agreed that his mismanagement of the Panic of 1837 was the chief reason for his political downfall, Van Buren was also widely criticized by Whigs for his extravagant presidential tastes. One famous attack, by

Pennsylvania congressman Charles Ogle, was dubbed the "Golden Spoon Oration" because it lampooned, in comically itemized fashion, the thousands of dollars Van Buren spent to decorate the White House and to entertain heads of state:

> Mr. Chairman, these three bills for table glass make, together, the clever sum of $2,596.50, an amount, I should suppose, sufficiently large to purchase the most democratic set of table glass in America. What, sir, will the honest locofoco say to Mr. Van Buren for spending the People's cash in 'FOREIGN FANNY KEMBLE GREEN FINGER CUPS,' in which to wash his pretty tapering, soft, white, lily fingers, after dining on *fricandeau de veau* and *omelette souffle*?[56]

The ideological, as well as gustatory, distance between "Squirrel Pie, Knickerbocker style" and "*fricandeau de veau*" should not be ignored. The congressman's outrage at Van Buren's lavish spending and "foreign" (read: European) tastes may be intensified by feelings of betrayal: surely this was not the homespun Dutch hospitality the nation had expected from a native son of Kinderhook, not to mention the handpicked successor to that paragon of rustic simplicity, Andrew Jackson? In fact, Van Buren, who was raised in reduced circumstances, was following the example set by Irving's hero Wolfert Webber, using his newfound fortune (in this case, taxpayer dollars instead of New York real estate) to achieve a nineteenth-century level of status and refinement. But no reporter dubbed Van Buren a Knickerbocker, and Irving's own reaction to the public critique of Van Buren may only be guessed at: when the president invited him to serve in his cabinet as the secretary of the navy, Irving declined, citing his fragile health.[57] The "Flying Dutchman" was not to become a part of the Knickerbocker brand.

Irving's final contribution to the Knickerbocker canon was *Wolfert's Roost*, a collection of miscellaneous writings published in 1855. The book brought Diedrich Knickerbocker full circle and settled the once-missing historian at a fictional homestead called the Roost, which had been the original name of the farmhouse Irving had enlarged and christened Sunnyside. The author repackaged the caricature that was now familiar to readers from countless portraits, appropriations, and advertisements, as well as from the *History*, by this time just shy of fifty years old. "Mementos of the sojourn of Diedrich Knickerbocker are still cherished at the Roost," Irving wrote, in a curious superimposition of narrator upon author, persona upon persona. "His elbow-chair and antique writing-desk maintain their place in the room he occupied, and his old cocked-hat still hangs on a peg against the wall."[58] Irving's new book of recycled sketches, this narrative implies, should also be cherished, as a further "memento" of the Dutch historian. But even as Irving took one final advantage of the market he created, he was still trying to control it. In one example, frustrated by the "vile caricature" of his historian published in an earlier edition that was, to his horror, subsequently "copied on all the Knickerbocker Omnibuses Steam boats &c. &c.," in the city, the author asked British illustrator Charles R. Leslie to submit a "pen or pencil sketch of Diedrich" that could be used for the frontispiece of the revised edition.[59] The illustrator duly sent G. P. Putnam & Sons "a pen sketch," begging pardon for its "slightness," but the publisher did not ultimately use Irving's preferred drawing. Even the historian's creator, it seemed, could not check the proliferation of his image and his name.

When Irving died in 1859, the newspapers reported that more than a thousand people waited outside Christ Church, the Episcopal parish in Tarrytown where he had served as vestry warden, hoping for the chance to pay their last respects to the first American literary celebrity. Surprisingly, the public statements of mourning focused almost exclusively on the milder repertory of Irving's Sunnyside years, or what Henry Wadsworth Longfellow would later characterize as "the bright Indian Summer of his fame" in his poem "In the Churchyard at Tarrytown."[60] Even the mayor of New York spoke only about his patriotic writings on Columbus and Washington, rather than the *History of New York*, "Rip," or "The Legend of Sleepy Hollow," prescribing "the genial products" of Irving's "pure and graceful pen" as "solace to the sick and weary." It mattered little that the mayor recast the writer as a literary Florence Nightingale, or that Longfellow, in his elegy, demoted him to the rank of "gentle humorist." After Irving's death, countless pilgrims still flocked to Sunnyside, only now they also stopped to pay their respects at Sleepy Hollow Cemetery, where he was buried. The marble headstone that marked the author's grave was so disfigured by visitors who had chipped away souvenir shards that it had to be replaced twice within fifty years.[61] These postmortem remembrances were not carved in memory of the "gentle" biographer of Columbus, John Jacob Astor, or other historical figures but in honor of the historian that Irving himself created, Diedrich Knickerbocker. In a city that contained more stories than the *Arabian Nights*, a fictional Dutchman was its first and best Scheherazade.

CHAPTER 3

FASHIONING A KNICKERBOCRACY

"We Want a National Name"

In the old world we are called a fast people, and the history of no spot in our vast confederacy is more impressed with the change that seems a normal condition of our republican life, than in this city. Its original landmarks are scarcely to be recognized; its population is utterly transformed; its resources indefinitely enlarged; nay, to the backward and loving gaze of a venerable Knickerbocker, its individuality is almost lost.[1]

The self-proclaimed "venerable Knickerbocker" who wrote this lament in 1858 was Dr. John Wakefield Francis, the founder of Rutgers Medical College and past president of the New York Academy of Medicine. From his vantage point, the "individuality" of what he dubbed Old New York must indeed have seemed on the brink of extinction, a belief that could only have been corroborated by the death of Washington Irving the following year. But the paleolithic perspective on the city's "original landmarks" shared by those born in the eighteenth century had begun to vanish with their passing. The territory of Old New York was soon thickly settled by chroniclers who derived political and social capital from the city's quicksilver history and found business opportunities in its self-lacerating nostalgia. The "fast people" of Gotham may not yet have given much thought to their landmarks, but they made a landmark out of Knickerbocker. With help from the eternal Dutchman, New York's past would be branded rather than buried.

One of the most historically significant Knickerbocker brands of the midcentury was that of Knickerbocker Baseball, the first organized baseball team in the United States. The New York club began in 1845 as an informal, privately run association of amateurs who played the game as it had been devised six years earlier by Abner Doubleday in Cooperstown, New York. Although the Knickerbockers lost their first official match, played at the Elysian Fields in Hoboken against the "New York Club," they went on to have a profound effect on the national pastime as it is played today. The club was founded by Alexander Joy Cartwright Jr., a firefighter who supposedly named his team in honor of the Knickerbocker Engine Company, of which he was a member. Cartwright was the first manager to codify the rules of modern baseball and to require players to wear a uniform to every game. The uniform of the Knickerbockers was a far cry from the "old black coat and cocked hat" of their namesake historian—instead, players wore white flannel shirts, blue trousers, and straw boaters, attire befitting their status as "gentlemen amateurs."[2] The Knickerbockers grew to a membership that was capped at forty players (each of whom paid annual dues of five dollars), they inspired the founding of rival teams, including the New York Mutuals, the Brooklyn Charter Oaks, and the Eclectics, and they organized baseball's first-ever conventions, in 1857 and 1858. The team was famous for its hospitable rituals: Knickerbockers serenaded their opponents before matches and hosted them for convivial postgame dinners. But the genteel decorum of the team was also its undoing. Unlike their stadium descendants today, the players refused to professionalize or to charge admission for games when pressured to do so, and their unwillingness to trade their amateur status for "pro" is often given as the reason for their disbanding in the 1870s. The sport had, for the foreseeable future, lost its Knickerbocker associations.

Four years after the team was founded, however, George G. Foster's *New York in Slices, by an Experienced Carver* presented Irving's historian as a different kind of "gentleman amateur." Foster's book and its sequels, *New York by Gaslight* (1850) and *New York Naked* (1854), were among the earliest examples of the "gaslight" genre in American literature, a form that built on the success of the penny dreadful, which was then enjoying tremendous popularity in Victorian England.

Gaslight books, like their descendant the dime novel, offered pruri-ent, purportedly "true" glimpses into the "sunshine and shadow" of a particular place, usually a city considered by the reading public to be equal parts charming and corrupt. The form was originated by a French socialist writer named Eugène Sue, whose series *The Myster-ies of Paris* was first published in English in the United States in 1843. Unsurprisingly, the primary focus of Foster's New York guides is the alluringly scandal-ridden precincts of the city best known to the vice squad, including the Five Points region and other dark and danger-ous corners: as we have already seen, more than a century before the publication of Herbert Asbury's *Gangs of New York*, these regions were attractions for thrill-seeking residents and tourists alike.

This is not to suggest that Foster neglects to comment on the customs and revels of those New Yorkers who made their homes on cleaner streets. His books devote equal time to lambasting the city's "addle-pated young 'aristocrats,' . . . merchant princes" and "fat wives of lean financiers."[3] By offering these behind-the-scenes glimpses of New York "society," the author was capitalizing on an emerging trend. New Yorkers (and others) wanted to know "who was whom" and who had what; they wanted, as Irving's real estate stories had shown, to be ranked and sorted, and to know where they stood in what was increasingly being known as the "Snobbish Ten Thousand" who made up the city's top social echelon. Just a year before, the *New York Sun* had issued a helpful pamphlet by Moses Yale Beach entitled *Wealth and Wealthy Citizens of New York City: comprising an alpha-betical arrangement of persons estimated to be worth $100,000 and up-wards, with the sums appended to each name. Being useful to Banks, Merchants, and others.* Beach's document of full disclosure may not have been the first of its kind in New York, but it certainly can be cred-ited with inspiring more than a century's worth of imitators, from the *Social Register* to the *Forbes* 400. It is surprising to see the ex-tent to which *Wealth and Wealthy Citizens* resembles a Knickerbocker family tree, with Dutch-descended families such as the Beekmans, Brevoorts, Joneses, Roosevelts, Schermerhorns, Stuyvesants, and Van Nests prominently listed. Affluent New Yorkers of English descent are also represented, including Clement Clarke Moore, the Chelsea landowner who was the author of *A Visit from Saint Nicholas*, and the diarist Philip Hone. The wealthiest man on the *Sun*'s list, however, had no distinguished ancestral connections, European title, or venerable New York associations. He was John Jacob Astor, a German immigrant and fur trader turned real estate mogul whose fortune the *Sun* underestimated in 1842 at ten million dollars. Even more than the fact of his stunning wealth, his presence at the top of this list was a harbinger of the shifting economic and social hierarchies of New York City and of the approaching Gilded Age that would set the Ten Thousand on its ear.[4]

It is interesting to read George Foster's accounts of "Knickerbocker" New York in the context of the *Sun*'s list. In a direct contradiction of the historian's own assertions about his simple, cabbage-tending ancestors, the gaslight books employ "Knickerbocker" as a synonym for "patrician" and shorthand for "elite and white." Inside a literary salon, for example, Foster finds "a handsome, intellectual-looking young man, evidently of the old aristocratic Knickerbocker blood," a hint to the reader that Dutch-descended New Yorkers, as indicated by the list in the *Sun*, still had the resources (at least the land, if not the liquidity) at midcentury to be considered "aristocratic" by the pulp press. In another book, Foster remarks with evident pleasure that "New York is undoubtedly the greatest place for dancing in all Anglo-Saxondom," because "nowhere else . . . has the light-toed goddess so many and such enthusiastic worshippers as in this staid old Dutch settlement of Gotham. There seems to be something in the intermixture of Puritan and Knickerbocker blood which gives peculiar activity to the heels and elasticity to the toes."[5]

A different kind of New York exceptionalism is at play in this argument, and the insistent repetition of "Knickerbocker blood" and admiring treatment of upper-middle-class city dwellers of English and Dutch descent may be contrasted with Foster's sneering description, in *New York by Gas-Light*, of "the descendants of Israel . . . as celebrated for fecundity as cats or Irish women," who live in the Five Points slums.[6] The New York of slum squalor and ethnic ghettos and the one Foster describes as the "staid Dutch settlement of Gotham" hardly seem to be the same city.

Foster's bigoted language reveals how effortlessly Irving's term could be linked to the idea of acceptable or authentic "stock" or "blood" and how the Dutch historian could be—and was—invoked to fuel the ever-increasing American preoccupation with ethnicity and race. Terms such as "blood" were by no means unique to Foster, or to the gaslight genre: despite its vaunted cosmopolitanism, nineteenth-century New York proved to be a critical hub for nativist sentiment in the decades leading up to the Civil War. In addition to the inter-racial and interethnic riots previously discussed, the city was the site of Samuel F. B. Morse's unsuccessful run for mayor on a nativist plat-form in 1836, and the virulent and powerful Know-Nothing Party had its beginnings there in the secret society known as the Order of the Star Spangled Banner. The Know-Nothings ran state and local cam-paigns as morality crusades; the party was anti-liquor, anti-Catholic, anti-immigrant, and anti-slavery, and by the mid-1850s they could claim more than one million followers in the Northeast and Mid-west.[7] The stated enemies of the group were Irish and German immi-grants: the former for their sinister-seeming adherence to "Papist" Rome, and the latter for their connection to the brewing industry and their economic and cultural objection to the restrictions of the temperance movement (in contrast, Know-Nothing Party members in California took the Chinese immigrants who served the mining and construction industries of that frontier state as their primary tar-gets). Anti-immigrant groups warned of the perils of liberal natu-ralization policies with inflammatory pamphlets such as *The Crisis! An Appeal to our Countrymen on the Subject of Foreign Influence in the United States!*[8] A *New York Times* crime blotter from this era demon-strates the prevalence of Know-Nothing bigotry: "the old Knicker-bocker families of Manhattan Island," the report begins, "through their generations still there, could boast of their industry and their purity . . . [but] there are some families of more recent standing which will hardly be able to leave to posterity such unsullied repu-tations." The family, in this instance, was the Fenian-supporting "O'Brians" of Washington Street, four Irish American brothers whose near-perfect record of murder and incarceration "constitutes one of the sad chapters of life in the Metropolis."[9] After the Civil War, it would be possible for the language of "blood" and "stock" to be co-opted by particularly liberal thinkers such as Walt Whitman, who wrote triumphantly of the "grand, common stock" of the United

States, and Henry Ward Beecher, who greeted the abolition of slavery by proclaiming that "the best blood of all nations will ultimate by and by in a better race."[10] But in prewar New York, Foster's "Knickerbocker blood" had a Know-Nothing ring. "Knickerbocker blood" was not meant to conjure the battered and rusty "cocked hat" of Irving's historian but rather the kid gloves of his "handsome, intellectual-looking," and most certainly patrician descendant, and to be of Knickerbocker extraction now meant to be ethnically above reproach, fully generations from the taint of "foreign influence" or the stigma of new money. The word was becoming ever more adaptable to the agendas of its appropriators, who substituted one form of nostalgia for another in an effort to rank and sort New Yorkers, since they couldn't arrest the city's continuous expansion altogether.

Against this backdrop, it is hardly a surprise that the first novel to describe a character as being a "Knickerbocker" was itself an explicitly kid-glove undertaking. In 1852, Charles Astor Bristed, a grandson of John Jacob Astor, published *The Upper Ten Thousand*, a novel "written entirely for the English market, without any expectation of [its] being generally read or republished here. This will account for [its] containing many things which must seem very flat and commonplace to an American reader, such as descriptions of sulkies and trotting-wagons, of how people dress, and what they eat for dinner, etc.; which are nevertheless not necessarily uninteresting to an Englishman who has not seen this country." It is, as the author advertises, quite literally a primer of Old New York, and a window, not unlike the one Edith Wharton would offer half a century later, on the customs and pretensions of the city's elite at play. In fact, the touristic element of Bristed's otherwise plodding novel is its only redeeming feature; unlike Wharton's novels, *The Upper Ten Thousand* is entirely unoriginal. Bristed borrows shamelessly from Cooper's New York trilogy, *The Chainbearers*, and from his domestic novel of Manhattan, *Home as Found*, as well as from Paulding's novel *The Dutchman's Fireside*, to compile his depiction of a family of patrician, Dutch-descended New Yorkers in Manhattan, at their country seat, Devilshoof (a blatant riff on Cooper's *Satanstoe*), and in Saratoga Springs. An English houseguest character serves the novel as a useful pedagogical device, allowing the protagonist (and, by extension, the

narrator) to play at being both gaslight guide and Diedrich Knickerbocker at the same time, while educating the reader about the particular totems of the tribe of Old New York. Sometimes this education
takes the form of a vocabulary tutorial, such as when Bristed's American protagonist helpfully exclaims to his English guest, "Oh, you
don't know what *stoop* means! It is a Dutch word we Gothamites
have retained. Well, then, come out on the front piazza"; or instructs
readers that "Kaatskill" is "the genuine Dutch orthography" for "Catskill."[11] In other instances, the narrator borrows Diedrich Knickerbocker's family trees, identifying *parvenu* families who were not, "in
point of birth, . . . related to the Van Hornes, the Masters, the Van-
derlyns, or any of the old Dutch settlers; nor, like Bell, Ludlow and
others of their set, sprung from the British families of long standing
in the city." Interestingly, Bristed himself had only recently allied his
own famous name (he was an Astor cousin) to one of the oldest of
the "old Dutch" families of New York; he had married a daughter of
Henry Brevoort Jr., a patrician son of New Amsterdam, and Irving
himself had attended the wedding.[12]

Perhaps the presence of this famous guest at his wedding inspired
Bristed to add the character of Phil Van Horne to his novel. Van
Horne, introduced to the reader as "the oldest and richest of the
groomsmen" at a wedding "above Bleecker," is described as a

> genuine Knickerbocker from the start[;] in the enjoyment of heredi-
> tary wealth, and fortunately without any turn for dissipation, he began
> by educating himself thoroughly, according to the American notion
> of the thing—that is to say, he learned a little of everything. . . . But
> all these accomplishments being grafted on a certain native Dutch
> solidity, he is by no means forward to display them, and will always
> let the rest of the company do the talking, unless you take consider-
> able trouble to stir him up and put him through his paces. . . . [H]e
> is tall and good-looking and decidedly ornamental, in addition to his
> other merits.[13]

Although Phil Van Horne is just a minor character in a minor novel,
his portrait was the first literary definition of a Knickerbocker, after
Irving. Up to this point, Knickerbocker references took the readers'

understanding of their meaning for granted, and newspapers referred
to Albany as "the capital of the Knickerbockers" or called for the
preservation of the Kip's Bay House, "last of the old Knickerbocker
residences," without clarifying explanation. Indeed, even the *Knickerbocker Magazine* never defined its name beyond the scope of its eponymous muse.[14] It is all the more disappointing, then, to find that
this first explicit inventory of "Knickerbocker" qualities amounts to
only education, accomplishments, and wealth, "grafted on a certain
native Dutch solidity." If this is indeed the sum of it, why should the
awkward moniker endure at all?

One answer may be found in the narrative's insistence that Van
Horne's inheritance is more important to New York society than his
personal traits—"the money first and the virtue last: I believe we have
enumerated the desirable qualities in their proper order"—because
Bristed slips, in this description, into the language of race and hered-
ity used by his Know-Nothing contemporaries.[15] Van Horne's "native
Dutch solidity" is the stock onto which the more ephemeral "qualities" are grafted in order to make him more eligible to the history-
blind, nouveau riche "upper ten thousand" of the novel's title. In fact,
the same year that Bristed published *The Upper Ten Thousand* in the
United States, another, less polished account of New York society
invoked Irving's creation to the same end. John D. Vose's *Fresh Leaves
from the Diary of a Broadway Dandy* is a pulp romance that details
the adventures of a genteel and wealthy New Yorker, raised "above
Bleecker," who ultimately renounces the "Hudson-street belle, the St.
Mark's Place princess, the Waverly Place beauty . . . [and] the Broadway heiress" in favor of his true love, a penniless girl "from the best
old stock of blood in the state—the real, pure Knickerbocker of the
old school—those days of Rip Van Winkle." Naturally, as in Irving's
own Knickerbocker tales, there is a silver porringer at the end of this
Dutch story: the young, seemingly destitute wife turns out to possess
not only "the best blood of New York . . . that genuine, whole-souled
Knickerbocker, Rip Van Winkle and Livingston stock," but also "property deeded in [her] name, which includes a block of stores in Pearl-
street, and a mansion in Ninth-street, on the west side of Broadway."
Like *The Upper Ten Thousand*, *Fresh Leaves* shores up its assertions of
Knickerbocker authenticity with proof of inherited wealth, the better

to maintain the readerly fantasy that New Yorkers of the "best blood" can indeed maintain their control of New York society, even if they cannot check the city's teeming population or contain its inexorable sprawl. The bachelor Van Horne and the bride of the reformed "dandy" may be advertised as "true Knickerbockers," but they are hybrid creations, and they reflect the hopes and concerns of their inventors more nearly than those of Irving's "genuine, whole-souled" 1809 original.[16]

This popular concept of Knickerbockerian "best blood" informs another pre–Civil War Knickerbocker usage, a minstrel song about New York stagecoaches entitled "The Stage Driver (On the Knickerbocker Line)."[17] The song, which was published in an 1859 volume entitled *Burnt Cork Lyrics*, riffs on the exclusivity of the private stagecoach companies, whose coaches charged a higher fare (and were thus less crowded) than the city's horsecar lines. "Now, White folks pay attention, Ise gwane to sing a song," the piece begins:

> I hope it's going to please you, though it isn't very long;
> It's about one of the old boys, so gallious and so fine,
> For he drove an omnibus on the Knickerbocker line,
> He was such a favorite wherever he went,
> And he never was known to knock down a cent.
> He slung a graceful whip, for he was bound to shine
> Like a high salary'd driver on the Knickerbocker line.

"The Stage Driver (On the Knickerbocker Line)" is evidence that the pleasingly polysyllabic, nonsensical word had already migrated to the music hall stage, where it offered the same freighted meaning to songwriters as it did to gaslight and society scribes (much as "Rockefeller" would in the early twentieth century). But with a difference: the song suggests that a Knickerbocker identity could be more universal than Irving had imagined and that the cosmopolitan associations of the word itself might be claimed by the African American "old boy" who drove the coach, just as it was by the wealthy white urbanites he drove.[18] Could a Knickerbocker sensibility be available to all New Yorkers, regardless of race and class? The answer is: potentially, but not yet. While "The Stage Driver" asserts the singer's participation in the characteristic rituals of daily life in antebellum New York, the song would hardly have struck its white audience as a challenge to the city's postslavery status quo. At the time, African Americans made up little more than 1 percent of the population of New York City, and they had few opportunities to try on Irving's talismanic word, which, exactly fifty years after its introduction, was still decidedly Anglo-Saxon in its connotation. The appropriation of Knickerbocker was a luxury that only elite New Yorkers could as yet afford.

Regardless of its genre or import, however, the mid-century "Knickerbocker" usage put increasing distance between the narrator and his creator, often detaching the name from the historian without preface or apology. "Knickerbocker," it seemed, now belonged solely to New York, not to Irving, and the ease with which it had been absorbed into the city's lexicon is illustrated by its first appearance in a dictionary. The word is listed for the first time in John Russell Bartlett's second edition of the *Dictionary of Americanisms: A Glossary of Words and Phrases, Usually Regarded as Peculiar to the United States*, which was published in 1859. It is surprising to find that Irving's signature term was not included in the first edition of Bartlett's *Dictionary*, which had been published in 1848, nearly forty years after the *History* and the same year that the Putnam's revised edition was released. It is possible that the popularity of the new edition prompted Bartlett to correct the omission, but his definition of "Knickerbocker" makes no mention of either the book or its elder statesman author.[19] In fact, Bartlett's "Knickerbocker" is not even connected to his fictional namesake but is simply and unambiguously "a descendant of one of the old Dutch families of New York." However, in the same edition, *Knickerbocker's History of New York* is listed—after a prefatory disclaimer by the author stating that the "etymology and meaning of some of the old Dutch words still used in New York" remains unsettled—as the primary source reference for an extensive range of Dutch-sounding terms that the dictionary deems "of purely American origin."[20] These include "Patroon," "Slap-jack," the essential "Oly-koek" and "Sour Krout," and "Stoop"—although for "stoop" the dictionary also credits James Fenimore Cooper.[21] Perhaps it was just the accumulation of Knickerbocker references in print (including the culinary and architectural terms pointed out by Bristed) that warranted the historian's inclusion in Bartlett's second edition, loosed from the moorings of Irving's text. Certainly, the dictionary's reliance on Irving as the Shakespeare of Dutch derivations is indicative of some degree of familiarity with the *History*, but the connection to its famous narrator goes curiously unsaid. The divorce of Knickerbocker from Irving and his Virgil of New Amsterdam was by no means complete, but it suggests that Bartlett had identified an independent role for "Knickerbocker," one that went beyond literary muse or party platform. As a bona fide Americanism, the word, and all that it stood for, now had national significance.

Knickerbocker's dictionary debut prefigured yet another attempt by New York at a redefinition of its own—this time precipitated by the Civil War. The war temporarily forced the city out of its recognized national role as an island of tastemakers and iconoclasts, polarized by vast differences in income and housing, not to mention by differences in language, ethnicity, and race. To be part of the Union, the city had to be unified itself, or at least to assemble a patriotic front. Such a front was a challenge to erect: the Panic of 1857 had smashed the financial markets, and commercial business everywhere—from the rail yards to the department stores to the pushcarts—ground to a horrifying halt. Southern states repudiated their New York debts, and Mayor Fernando Wood, searching for a way to preserve the interests of his island, at one point even put forth a motion for the city's secession from the nation altogether. Nevertheless, by the spring of 1861 the city was largely united as an enthusiastic participant in the Union cause, and its most prominent citizens organized massive rallies and instituted a Union Defense Committee to help fund the war. The course of this new patriotism did not run entirely smooth. Morale plummeted when the Confederates invaded the North; the 1863 Draft Riots terrorized African American New Yorkers and saw the city ransacked over four days of uncontrollable mob violence; and Copperhead conspiracy plots (including a fire in thirteen major hotels, as well as at docks, lumberyards, and Barnum's Museum, that did hundreds of thousands of dollars' worth of damage) kept New Yorkers on the alert for goldbugs and Confederate spies. But even in confusing times, no one threw a better party than New York, and in 1864 both Manhattan and Brooklyn did just that, hosting ambitious, multi-pronged "Metropolitan Fairs" to benefit the U.S. Sanitary Commission, a federally sanctioned outgrowth of the Women's Central Association of Relief that supported the Union army with volunteer nursing and fund-raising. Although the New York and Brooklyn fairs were just two among many being held across the Northeast, newspapers across the United States reported on the highlights of the city's dueling benefits with wonder and more than a little envy. Both fairs, it was announced, would feature "Knickerbocker" buildings, constructed expressly for the occasion. Brooklyn's February fair showcased a "Knickerbocker Hall" and a "New England Kitchen," constructed on empty lots adjacent to the Brooklyn Academy of Music (then on Montague Street in Brooklyn Heights). From this prominent and fashionable vantage, just a few blocks from Henry Ward Beecher's Church of the Pilgrims, the Knickerbocker Hall offered "meals . . . in all varieties, and in the style of the very best city restaurants," including green turtle soup for thirty-five cents a serving. The New England Kitchen, in contrast, served a more rustic repast, including bowls of chowder. To reinforce the restaurant's patriotic, unified message, the servers at Knickerbocker Hall wore red, white, and blue uniforms. But the food of the "best city restaurants" in Brooklyn could not compete with Manhattan's "Knickerbocker Kitchen," which captured the national imagination during that city's Metropolitan Fair, held for three weeks in April of 1864.[22]

The Manhattan Sanitary Fair was headquartered at Union Square, a fashionable address close to the Academy of Music, the favorite see-and-be-seen venue for the city's privileged class. From this prominent vantage, the Knickerbocker Kitchen dispensed fine cuisine in a setting of pitch-perfect nostalgia. The ladies at the helm of the Metropolitan Fair Committee had taken great pains to replicate an eighteenth-century Dutch farmhouse kitchen in the available space, and the restaurant was, from all accounts, a curatorial marvel, featuring an open hearth and low beams festooned with "dried apples, rows of dip-candles, seed-corn and bright red peppers." The kitchen's dining tables were set with vintage "blue china, steel forks, and all the good things that were found on the Knickerbocker bill of fare," a menu that included "such viands as would have delighted [Dutch]

ancestors," including "ham and head cheese, spiced beef and veal, rul-
lichies, waffles, . . . olykoeks, krullers, and the many preserves and
pickles that are so nearly lost to our present civilization." In addition
to its heirloom recipes, the kitchen also featured actual Dutch heirlooms, on loan from patriotic Old New York families. The talismanic
items on display included the "mirror that had belonged to Governor Stuyvesant, brought over, it is said, in the same vessel that bore
the Governor to his faithful colony," as well as the Beekman family
cradle, dating from the 1750s. The all-female organizing committee
of the restaurant was itself on display, since it was "composed exclusively of representatives from the oldest Dutch families in the State"
and included the wife of Congressman James J. Roosevelt, née Van
Ness, and Mrs. William Schermerhorn (famous for inviting six hundred guests to her costume balls), among others. These well-heeled
Ladies Bountiful supervised the Knickerbocker Kitchen's operations
dressed in "the costume of [their] great-grandmothers," with all the
petticoats that historical accuracy required, while "Chloe and Caesar,
respectable people of color," provided musical entertainment for the
diners. Visitors to the kitchen did not seem to be disturbed by this
tableau vivant of slavery (or, at least, domestic servitude) taking place
in a free state, and, according to the committee's report, the only com-
plaint voiced about the restaurant was that it was not big enough to
hold all those who wished to take lunch or tea among its evocative
relics of the past. Diners might even have paid for their meal with
Knickerbocker tokens, coins stamped with a portrait of a man in
colonial dress and walking stick framed by the words "Knickerbocker
Currency." These lightweight one-penny pieces were among the many
tokens privately minted by Union merchants during the war, when
monetary metals were scarce and often hoarded.[23]

Regardless of how the guests paid their bills, the restaurant grossed
over twelve thousand dollars for the Manhattan Sanitary Fair, which
itself raised a total of $1.3 million for the Union cause. The kitchen's
popularity cannot be entirely due to New Yorkers' nostalgia for head
cheese and Irving's "olykoeks." Despite its borrowed antiques and
well-researched artifacts, the kitchen, as the organizers readily admitted, was more fantastic than it was factual. "Perhaps at first glance
the learned Diedrich might have thought that his pictures had been

somewhat idealized in this copy," the organizers of Manhattan's Metropolitan Fair noted wryly in their *Report*, "for here was not only the solid comfort of the burgomaster, but something of gubernatorial splendor was superadded." The appeal of the kitchen was its highbrow nostalgia, which had scrubbed and polished the homely landscape of Knickerbocker's New Amsterdam and populated its rooms with "gubernatorial" elites. The kitchen employed Knickerbocker's identifying symbols of New Amsterdam simplicity and plenty to draw New Yorkers—and all Americans—together during a time of crisis and presented a lexicon of tastes and remembrances that all could share, even if they originally belonged to someone else.[24]

"We've neither a legendary past nor a poetic present," George Templeton Strong had lamented of New York in 1837, little knowing what transformations lay in store for his hometown.[25] By the close of the Civil War, the city had become a place of tremendous cultural and social differentiation, an island where the Philharmonic could coexist with P. T. Barnum's "Great Model of Niagara Falls" (featuring "real Croton water" from the upstate reservoir); where oysters, New Yorkers' universally beloved snack, could be consumed on the go from street carts or while lingering over a "great bowl of sauterne punch" at the Century Club; and where the Sunday ritual ranged from watching the elite mingle at fashionable Grace Church to witnessing the parade of humanity on the popular *Knickerbocker* steamboat, one of several in a fleet that ferried over ten thousand day-trippers to and from Hoboken and other New Jersey vacation spots during the summer months.[26] In fact, the many appropriations of Knickerbocker at midcentury reflect the points at which these various New Yorks met and coexisted, as uneasy and never-ending as that process of coexistence may have been. And the safe—and safely vanished—world of the Dutch gave to all these New Yorks the "legendary past" that Templeton Strong hoped for, as apocryphal as it might actually be. "We want a NATIONAL NAME. We want it poetically, and we want it politically," Washington Irving had written in the *Knickerbocker Magazine* in 1839, bewailing the "Old World" implications of the name of "New York." By the close of the Civil War, his readers and fellow Gothamites had chosen a name, and it was Knickerbocker.

Goede Vrouwen and Social Climbers

"WHERE ARE THE KNICKERBOCKERS?" demanded the headline in
the January 1871 issue of the *Genealogical and Biographical Record,*

> Where are the Dutchmen of the olden time
> Who saw an ancient city in its prime?
> The Bleeckers, Brenckerhoffs, Van Hornes, and Dyckmans,
> Van Hooks, Van Bummels, Vanderpoels, and Ryckmans,
> Van Rensselaers, Ten Broecks, Van Pelts, and Hoppers,
> The Vander Spiegles, Vander Hoofs, and Cloppers? . . .
> Where are they all, these men of sounding name,
> Of pipe, knee-breeches, and round-headed fame?

The poem, billed as a "New Year's address," had originally been
printed in the *Albany Dutchman.* For the *Record,* the journal of the
nascent New York Genealogical and Biographical Society, the poem
may just have been a charming "find," a feat of versification (a total
of sixty-five Dutch surnames were included in rhyming couplets)
and an advertisement for the genealogical services of its professional
and amateur members, who could help readers to find their own
"Dutchmen of the olden time." But it was also a timely question to
ask of postwar New York. Where *were* the Knickerbockers? Who could
claim that "sounding name" now? And what was left of the "ancient
city" Irving's historian had celebrated?

Even though the battles of the Civil War had not taken place in
New York, as had those of the Revolutionary War, the conflict nonetheless shattered and reassembled the city's financial and social organization in dramatic and unforeseen ways. The first national system
of currency had been imposed during the war, and the U.S. government borrowed from New York's banks to pay for this infusion of
"greenbacks." As Burroughs and Wallace have pointed out, the city
lost no time in building a fitting monument to its new role as banker
to the nation, erecting a marble-and-steel New York Stock Exchange
on Wall Street in 1865.[27] The Stock Exchange could just as easily have
served as a signpost, pointing visitors in the direction of New York's

new money: wartime industry and speculation had created a class of Gothamites who seemed to wear their net worth on their ostentatious sleeves. This group (and many of them were recent arrivals to the city, as well as recently rich) was dubbed a "snobocracy" by *Harper's* magazine, perhaps to distinguish it from Nathaniel Parker Willis's "Knickerbocracy," his 1855 coinage for the landed gentry of the Hudson River Valley. Some New Yorkers found the influx of these reverse carpetbaggers to be socially toxic and complained that while in Philadelphia "people asked you *who* you were," in New York they asked "how much you were worth."[28] The Civil War had indeed made New York the economic epicenter of the nation, irresistible to real estate developers, manufacturers, and bankers, as well as to successive and increasing waves of European and Asian immigrants looking for personal freedom and for work. This swell in commerce and population corresponded to a renewed interest in municipal reform programs and cultural uplift movements like those instituted by wealthy native sons such as DeWitt Clinton after the Revolutionary War. This time, however, Manhattan's newly anointed captains of industry led the charge for greater public access to the arts, rather than the Emersonian "statesmen, scholars and divines" who had organized the Historical Society and other founding institutions of the city.

An astonishing number of New York City's most treasured cultural resources were incorporated in the decades that immediately followed the Civil War, and many of them could be found on the residential avenues that framed Central Park, hard by the Beaux Arts homes of their chief patrons. Among the institutions founded at this time were the American Museum of Natural History on Central Park West (1869), the "Ruskinian Gothic kernel" designed by Calvert Vaux that would grow into the present-day Metropolitan Museum of Art (1872), the Metropolitan Opera House (1880), and the New York Public Library (1895).[29] In addition to bringing beauty and learning into the lives of many, these "people's palaces" were indispensable to New York as it strove ever harder to remain not just the largest city in the United States but a marketable phenomenon and tourist destination without peer. It was certainly the nation's best hope to rival the cultivation and built environment—if not the voluminous history—of

Paris, London, or Rome. In fact, the Romanesque Revival and Neo-Renaissance edifices of the city's temples to art and culture themselves had a purposefully Old World look, weighted down on their massive lots with classical columns, friezes, and other inspirational statuary. But the antiqued marble of these shiny new urban playgrounds only camouflaged the intensely modern ambitions of their founders, serving as an elegant screen for what Henry James called the "foredoomed *grope* of wealth, in the conquest of the amenities."[30] The noble purpose and graceful lines of New York's new museums and concert halls and libraries helped to launder, or at least legitimize, the amoral profiteering that paid for much of their construction in the first place. Several of the city's most beautiful Gilded Age structures (including the Metropolitan Opera, which James referred to as the "great vessel of social salvation," and the by-invitation-only Metropolitan Club) were built for the express purpose of assuaging the feelings of nouveau riche names (such as Vanderbilt, Morgan, and Gould) who had been denied admission to the venerable institutions of their established rivals. Indeed, in order to avoid being dismissed as a whim of this stratum of inflated arrivistes, the founders of the Metropolitan Museum of Art had borrowed important social capital to build their first board of trustees, choosing more than half its members from the unimpeachable, time-honored roster of the New-York Historical Society.[31] Certainly, the identification of particular New York families with certain civic institutions (or political administrations) was nothing new: since the founding of the Historical Society itself, the presence of certain recognizable surnames was understood to imbue a charitable group or cultural venture with all the dynastic authority of the family itself. But now, with increasing inevitability, and in a diverse array of circumstances, the remnants of such dynasties of Bleeckers, Fishes, Livingstons, Schermerhorns, Van Rensselaers, and the like were collectively referred to as "Knickerbockers."

It was a name, as we will see, that some Manhattan mandarins embraced and others rejected, but in any case, there seemed to be no escape from it. For a city accustomed to making distinctions and inspiring superlatives, a set of "First Families" was essential, and it had to encompass the very loftiest and most historic names. The keepers of these names might also be dubbed the "Bourbons of New York," or they might be dismissed by Walt Whitman as "Fifth Avenoodledom," but it was as "Knickerbockers" that they were tacitly encouraged to oversee New York's postwar civic culture and mediate the disputes of an evolving high society. It was no coincidence that when a group of disaffected younger members of the Union Club, the oldest and most exclusive private club in New York, chose to form their own splinter organization in 1871, they named it for Irving's historian. The Knickerbocker Club wasted no time siphoning members from the city's existing clubs, and within a decade the length of its waiting list for membership had reached fabled proportions.[32] The Knickerbocker name was as easily converted into cash as it was into cachet: as they had during the writer's lifetime, several large-scale commercial enterprises in the Gilded Age exploited Irving's narrator to give their business a privileged, "New York" gloss. By the 1880s, the Knickerbocker Ice and Knickerbocker Steamboat companies that the author had mentioned in his "Apology" were joined by the Knickerbocker Trust Bank, the Knickerbocker Gas-Light Company, and the Knickerbocker Apartment Company (which had purchased the original site of the Knickerbocker Club in order to build a million-dollar "apartment house of the first class").[33] On the consumer side, New Yorkers could patronize the Knickerbocker Cottage restaurant or purchase a Knickerbocker-model combination billiard table for their home (which was manufactured in Ludington, Michigan). But "Knickerbocker" was much more than just a convenient and profitable moniker for the city, its "patriarchs," and those who wished to sell to them. Diedrich Knickerbocker, along with the constellation of urban artifacts, Dutch names, and nostalgic tableaux that were his acknowledged trademarks, was integral to the self-fashioning of Gilded Age New York. Preservationists and genealogists who struggled to discover and conserve the city's past saw an ally in Knickerbocker. Society memoirs, social registers, and advertisers shamelessly appropriated his dynastic families. Novelists borrowed his imagery wholesale or endowed their characters with a Knickerbocker sensibility. Always, however, without exception, Knickerbocker's turn-of-the-century proponents took their cue from the Sanitary Commission's Knickerbocker Kitchen and so gilded and bedecked Irving's original until it seemed that only a wooden leg separated the imaginary historian from Governor Stuyvesant himself.

The horrors and dislocations of the Civil War inspired many Americans to look to the past for reassurance and a sense of community. In the Gilded Age, this look back increasingly took the form of genealogical societies, some of which held to strict rules of lineal descent from the ancestors in question. Before the war, only a handful of these groups existed in the United States, and most of them fell into the category of the ethnic or religious "benevolent" associations (such as the previously mentioned New England Society) or were outgrowths of support for war veterans and their families (such as the Military Society of the War of 1812, founded in 1826). However, after the war, the American interest in genealogy became a positive craze: between 1867 and 1905, more than fifty new genealogical and patriotic societies were founded in the United States. These included veterans' groups (the Sons of Union Veterans of the Civil War and the United Daughters of the Confederacy, among others), some of which had overlapping or rival constituencies (for example, New York City embraced not only the National Society of Colonial Dames and the Colonial Dames of America but also the Daughters of the American Revolution and the Daughters of Holland Dames), organizations celebrating dissenting ancestors (the Huguenot Society of America, the General Society of Mayflower Descendants, the Pilgrim John Howland Society) and those for pioneering ones (the Sons of the Republic of Texas, the Daughters of Hawaii), and, for utmost exclusivity, clubs that celebrated a pedigree few Americans could actually prove (such as the Baronial Order of the Magna Carta and the Plantagenet Society—this last was for descendants of the Plantagenet kings of England, including the Houses of York and Lancaster).[34] Amateur genealogical organizations sprang up to support those in search of the family trees necessary for admission into these exclusive groups, and by 1876 there were already seventy-eight state and local genealogical societies across the United States, including the aforementioned New York Genealogical and Biographical Society, founded with a mandate to "collect and make available information on genealogy, biography and history, particularly as it relates to the people of New York State." Both T. Jackson Lears and Sven Beckert have argued that the Gilded Age mania for genealogy "merged class-consciousness with racism" and have proposed that the founding of ancestor societies such as the Saint Nicholas Society or the Sons of the Revolution was, along with family coats of arms and the Arts and Crafts movement, one of the "antimodern" fads that wealthy Americans employed as proof of the "Nordic purity supposedly guaranteed by medieval antecedents."[35] Nowhere was the gathering of ancestral proofs more popular than in New York City, where the percentage of foreign-born residents in Manhattan hovered around 42 percent by 1875, and newly minted tycoons from beyond the Hudson River seemed to increase in number and visibility daily. As early as 1853, the *North American Review* had noted with relief that the roll call of the Society of the Cincinnati, that group of descendants of George Washington's regiment that had been founded before Irving published the *History*, still contained a "goodly array of old Knickerbocker names."[36] It didn't matter to the *Review* that Knickerbocker was himself a fiction, because his warning about the possibility of extinction for the "old names" was quickly becoming fact. In this unsettled new regime, any index that could ascertain the native, authentic status of a New Yorker—and certify his or her right to be known as such—was, increasingly, of paramount importance.

The snobbish status that accrued to these patriotic and historic groups did not go unremarked in the media. One gentle spoof in an 1884 issue of *Harper's* magazine chided city tennis clubs for "'squatting' in the militia armories," disguised as genealogical groups under the name of "the 'True Knickerbocker Tennis Club' or the 'Original Mayflower Racketeers.'" An actual tennis club called the Knickerbocker Field Club would be organized several years later in the Flatbush section of Brooklyn, but *Harper's* likely had a different target in mind for this mild satire: the Knickerbocker Greys, a junior cadet corps for boys "from well-known New York families" that had been founded in 1881 and is still active. Prompted, perhaps, by the example of the Iron Greys, a Revolutionary War independent militia company that, along with the New York Hussars and the Neptune Corps of Sea Fencibles, had been reactivated in New York during the War of 1812, a well-connected New York mother named Mrs. Edward Curtis began offering regular military drills for boys in the Seventh Regiment

Armory on Park Avenue. The drills had the stated goal of instilling a "sense of personal responsibility, an instinct for leadership, the habit of dependability, and the self-assurance which follows mastery of these steps to useful citizenship" in members of the corps, and the early membership of the Knickerbocker Greys suggests that many of Mrs. Curtis's charges were already well on the path to City Fatherhood: the alumni roster includes a variety of well-known New York surnames, including a Bleecker, a Vanderpoel, a Forbes, and the namesake son of Stuyvesant Fish, a society leader, onetime president of the Illinois Central Railroad, and distant descendant of the Preserved Fish whose awkward moniker was spoofed in Irving's *History*. Unlike the Saint Nicholas Society, the Greys did not explicitly require Dutch or Old New York ancestry for admission, but that hardly kept the drill class from being exclusive: two letters of sponsorship were required, and the troop was limited to American citizens "of good character" who were, crucially, "at least eight years of age."[37]

Another way in which self-proclaimed Knickerbocker New Yorkers demonstrated their native prerogative during this era was by literal repossession of what, as we have seen, was increasingly referred to as Old New York. Before the Civil War, few sites of national significance had been given protected status by the federal government, and Americans as a nation took limited interest in the subject of historic preservation. New York, characteristically, was the exception: in 1850 the state government purchased and dedicated Hasbrouck House, a Dutch house in Newburgh that had served as a wartime headquarters for George Washington from 1782 to 1783. Hasbrouck House may have had a particular resonance for proud New Yorkers, not just for its patriotic associations but also because it resembles the dwellings described by the nation's first storyteller, Knickerbocker. The ancient house, with its Hudson River vista, inviting fieldstone walls, and quaint, sloping roof, would not be out of place in Tarrytown, Sleepy Hollow, or any other place of Irving's imagining. Nor would any of the subsequent historic homes and structures that moneyed New Yorkers (and their peers in other cities) rallied to preserve during the Gilded Age. In fact, many of the historic properties rescued in the late nineteenth century were from the time of the Dutch settlement, once more giving the lie to the Historical Society's original protestations. In the city, the preservation and purchase of these structures was often the result of intercessions by the American Scenic and Historical Preservation Society, a precursor to the city's Landmarks Preservation Association that had been created and was led by the visionary parks commissioner and city planner Andrew Haswell Green. But there were privately funded campaigns as well, which saved the Grange, Alexander Hamilton's Harlem home, from demolition; preserved a window from the Rhinelander Sugar House, once a British prison for American soldiers; and fought to keep the original City Hall intact. Some rescues were done in partnership with the city: the Van Cortlandt House, a stately Georgian manor house and farm in the northwest Bronx, exemplifies the kind of historic structure that interested this first wave of deep-pocketed preservationists. The property, which had been home to the Van Cortlandt family since the late seventeenth century, was licensed to the National Society of Colonial Dames by the City of New York in 1896, for architectural restoration and use as a public museum and educational resource. The Dames later renovated the house interior in the popular Colonial Revival style. Others, like the Dyckman Farmhouse on upper Broadway, another colonial Dutch estate, were "bought back" and restored by the descendants of the original owners who had themselves moved to more stylish addresses farther downtown.[38] However these saving missions were accomplished, they all were crucial: Americans have since come to take the continuity of historical landmarks for granted, but the preservation of New York's oldest extant structures was not a commonplace activity at the time. The decisions to spare decrepit old buildings from the perpetual cycle of redevelopment and to fund their restoration for public use were based on more than mere funds; they were based on a postwar understanding of the fragility of the city's built environment and, as important, on the new realization that in addition to having a "history" the city was, in fact, old.

Reawakened by preservationists and amateur genealogists to the fact of their city's vanishing past, many New Yorkers once again proved as anxious to sell their famous town as they were to save it. Diedrich Knickerbocker had set the example for a new literary trend, in which nostalgia signaled familiarity: if you could speak about Old

1. Engraving from book 1, chapter 1 of *A History of New York*, 1848 edition. Note the long pipes and tankards of Knickerbocker's audience: the stereotypes of Irving's easygoing Dutchmen were firmly in place by this time. General Research Division, The New York Public Library, Astor, Lenox and Tilden Foundations.

2. "A small elderly gentleman, dressed in an old black coat and cocked hat, by the name of Knickerbocker." A rendering of Diedrich Knickerbocker from *Valentine's Manual*. Undated. Print Collection, Miriam and Ira D. Wallach Division of Art, Prints and Photographs, The New York Public Library, Astor, Lenox and Tilden Foundations.

The author's apology

The following work, in which, at the outset, nothing more was contemplated than a temporary jeu d'esprit, was commenced in company with my brother the late Peter Irving Esq. Our idea was to parody a small hand book, which had recently appeared, entitled "A Picture of New York" like that our work was to begin with an historical sketch; to be followed by notices of the costumes, manners and institutions of the city;

3. "A temporary jeu d'esprit." First manuscript page of the "Author's Apology" to the 1848 edition of *A History of New York.* Washington Irving Papers, Manuscripts and Archives Division, The New York Public Library, Astor, Lenox and Tilden Foundations.

4. A lithograph of Sunnyside, Washington Irving's Westchester home, made in 1860. Just one year after his death, Sunnyside had already become a place of pilgrimage. Print Collection, Miriam and Ira D. Wallach Division of Art, Prints and Photographs, The New York Public Library, Astor, Lenox and Tilden Foundations.

5. "Washington Irving's Grave, Sleepy Hollow, Tarrytown, N.Y." So many fans of Irving's work chipped souvenir shards from the author's tombstone that it had to be replaced twice within fifty years of his death. Photography Collection, Miriam and Ira D. Wallach Division of Art, Prints and Photographs, The New York Public Library, Astor, Lenox and Tilden Foundations.

6. The Knickerbocker and Excelsior Baseball Clubs, 1858. The Knickerbocker team is widely recognized as the first organized baseball team in the United States. Photography Collection, Miriam and Ira D. Wallach Division of Art, Prints and Photographs, The New York Public Library, Astor, Lenox and Tilden Foundations.

7. The steamboat *Knickerbocker* at Albany, depicted by Currier & Ives. One steamboat named *Knickerbocker* sank near Fort Montgomery (Orange County), New York, in 1855; all the passengers were rescued by nearby boats. Undated (possibly 1850s). Collection of the author.

8. A view of the popular Knickerbocker Kitchen at the Metropolitan Fair in Union
Square, featuring Dutch colonial décor and reenactors portraying African American
household servants of indeterminate status, obliquely described by the Sanitary
Commission as "Chloe and Caesar, respectable people of color." From *Harper's
Weekly*, April 23, 1864. Picture Collection, The Branch Libraries, The New York Public
Library, Astor, Lenox, and Tilden Foundations.

9. A full-page advertisement for Knickerbocker, an eight-year-old stallion "of a rich mahogany color . . . very stylish and fast." J. B. Beers & Co. County Atlas of Orange, New York, by F. W. Beers, 1875. The Lionel Pincus and Princess Firyal Map Division, The New York Public Library, Astor, Lenox and Tilden Foundations.

10. Father Knickerbocker proposes consolidation to Miss Brooklyn. "Selfish Objections to a Good Match," *Puck*, January 18, 1893. Courtesy of Michael Miscione.

11. Another perspective on the consolidation of Brooklyn and Manhattan. "The Adopted Son—He Thinks He Is Bigger than the Old Man," *Puck*, December 29, 1897. Courtesy of Michael Miscione.

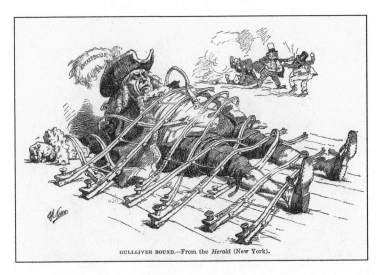

GULLIVER BOUND.—From the *Herald* (New York).

12. Knickerbocker faces municipal challenges after the consolidation of Greater New York. "Gulliver Bound," *New York Herald*, 1897. Courtesy of Michael Miscione.

13. Dust jacket for *The Last of the Knickerbockers: A Comedy Romance*, by Herman Knickerbocker Vielé (1901). Illustration by Edward Penfield. Knickerbocker Vielé was a descendant of U.S. Representative Herman Knickerbocker of Schaghticoke, New York, whose surname Irving appropriated for his famous historian. Art and Architecture Collection, Miriam and Ira D. Wallach Division of Art, Prints and Photographs, The New York Public Library, Astor, Lenox and Tilden Foundations.

The
Knickerbocker
Charity Ball
December twenty-seventh, 1905
Waldorf-Astoria

Menu

PAMPLEMOUSSE

CONSOMMÉ, BELLE VUE, EN TASSE

COQUILLES À LA KNICKERBOCKER

PIGEONNEAUX GRILLÉS
SALADE DE LAITUE

GLACES DE FANTAISIE

PETITS FOURS

CAFÉ

MOET & CHANDON, WHITE SEAL	$4.00
MOET & CHANDON, IMPERIAL BRUT	4.50
APOLLINARIS	0.40

DEMPSEY & CARROLL, N. Y.

14. Menu from a charity ball held by the Knickerbocker Club at the Waldorf-Astoria in 1905. Rare Books Division, The New York Public Library, Astor, Lenox and Tilden Foundations.

15. Hotel Knickerbocker, southeast corner of Forty-second Street and Broadway, 1912. In 2006, the building was purchased by the royal family of Dubai with the stated goal of restoring it as a luxury hotel. Museum of the City of New York, Byron Collection 93.1.1.6293.

16. Bar of the Knickerbocker Hotel, featuring the Maxfield Parrish mural entitled "Old King Cole" in its original location. Byron Company (New York, NY) / Museum of the City of New York, 93.1.3.1425.

17. A Knickerbocker Grey cadet in uniform, 1910. Courtesy of the Knickerbocker Greys.

Price, net. $3.50

Washington Irving's classic chronicle of the early days on Manhattan is a surprisingly modern tale in this spirited new edition, edited by Anne Carroll Moore and illustrated by James Daugherty.

Not a word of the text has been changed—but with the omission of the long soliloquies and digressions typical of the time in which the book was written it appears modern in its manner of writing, its feeling and its humor. . . .

It is our own history, as American as New York, the Woolworth Tower, the Statue of Liberty and the stones on which Manhattan is built.

It starts right out with Hendrik Hudson and ends with Peter Stuyvesant. It is a pageant of Dutch life—showing the gradual infringements by the Yankees and the final capitulation.

The Daugherty illustrations animate this pageant with a boisterous gusto. Mr. Daugherty has done more than depict characters and scenes with historical accuracy—he has caught the very essence of the spirit of these hardy, vigorous Dutch forefathers.

19. *Knickerbocker's History of New York* book jacket, 1928. With their elaborate ruffs, Knickerbocker's "patriarchs" here resemble a painting by Frans Hals or Rembrandt van Rijn. Doubleday has chosen to title the book *Knickerbocker's History of New York by Washington Irving*, a reminder that the historian was now as inextricably linked to the work as its author. General Research Division, The New York Public Library, Astor, Lenox and Tilden Foundations.

20. A 1934 view of the Knickerbocker Village complex under construction at the intersection of Cherry and Catherine streets. Milstein Division of United States History, Local History & Genealogy, The New York Public Library, Astor, Lenox and Tilden Foundations.

21. Panoramic view of New York City, sponsored by Ruppert's Knickerbocker Beer. The Lionel Pincus and Princess Firyal Map Division, The New York Public Library, Astor, Lenox and Tilden Foundations.

22. An advertisement for Knickerbocker Beer. Undated. Collection of the author.

23. "Famous New York Traditions of Father Knickerbocker: Dutch Landing at Communipaw." Part of the series of 1954 Knickerbocker Beer advertisements featuring passages from Irving's *History* and illustrated by the muralist Lumen Martin Winter. Collection of the author.

24. Original logo of the New York Knickerbockers basketball team, used from 1946 to 1964. The NBA member team identification is the intellectual property of the New York Knicks. Printed with permission from NBA Properties, Inc.

New York, the publishers' reasoning went, you were *of* Old New York. While the personal reminiscences of native-born city dwellers had been a staple of editorial columns and New-York Historical Society dinners for decades, the preoccupations of the Gilded Age gave rise to a cottage industry of New York histories, memoirs, and guidebooks. These narratives emphasized the singularity of the New York experience, regardless of whether the writer's focus was on the city's bright future or the sepia tones of days gone by. Following on the heels of *Valentine's History of New York* came a variety of books designed to appeal to casual tourists and know-it-all natives alike. Works with titles like *In Old New York* encouraged readers in their personal quest for "signs and relics of a truly interesting past," promising "a flood of genuine antiquarian joy" to those who seek out "traces of old-time by-ways" such as the Dyckman farmhouse, or imagined the ghosts of "Dutchmen of Manhattoes, [who] discreetly smoke their pipes and drink their schnapps" just outside our view. Other chroniclers in this genre reject such reveries and sound the death knell for Old New York altogether (one author puts it at 1825, after the completion of the Erie Canal), all the while calling urgently, like Irving's historian, and like the Historical Society before him, for the preservation of any relics from this irretrievable past. These lingering totems, inevitably Dutch, included the Stuyvesant Pear Tree, "the last visible link which connected the present generation directly with the time of the Dutch dynasty," as well as the old Middle Dutch Church, now the Nassau Street branch of the U.S. Post Office (and a very early example of adaptive reuse).[39] That "old shrine of the Knickerbockers," one historian marveled, had become the

> busy brain of the nation and the world, [receiving] some forty tons of thought a day. What would one of those old Rip Van Winkles of 1729 have thought, if he could have prolonged his Sunday afternoon nap in one of those ancient pews till now, and awoke to watch the day's mail, with news by the last steamer and the Atlantic cable for all parts of the great continent?[40]

Despite the fact that Rip Van Winkle was a product of 1819, not 1729, he and the rest of Irving's Dutch patriarchs (whether real or fictional) had become part of New York's collective historical memory, and no account of "the olden time" was complete without them.

Not every aspect of New York warranted celebration by these self-appointed curators. Like the nativists before the war, the latest wave of city chroniclers deplored the presence of "undesirable" immigrants and blamed the "suicidal laissez-faire" emigration policies of the American government for the ever-increasing numbers of newest New Yorkers.[41] Crowded into tenements and ghettos, the writers argued, these recent arrivals marred the picturesque effect of some of New York's oldest and most storied quarters with their public displays of poverty and need. "On the east side," the author of *In Old New York* quite literally sniffs, "even the bad smells have foreign names."[42] The bigotry among would-be preservationists was not always this muted. The *Record*, the journal of the New York Genealogical and Biographical Society, headlined an 1881 issue with an essay entitled "Race in Genealogy and the Chinese Emigration" in which the author exhorted his audience to improved "self-protection" against the influx of immigrants from China, in order to avoid "degrad[ing] *our* condition, and that of the *age* in which, and the *people* among whom, we live."[43] More typical of the *Record* is an editorial call for proof of the "oldest New York family now represented in the City," which received a flood of sharp-elbowed responses from readers determined to prove the superior staying power of their (unquestionably Anglo-Saxon) ancestors.[44] The coexistence of these two ways of asserting race prerogative (one openly racist, the other more oblique) is evidence that many New Yorkers did indeed consider immigration to be a serious menace to their tidy, rose-colored vision of the city, and one that must be held at bay with their own increasingly tribal identifications—including, if necessary, their own private militias, like the Knickerbocker Greys.

The new industry of Old New York naturally turned to "Knickerbocker" and "the Knickerbockers" as talismans, again using Irving's terminology to xenophobic ends. Some writers even volunteered to speak on behalf of these revered citizens of the past. In their hands, "Knickerbocker" became a synonym for "New York as It Never Was": a cultural and ethnic monolith, perfectly genteel and self-sufficient (and Dutch in the nicest possible way), aesthetically pleasing, and just aristocratic enough. These included Abram C. Dayton's 1871 *Last Days of Knickerbocker Life in New York,* which compared a dystopic vision of contemporary Manhattan to an "ancient and venerable" city of his own devising, which, while ostensibly "Knickerbocker," is leached of all the joy and mischief of Irving's creation. "History scarcely presents the parallel of this sudden, marked transition from Dutch Gotham, with its noiseless, steady routine," Dayton laments, "to metropolitan New York, with its bustling, flighty excitement." In fact, as we have seen, there was nothing "sudden" about the city's "transition"—Dayton ignores the fact that New York has always been changing and that its citizens and visitors have always been marveling at the change. Indeed, Dayton's "Dutch Gotham" is not, it turns out, New Amsterdam at all, but rather the New York of "forty years ago," when "home with its legitimate influences reigned supreme." The Knickerbockers who people this vision of the "legitimate" 1830s are stern, exacting, temperate "in every thing," and "*stickler*[s] for systematic routine." Dayton's joyless, revered "progenitors" are both Anglo- and Dutch-descended, and they merge the families listed in the *History* with Irving's contemporaries: "Allen, Brown, Lee, [and] Clinton" together with "Paulding, Ten Eyck, De Peyster, [and] Van Cortlandt." However, Dayton's portrait of the Knickerbocker home, which is offered in open contrast to what he calls the "Seclusion Coterie" of contemporary high society, has all the hallmarks of convivial Dutch living as Irving portrayed it. Dayton's midcentury burghers offered their guests "heavy stubby decanters filled with Madeira and Santa Cruz," while their wives and daughters put forth "silver baskets each day replenished with fresh doughnuts and crullers, as a real earnest of hospitality."[45] Doughnuts and "systematic routine," Madeira and moderation? It is in these moments of nostalgic inconsistency that Dayton's oddly puritanical "patriarchs" have something to offer the contemporary reader. They are the author's anxious hints that upper-class New York, caught up in a fearful and imitative "Seclusion Coterie," may have forgotten how to emulate Knickerbocker's easygoing, liberal-handed Dutch heroes like Wouter Van Twiller or Dolph Heyliger. How can they be thoughtful citizens of their exalted city, if they cannot be gracious hosts?

Another, more prolific New York chronicler argues Dayton's point more vehemently and insists that social and civic leadership are inherent founding traits for the Dutch colony. In *New Yorkers of the XIX Century* (1897) and *The Goede Vrouw of Mana-ha-ta at Home and in Society, 1609–1760* (1898), Mrs. John King Van Rensselaer offers a genealogy and a chronological series of portraits of the "chief families of the city of New York" in which she details the heroic achievements and cosmopolitan graces of Dutch clans including her own (she is descended from Killiaen Van Rensselaer, the patroon of Albany) and pointedly distinguishes the "social organization," as Edith Wharton would describe it, of these colonial dynasties, from that of Manhattan's current boldfaced names. While *New Yorkers of the XIX Century* is a kind of Dutch American *Debrett's Peerage*, offering a catalog of "nearly all the prominent people" of the city at midcentury (and drawn from the author's own "family visiting lists"), *The Goede Vrouw of Mana-ha-ta* looks back even further, to the ancestral matriarchs of many of the same families, and traces the arcs of their influence from the New Amsterdam settlement to the eve of the Revolutionary War.[46] Even under the yoke of English rule, Mrs. Van Rensselaer points out, her subjects remained staunchly Dutch in their traditions and their values, "imbued with all the doctrines of the pioneer women of Mana-ha-ta," and contemptuous of the "new customs and innovations that had been introduced by the English rulers." Although, the author acknowledges, the Dutch colony's mercantile hierarchy had dissolved, the descendants of the original "vrouwen" had "not so easily relaxed their grasp on the reins of social power as their husbands had on the political supremacy that they had wielded . . . [but] persisted in upholding the cherished Dutch customs" until the 1760s, when "the intermarriages of the young people of the colony with persons of other nationalities infused a new flavor into the ethics of the social life of Mana-ha-ta."[47] No further information is given to the reader about what the "new flavor" of Manhattan "ethics" might be, but it is difficult to miss the author's implication that the city's earliest "upper ten thousand" went to hell in a handbasket shortly thereafter. According to Mrs. Van Rensselaer, miscegenation has been the undoing of New York.

Van Rensselaer mentions Diedrich Knickerbocker only as the inventor of a nonsensical meaning for "Mana-ha-ta," and, as an aristocratic Dutch American herself, she declines to characterize her heroines as Knickerbockers. Another work designed to extol the virtues of Dutch women and the impact of their descendants on the culture of New York was less fastidious. It is a measure of how popular New Amsterdam nostalgia was at the turn of the century that younger readers could have simultaneously encountered Van Rensselaer's "goede vrouwen," in the pages of an 1898 children's book entitled *A Little Colonial Dame: A Story of Old Manhattan Island.* Agnes Carr Sage's story haphazardly combined elements of Irving, Paulding, James Fenimore Cooper, *Little Women,* and *Hans Brinker and the Silver Skates* to tell (sometimes in mock Dutch) the story of Rychie Van Couwenhoven (the "colonial dame" of the title) and the "wholesouled hospitality" of the "worthy Knickerbockers" of New Amsterdam among whose number the demure young Rychie could be safely counted. Sage dedicated the book to the Colonial Dames of America, a gesture that reminds the reader of the pervasiveness of genealogical societies at the turn of the century and suggests that the book, as well as Sage's companion work, *A Little Daughter of the Revolution,* may be used as a pedigree primer for the young and gently bred.[48]

The potential value of Dutch New York and its descendants was not lost on more dispassionate observers of the Gilded Age, either. Considering "New York as a Field for Fiction" in the *Century,* the critic H. C. Bunner remarked on the literary possibilities to be found in Dayton's and Van Rensselaer's stalwart, understated clans. "To me it has always seemed that there is one class in New York that sits guard over a past full of romance and quaint color," he wrote in 1883:

> This is what I suppose must be called, conventionally, the Knickerbocker class—not those uncommonly proud Vans and Vanders who stalk loftily through Mr. Augustin Daly's American vaudevilles from the German, but the agreeable relics of the simple provincial society of two generations ago. A class not unthrifty, not extravagant, yet not well fitted to make or hoard money, they live in a golden mean of comfort, perhaps in an atmosphere of mild luxury, on the borders of the world of fashion.[49]

Here is a call to revive the "Knickerbocker class," the city's forgotten guardians: those keepers of "a past full of romance" and inheritors of a "golden mean of comfort" whose simplicity profits by comparison to the extravagant times in which New Yorkers now lived. While the critic's call for a Knickerbocker literature had arguably already been answered by writers like Dayton and Van Rensselaer, the prize must be given to *The Last of the Knickerbockers* (1901), a "comic romance" that followed the fortunes of Alida Van Wandeleer, a native, Dutch-descended New Yorker graced with "the sublime provincialism that marks the metropolitan," and a young woman with "the aura which is the heritage of [being] born between the Three Rivers. . . . [M]eeting her anywhere upon the planet would say at once, 'New York.'" While Alida's family barely achieves Bunner's "golden mean of comfort," her "social talent," "perfect breeding," and affection for New York, along with her recognizable surname, ensure that hansom cab drivers and titled nobility alike instantly identify her as "a real, live Knickerbocker." The author of the novel was himself a "real, live Knickerbocker": Herman Knickerbocker Vielé was a lineal descendant of the "Knickerbockers of Schagticoke" from whom Irving had "borrowed" his historian's name. With this advantage, he is in a position to undermine the authority of his more famous, fictional "cousin," but the author chooses instead to authenticate his heroine's pedigree by using Irving's book as Irving himself so often did: as a kind of circular proof. When asked if she has ever read Irving's *History of New York*, his heroine replies: "Oh, yes . . . I am descended from nearly everybody mentioned in it!" Unlike her real-life, Dutch-descended counterparts such as Mrs. Van Rensselaer or Giulian Verplanck, the fictional Alida is proud to be associated with her city's semi-apocryphal founding text.[50]

While Knickerbocker Vielé's portrait of New Yorkers with a "burgher's birthright" does chide his subjects for being "closemouthed," implying that Bunner's "agreeable relics" diminish their own influence by remaining as private and clannish as the animal on New York's city seal, "the beaver who builds his house impregnable and keeps its one door hidden," his novel is nonetheless unquestionably a love letter to the "old stock," and a primer in historical consciousness for the "new people, whose names mean absolutely nothing, and [who are] frightfully overdressed." And Knickerbocker Vielé's characters remind the reader time and again that the Dutch inheritance is, in fact, history. "But I am not like you, I have no traditions to fall back on," a Peoria-born "dollar princess" says to Alida, more in wistfulness than in envy. "You are born knowing things we have to learn." Even in their reduced circumstances, this latest clan of authenticated Knickerbockers luxuriate in their traditions and are downright ambassadorial about the city of their birth; they call Croton water their "vin du pays" and try to educate strangers to the subtle delights of New York, encouraging them to look beyond its advertised "theaters and department stores and noise." Ultimately, the charming Alida finds another "last" Knickerbocker to marry, one who has grown conveniently rich by prospecting in the mythical mining town of "Oro City, somewhere in the Rocky Mountains," but who still values the singular New York identity, as she does. With this intercession, Knickerbocker Vielé concludes his valentine to the city, having rescued his postcolonial dame from the genteel poverty that would undo one of the most famous heroines of another New York novelist, Edith Wharton.[51]

"For the first time, the veil has been lifted from New York society," the dust jacket of the first edition of *The House of Mirth* announced, promising that Edith Wharton's 1905 novel would truly be an insider's account of the "Upper Ten Thousand." Although Wharton apparently insisted that Scribner remove the statement from future editions of the book, it was by no means the last time that such a claim would be made about her work. From a commercial perspective, Wharton's Old New York pedigree and Four Hundred status made her the ultimate tour guide to the Gilded Age. "On both sides," Wharton acknowledged in *A Backward Glance*, "our colonial ancestry goes back for nearly three hundred years, and on both sides the colonists in question seem to have been identified since early days with New York." She was born into the world she described, so how could the Manhattan under her microscope not be more precise than the one promised by lesser chroniclers?[52] And yet unlike Herman Knickerbocker Vielé, Wharton make a great point of never describing her New Yorkers as "Knickerbockers" or "Old New Yorkers," and her Manhattan "tribes" consistently deny that their own tribal identifications even exist:

"Don't tell me," Mrs. Archer would say to her children, "all this mod-ern newspaper rubbish about a New York aristocracy. If there is one, neither the Mingotts nor the Mansons belong to it; no, nor the New-lands or the Chiverses either. Our grandfathers and great-grandfathers were just respectable English or Dutch merchants, who came to the colonies to make their fortune, and stayed here because they did so well. One of your great-grandfathers signed the Declaration, and another was a general on Washington's staff, and received General Burgoyne's sword after the battle of Saratoga. These are things to be proud of, but they have nothing to do with rank or class. New York has always been a commercial community, and there are not more than three families in it who can claim an aristocratic origin in the real sense of the word."[53]

These protestations from *The Age of Innocence* are echoed by Whar-ton's own story. She recalls her mother expressing the same "hearty contempt for the tardy discovery of aristocratic genealogies" as Mrs. Archer, and the author asserts that her own family's antecedents were "purely middle class . . . merchants, bankers, and lawyers."[54] How-ever, while Wharton's novels adhere to the letter of these inclusive, republican principles, they universally depart from them in spirit and painstakingly enumerate the inherited attributes that comprise a particular kind of New York aristocracy, closely resembling the one all her literary and tabloid peers were calling "Knickerbocker."

The gently born descendants of the "purely middle class" Dutch and English merchants whose lives are portrayed in novels such as *The House of Mirth, The Custom of the Country*, and *The Age of Inno-cence*, as well as in the novellas that make up the collection *Old New York*, derive their authority over their respective New Yorks from what Pamela Knight has called "the welter of trifles, the matrix of social knowledge" that they, as an elite group, have accumulated through successive generations.[55] These "trifles" range from ances-tral homes and portraits to the provenance of the family wine cel-lar to an innate grasp of the fine-grained linguistic and aesthetic cues—what one Wharton character describes, with airy assurance, as "certain nuances."[56] The crucial importance of these nuances is most keenly felt in *The House of Mirth*, where wealthy climbers ask for Lily Bart's help in fine-tuning their "flamboyant copy" of high society:

> The people about her were doing the same thing as the Trenors, the Van Osburghs, and the Dorsets: the difference lay in a hundred shades of aspect and manner, from the pattern of the men's waistcoats to the inflexion of the women's voices. Everything was pitched in a higher key, and there was more of each thing: more noise, more color, more champagne, more familiarity.[57]

The inability of New York's nouveaux riches to get the details of "aspect and manner" right is handled with a Jamesian allusiveness by the narrator, thus suggesting that the reader, like Knickerbocker Vielé's Alida Van Wandeleer, is familiar with the requirements of "perfect breeding" and needs little prompting to understand how the "social Coney Island" Lily Bart has fallen into can be so near and yet so distant from the island of "Fifth Avenoodledom"—Manhattan.

Above all, however, the evidence of the reach of Wharton's clans, of their right to be called "Society" by Scribner and others, can be found in the complex hierarchy of their inherited, nearly interchangeable names. While Wharton's interest in primitive cultures is well known, her ordered, finite list of Anglo-Dutch family names (sometimes alongside their attributes) owes as much to the "dynasty" of Irving's *History* as it does to her study of the work of anthropologists such as Franz Boas. Claire Preston has noted that Wharton's endless loop of names "reinforces the sense of tribal enclosure and genetic inevitability" in the novels, rendering the cousinships she describes "inscrutable to all but the initiated," as *The Age of Innocence* abundantly shows:

> Mrs. Archer ran thoughtfully over the list, checking off each name with her sharp gold pen.
>
> "Henry van der Luyden—Louisa—the Lovell Mingotts—the Reggie Chiverses—Lawrence Lefferts and Gertrude—(yes, I suppose May was right to have them)—the Sefridge Merrys, Sillerton Jackson, Van Newland and his wife. (How time passes! It seems only yesterday that he was your best man, Newland)—and Countess Olenska—yes, I think that's all. . . ."[58]

Much like Knickerbocker's exegesis of his cherished Dutch warriors' names, this set of reversible names would be opaque to the point of incomprehensibility except for Mrs. Archer's helpful intercessions. In this way, Wharton's names are as useful to the narrative as they are to the individuals who use them as objects of cultural exchange and genealogical calling cards. As the city grows, the names become a necessary substitute for the social cues once conveyed simply by an address. "'When I was a girl,' Mrs. Archer used to say, 'we knew everybody between the Battery and Canal Street; and only the people one knew had carriages. It was perfectly easy to place any one then; now one can't tell and I prefer not to try.'"[59]

Wharton's novels ask Mrs. Archer's question again and again: how can social authority be fixed in a city where the contours of fashionable neighborhoods are perpetually in flux? The New York native who narrates "New Year's Day" comments with rueful clarity that his "pioneering" grandfather, who built in West Twenty-third Street "in days when people shuddered at the perils of living north of Union Square," had, through his forward-thinking real estate purchases, doomed his descendants to "a dullish back-water between Aristocracy to the south and Money to the north." If one's address is not an index of inherited social authority, what is? The answer, for Wharton, is social responsibility. "Delia Ralston sometimes asked herself," the narrator of "The Old Maid" confides, "whether, were she to turn her own little boy loose in a wilderness, he would not create a small New York there, and be on all its boards of directors." This throwaway remark is an uncanny echo of one made in *The Last of the Knickerbockers*, when a non-native New Yorker declares that if a member of the Van Wandeleer family had been born "on the prairies" of the Midwest, instead of in New York City, "he would have taken to civilization like a duck to water. He would have even invented it for himself."[60] It is also shorthand for what was fast becoming a particularly "Knickerbocker" creed. The guiding principles of civic duty and moral obligation to the ancestral city are most evident in *The Age of Innocence*, with its patrician native sons whose every solemn action takes on the significance of a religious rite.[61] Unlike Henry James's New Yorkers, who "stood off, in the awful modern crush" whenever they could, or retreated to what remained of "their quite far-away and antediluvian social period and order," Wharton's characters do their best to see by the "cynical light of New York," cope with its transformations, and do good work on its behalf:

> [Newland Archer] had been, in short, what people were beginning to call a "good citizen." In New York, for many years past, every new movement, philanthropic, municipal, or artistic, had taken account of his opinion and wanted his name. People said: "Ask Archer," when there was a question of starting the first school for crippled children, reorganizing the Museum of Art, founding the Grolier Club, inaugurating the new Library, or getting up a new society of Chamber Music.[62]

By retrospectively inserting the fictional Archer into the real monuments of fin de siècle New York culture and municipal improvement, Wharton connects the code of Old New York to the philanthropic playing field of the modern city. First (and nearly alone) among her "tribal" protagonists, Archer lives out the rest of his life in complete accordance with the genteel ethical code of his literary, as well as historical, ancestors.

Could money create a Knickerbocker? Was the Gilded Age creating "small New Yorks" out of the wilderness, as both Knickerbocker Vielé and Wharton propose? The city's most opulent social institutions at the time of their writing were organized around principles of purchased inclusion: those excluded from the dances held by the "Society of Patriarchs" or blackballed from the Union Club retaliated by throwing "Silver," "Gold," and "Diamond" dinners at Delmonico's Restaurant (such as those hosted by Leonard Jerome, a founder of the Belmont Racetrack and future grandfather of Winston Churchill), by constructing ballrooms of their own in their limestone Fifth Avenue châteaux, and by organizing and presiding over ever more opulent city, yacht, racing, and country clubs. They also availed themselves of the newspapers, which had not stinted, since the days of Moses Beach's list of top earners, in offering help to New Yorkers looking to rank themselves and their neighbors in calling-card hierarchies. As Arthur M. Schlesinger has pointed out, the increased self-consciousness of the urban elite during the late nineteenth century was largely the responsibility of the media, which capitalized on the fact that New York's social as well as economic primacy had become a subject of national interest.[63] In tabloids, supplements, circulars, and "exclusives," confidants with blue-blooded pen names claimed the authority to translate the grammar of society for those living beyond its reach. The dish and drama of upper-class New York had become gilded commodities, and tabloids and respectable publishers alike sold them nationwide, as well as back to the self-conscious "ton" who had manufactured their news in the first place. Chief among these recyclers was the society tabloid *Town Topics*, founded in New York in 1885 under the banner "Able, Fearless, Truthful: A Trustworthy Chronicle of Events in the World of SOCIETY." Such events, according to the paper, included "Art, Literature, Music and the Drama," as well as, naturally, "Other People's Money: Hints for Bulls and Bears." When not delivering the latest blind item about upper-crust extramarital relations, *Town Topics* critiqued the parties from Tuxedo to Chicago, offered comments on the throng at the Metropolitan Opera (fashionable New Yorkers were particularly fond of two high-profile divas, Christine Nilsson and Adelina Patti), and posed the occasional ontological question, such as "Have We an Aristocracy?" The magazine even had a cameo appearance in Wharton's novel *The Custom of the Country*, where it was referred to as *Town Talk* and was chief among the tabloids that enabled the heroine, Undine Spragg of Apex City, to arrive in Manhattan knowing "all of New York's golden aristocracy by name," particularly "its most distinguished scions . . . made familiar by passionate poring over the daily press." But Irving's clans did not figure in the tabloid tales of *Town Topics* except as a footnote, when a nostalgic or moral point is to be made. To this end, a discussion of etiquette classes for children is punctuated by the remark that "fashionable kindergartens" have been sadly overlooked "ever since, in fact, the days of the Knickerbocker regime," and a social note spoofs Knickerbocker Club members' habit of sitting in the club window, suggesting that their "stolid immobility" has led the neighborhood children to believe that "the club keeps an assortment of stuffed dudes to show the public." Occasionally, a bona fide descendant of the Knickerbockers of Schaghticoke makes an appearance in the tabloid, such as when it is noted that one Mr. Henry Knickerbocker has been glimpsed in his box at the Metropolitan Opera. How can these competing invocations of Knickerbocker be reconciled? Is the "regime" really over if actual Knickerbockers still make their social authority felt at the most fashionable venue in town? What Knickerbocker might mean to New York's popular press is suggested by a long editorial entitled "The Views of a Fossil: Society as It Was and Is," which digs a grave for "Irving's peerage with its array of Vans and 'broecks'": "We have somehow lost our connection with the colonial days. The savor of them has departed. I think it must be owing to the advent of *nouveaux riches* of the eager, pushing sort, who have reached the top round of the ladder, and have driven into comparative obscurity the old names and the old people. [They] have no traditions." The "Fossil" flatters his reader, who, it is assumed, will understand the import of this provocative lament and share his disapproval as well as the nostalgia that has become the stock in trade of so many New Yorkers by the late nineteenth century. Not surprisingly, the "Fossil" neglects to mention that "Irving's peerage" is a fabrication, not unlike the "pushing" clans vying for a place in *Town Topics.* Like Herman Knickerbocker's Peoria princess, the tabloid denies the possibility that the new families at the "top round of the ladder" could bring any authentic "traditions" of their own to high society, or, for that matter, show any manners.[64]

Other "trustworthy chronicles" of Fifth Avenue were more sanguine, proposing that "the old names and old people" should be preserved for much the same purpose as the Van Cortlandt House: to lead the striving arrivistes by their dignified example. This is the mantra of social arbiter Ward McAllister, whose 1890 memoir, *Society as I Have Found It,* describes his founding of the city's famous "Patriarchs' Ball" and included the original list of Mrs. Astor's famous "Four Hundred" (supposedly the number of guests who would fit in her Manhattan ballroom, and hence the inexorable measure of true New York "society"). His decorous tell-all dropped hints on how that storied roster came into existence and gave readers a little hope that they might infiltrate the "Bourbon" class themselves: "You could but read the list of those who gave these balls, to see at a glance that they embraced not only the smart set but the old Knickerbocker families as well; and that they would, from the very nature of the case, representing the best society of this great commercial city, have to grow and enlarge."[65] McAllister presumes that his readership will immediately grasp the implicit distinction between the "smart set" and the "old Knickerbocker families" and that they will comprehend, as he says Mrs. Astor does, the "value of ancestry" in establishing a lasting, organized American gentry. While the Astor Four Hundred has since come to serve as shorthand for the idea of a delimited, self-proclaimed New York society, it was by no means the last list of its kind.[66] McAllister's competition included *The Season: An Annual Record of Society* (1883), *King's Notable New Yorkers*, which began publication in 1899, *The Ultra-Fashionable Peerage in America: An Official List of People Who Can Properly Be Called Ultra-Fashionable in the United States, with a Few Appended Essays on Ultra-Smartness* (1904), and its update, *469 Ultra-Fashionables of America: A Social Guidebook and Register to Date* (1912).[67] These last two catalogs were the arch, semi-serious offerings of Charles Wilberforce DeLyon Nicholls, self-proclaimed "Governor General of the National Society of Scions of Colonial Cavaliers," who urged "ambitious" readers to "employ a press agent at once," the better to increase their visibility on the city scene. Part etiquette manual, part *Debrett's Peerage*, Nicholls's books signal their author's understanding of the intricate and shifting ranking system that codified New York's established elite, even as he argues for their increasing irrelevance in a post–Mrs. Astor environment, one where social decisions were driven largely by sheer quantities of cash. In Nicholls's "five descending degrees of fashionable precedence," the "Vicereagal leaders of the '150'" come first, and "colonial and Knickerbocker families" only fourth. Despite this profane relegation, his Knickerbocker families are not so different from those of Wharton, Knickerbocker Vielé, or even Mrs. Van Rensselaer herself; they are characterized, he tells the uninitiated, by "an innate shrinking from the seeming vulgarity of great wealth," and a penchant for "sit[ting] apart [from society] like the gods upon Olympus."[68]

The most enduring of these directories was the *Social Register*, a privately managed and published annual list that was founded in 1887 by the Social Register Association of New York and has been continuously published since that time. A self-proclaimed "record of Society, comprising an accurate and careful list of its members, with their addresses, many of the maiden names of the married women, the club addresses of the men, officers of the leading clubs and social organizations, opera box holders, and other useful social information," the *Register*'s first edition included sections with the titles "departures and foreign addresses," "engaged," "married," "deaths," and "club elections" (the Knickerbocker, Union, Century, and Tuxedo clubs were among those the *Register* deemed "leading clubs").[69] No definition of "society" has ever been offered by the Social Register Association, nor has the organization ever publicly explained by what science or art it arrives at its "accurate and careful" list. Perhaps this is why the *Register* endures: like Wharton's "certain nuances," it derives its lasting influence from its ineffability.

Whether serious or in jest, all of these taxonomies, like Wharton's tangled, interchangeable genealogies, derive their structure and first authority from Irving's primordial list of "patriarchs" and appropriate the language of his narrator to define and limit the ranks of the "American aristocracy" whose existence Mrs. Archer had so vehemently denied. By the time the *Social Register* was published, New York City had assembled a fairly complete portrait of itself. Through guidebooks, memoirs, and novels, white New Yorkers, native and immigrant alike, had been given the tools to reminisce convincingly about a past they may not have shared. The aspirational among them memorized and invoked the names on the city's social roster, even as that exalted pantheon continued to shift. They commissioned family trees, designed ancestral crests, and preserved historic homesteads, the better to prove their authentic connection to Irving's "real lords of the soil." And in the never-ending effort to get into (and stay in) Manhattan's "Knickerbocracy," they had become increasingly philanthropic and civic-minded. But the Gilded Age had sanitized the Dutch champion, leaching the earthy hilarity and quixotic pride from his trademark clans on the losing side. In fact, Knickerbocker himself seemed to be no longer a Gotham trademark but a hasty footnote on the society page, an insider's reference to burgher values and old-fashioned pastimes. The Knickerbocker name, much like his eponymous Civil War currency, had been sadly devalued.

CHAPTER 4

KNICKERBOCKER IN A NEW CENTURY

KNICKERBOCKER, PATERFAMILIAS

"DAMP DAYS FOR OLD NEW YORK," announced the *New York Times* headline on January 1, 1898. "Father Knickerbocker's Last Day as a Bachelor Was Spent under an Umbrella." The plan to consolidate Manhattan (known primarily as New York City), Brooklyn, the Bronx, Queens, and Staten Island into the five boroughs of "Greater New York" was coming to fruition in a downpour. The credit for this once impossible partnership was due to the redoubtable Andrew Haswell Green, the previously discussed champion of landmarks and commissioner of parks. But consolidation was no easy task: at the time, Brooklyn was an economic rival to Manhattan, while the Bronx was known as the "Annex," more than fifty-seven square miles of small towns and farmland, formerly part of Westchester County, that was officially under the jurisdiction of Green and his Parks Department. It would take seven years for Green, then-Mayor William L. Strong (who ran on the borough "Fusion" ticket), and numerous city bosses to come to an agreement for these disparate regions. "The Imperial city has won an honorable renown throughout the world," Green declared, in an attempt to convince New Yorkers of the wisdom of his grand design, "which all her colonies may proudly inherit and which they cannot avoid accepting."[1] Green's "imperial" philosophy of New York City was the guiding force behind the consolidation plan and inspired its brand-new mascot: "Father Knickerbocker."

Suddenly, Knickerbocker was more popular than he had been since 1809. During the seven years that it took to push the Greater New York

113

initiative through the legislatures of Manhattan and Brooklyn, the Dutch historian was resurrected almost as frequently as he had been during Irving's lifetime. Cartoons of his likeness became a popular staple of daily newspapers and satirical magazines such as *Punch*. But there was a crucial difference: the former spokesperson for the vanquished, the offbeat, the self-segregating, or the nearly extinct had become the captain of the winning team. As Commissioner Green lobbied to connect the diverse islands and territories that comprised his ideal New York, the media image of his unifying "Father" figure grew ever more patrician and powerful. In fact, this new consolidation icon can be best described by what he was not. He was not Irving's retiring historian, Diedrich, "cousin-german to the Congressman" at Schaghticoke. He was not a muse, a paranoid nativist, a vestigial member of the fading "Knickerbocracy," or an advertisement for New Year's cakes, billiard tables, or baseball. This new Knickerbocker did not resemble the Irving-approved F.O.C. Darley sketches of Knickerbocker the historian, slight of frame and quizzical of expression, wearing his battered hat and shabby cloak (one appears on the cover of this book). Nor could Green's mascot be mistaken for the popular illustrations of Rip Van Winkle—by now a near-canonical text for American children—who was universally depicted as in need of a wash and a beard trimming, after his twenty-year sleep in the Catskills. This Dutchman, in contrast, was polished and political, and he seemed never to sleep. In fact, there was little that looked "Dutch" at all about the consolidation-era Father Knickerbocker, and yet he was understood, by admirers, invokers, and the readers of *Punch*, to still be that Virgil of Gotham that New Yorkers knew as Knickerbocker.

It is difficult, from more than a century's distance, to see a resemblance to Irving's 1809 original in the Father Knickerbocker of 1898. He was Gilded Age New York's idea of a colonial founding father—strapping, portly, and with powdered curls. In the cartoons that charted his consolidation travails, only Knickerbocker's physiognomy changed with the political situation: if he was victorious, it was round and beatific, not unlike the beaming William Penn look-alike whose portrait graced contemporary packages of Quaker Oats.[2] Or, if he was under siege, Knickerbocker's curls grew longer and his face more severe, until he resembled an earlier and more quarrelsome city champion, Peter Stuyvesant.[3] But even when his expression and coiffure changed, his uniform was consistently grand, befitting Green's imperial consolidation mission. Father Knickerbocker's cutaway coat was nearly always trimmed with gold braid, and his buttons and shoe buckles had been upgraded to gold, too. His cuffs and jabot were usually ruffled, and he might also sport a lace handkerchief, handily embroidered with the logo "New York City" or "Knickerbocker," tucked into a breast pocket. The identifying label was essential to the newspaper depiction of the historian—if the occasion didn't call for a handkerchief, a plume embellished with "Knickerbocker" would wave from his tricorn hat. And the Fusion Father Knickerbocker stayed on message: whether beset by Tammany bosses or Brooklyn partisans (often shown trying to lash him to Manhattan with railroad ties or, in the form of Lilliputians, nipping at his Gulliver-like heels), he always brandished a beribboned parchment charter for Greater New York's consolidation. In short, the image of the Father of Greater New York was as genteel, responsible, and sanitized as any of his self-appointed caretakers could wish. After consolidation legislation was finally passed in 1898, New York's new mascot grew magnanimous in victory, as his ancestors had never had the opportunity to be. He changed from the ardent suitor of "Miss Brooklyn," who had been represented, during the consolidation negotiations, by the cartoon of a pretty young woman, weighing the merits of Knickerbocker's proposal while anti-consolidation advisors railed behind her, to the tolerant father of "little Brooklyn," an obstreperous boy in tam-o'-shanter and short pants. And finally, he was depicted as the triumphant, avuncular head of a peaceable, five-borough family, each borough represented, as Brooklyn had first been, by a young woman of Gibson Girl proportions, dressed in flowing Columbian robes and draped in a stars-and-stripes sash.

Although these early twentieth-century invocations swaddled Irving's creation first in layers of Gilded Age pretension and then in consolidation's red tape, they did not entirely erase the scrappy, cheeky personality that had captivated readers nearly a hundred years before. By the turn of the century, the Knickerbocker name was well-established shorthand for New York itself, and the long memory of his proud Gothamites would not allow it to be entirely supplanted with the staid, imperial architect of 1898. Instead, after consolidation the Father Knickerbocker icon was sent back into the ring, to become synonymous with a city under siege by the competing interests of local and state governments. He was pressed into service as an emblem of civic probity and honor, the long-suffering and incorruptible advocate for the five boroughs, foe of big business and bosses with "predatory plans." "Father Knickerbocker needs to keep a sharper lookout than ever," warned a 1903 pamphlet entitled *Greater New York Government, 1902–1903: Father Knickerbocker Adrift.* "His rickety 'Fusion' raft is in more danger than that of helpless drifting. There are political pirates about whose purpose is to capture him and to deliver him into the hands of his enemies." In a reversal of Irving's original Dutch iconography, the media occasionally depicted the state government at Albany as Knickerbocker's chief opponent: "It is when he takes a drink that Father Knickerbocker gets it the worst from the State government that favors its farmer friends. Whether the New Yorker drinks much or little, seldom or often, whether he takes wine, beer or whiskey, he pays heavily in this indulgence toward relieving the tax burdens of the inhabitants of the rest of the State." Other observers suggested that New York's consolidator had some fight left, like his Dutch antecedents, and would soon revolt against the unsophisticated tyranny of state government. "They are independents, these New Yorkers," Rupert Hughes wrote in *The Real New York,* "and are constantly talking of forming a State of their own as a release from the truly rural rule of Albany. 'Secede from Hayseed' would doubtless be the war cry. But for the present, Father Knickerbocker must be content with *J'y suis, j'y reste.*"[4]

It turned out that Father Knickerbocker did indeed need to be vigilant: in 1907, the Knickerbocker most often in the news was the Knickerbocker Trust Bank, which had closed its doors after the news of a failed copper mine speculation led to a run on the bank and created a large-scale financial panic that nearly shut the New York Stock Exchange.[5] In the wake of this significant destabilizing incident in the city's history, we discover Father Knickerbocker presiding over the Hudson-Fulton celebrations that took place in 1909, to mark the three hundredth anniversary of Hudson's discovery and the centennial of

Fulton's successful steamboat demonstration (as well as Knicker-bocker's own hundredth birthday). Across New York state, numer-ous tricentennial celebrations featured flotillas bearing individuals costumed as Knickerbocker, and the five boroughs of Greater New York organized a "Children's Fete" reminiscent of the Knickerbocker Greys, in which an anticipated two hundred thousand New York chil-dren would be "drilled" at "training camps in Van Cortlandt Park" for their role in a celebration that included representing "a congress of nations . . . [expressing] their loyalty to Father Knickerbocker."[6] However, the mythic associations of the fictional Dutchman ultimately could not postpone the challenging realities of twentieth-century New York. Irving's famous moniker was now freighted with rival mean-ings and memories, and even the patrician financier J. P. Morgan, emblem, to some, of Knickerbocker-style living in New York's Gilded Age, couldn't keep the Knickerbocker Trust from failing after the new century had turned. The "authentic" historian and city champion was now irrevocably in the fray, as likely to be co-opted by working New Yorkers as by politicians or self-segregating elites. "*Wake Up! Father Knickerbocker*—Your Library Needs You" blazed the headline over the picture of a man in tricorn hat and knee breeches curled in sleep at the foot of one of the New York Public Library's marble lions. The illustration might have been whimsical, but the message was urgent. "Nearly 1,000 Public Library Employees" had borrowed the Dutch historian's image for the cover of a 1924 labor rights pam-phlet, in order to make a vivid point about the city's increasingly negligent treatment of cherished resources such as the public library system. New Yorkers should not allow this decline in city support for a public amenity to go unchallenged, the pamphlet exhorted; "express your opinion to your local Democratic leader, to the members of the Board of Estimate, and through the columns of the press."[7] In other words, use every muckraking reporter and urban reformer at your disposal to remind the city of its founding principles and to wake Father Knickerbocker from his negligent nap.

The librarians' irreverent, slightly disapproving invocation suggests that while Irving's historian (in his paternal role) was still considered to be New York's "mediator and advocate," the exalted associations that "Knickerbocker" had enjoyed in the late nineteenth century had already faded. The opera-box hierarchies and club fiefdoms that governed Knickerbocker Vielé's and Wharton's brownstone-clad "Old New York" had been replaced by a Jazz Age variety show, one whose electrified syncopations fueled the work of F. Scott Fitzgerald, John Dos Passos, and Langston Hughes and seemed, at first glance, to lack all sense of stratification, not to mention history. New Yorkers were imbued "not only with no history, but with no credible possibility of time for history," Henry James had complained in 1907. "One story is good only till another is told . . . and the consciousness of that truth, the consciousness of the finite, the menaced, the essentially *invented* state, twinkles ever, to my perception, in the thousand glassy eyes" of the skyscrapers he observed with open dismay.[8] How could Knickerbocker be expected to keep pace with this new urban rhythm, whose tempo was so different from all that had come before? Would he—or should he—survive the transition? New York was no longer in Washington Irving's century, and fewer and fewer writers and city chroniclers looked to Knickerbocker's fabled ancestors for reassurance of respectability, or a link to the Old World. As Wharton had demonstrated in her last, unfinished work, *The Buccaneers*, what were now called Manhattan's "dollar princesses" hunted down their proxy pedigrees in Europe, rather than among the family trees of New Amsterdam, while those who were not already in Mrs. Astor's Four Hundred didn't seem to care.

But Greater New York's first century did find new uses for Knickerbocker, and if Irving's creation did not feature in many of the literary productions of the time, his name and composite image were still sent to work, to play, and to war, sometimes all at once. Knickerbocker supported the New Deal and Uncle Sam, drank beer and played basketball, marketed large-scale investments and low-income housing projects, and kept watch over the dwindling number of his genteel descendants and their debutante daughters. These invocations could seem as kinetic and fractured as their historic moment, and they ranged from casual references and elastic generalizations to grave petitions and manifestos of rigid exclusivity. Sometimes the Knickerbocker name was used in the context of Dutch culture and heritage, but more often than not the twentieth-century usage was related to the historian's other famous trait—his New York exceptionalism.

As we have seen, the Knickerbocker works in Irving's oeuvre all invariably return to the theme of superiority; the tolerant, stable, and fun-loving New Amsterdammers and their descendants always claim the moral victory over their English invaders or Yankee neighbors, and no matter what calamity overtakes them, the "genuine lords of the soil" ultimately triumph, sometimes in spite of themselves. By virtue of being "authentic" New Yorkers, in the Knickerbocker parlance, they are, as the historian represents them, impervious to the encroachments of change and modernity, and the city nurtures their secret ambitions much as Wolfert Webber tended the desperate cabbages that would be his literal "cash crop" in the end. This Knickerbocker philosophy could not help but appeal to the imaginations of twentieth-century New Yorkers in a wide spectrum of economic and cultural circumstances, as they met the unthinkable challenges of economic depression, war, and hectic modernization. Who would not want to claim that privileged authenticity for himself, or to advertise his right, whether innate or earned, to be a citizen of this exhilarating, overwhelming metropolis? Knickerbocker was also offered to out-of-towners as a goodwill ambassador, a personality for the impersonal Empire City. One guidebook for investors, *Father Knickerbocker; or, Bag-dad on the Subway,* hawked the city like a sideshow attraction: "One City With a Demand to Equal Ten Western States!"[9] This extrapolation from Irving's original suited the demanding city quite well, too; New York's project was no longer one of self-fashioning but one of self-promotion, and Knickerbocker, woken by the librarians from his complacent slumber, was the ideal symbol for this ambitious new campaign.

The advent of this new, exceptionalist Knickerbocker coincided with the shuttering of one of the city's most elaborate—if short-lived—Gilded Age temples: the Knickerbocker Hotel. Built by John Jacob Astor IV in 1905 at the corner of Forty-second Street and Broadway, the Knickerbocker was an instant landmark. The sixteen-story wedding cake of terra-cotta and limestone with an imposing mansard roof presided over the dizzy bustle and glamour of Times Square with queenly grandeur. When it opened, the hotel boasted unheard-of luxury, including individual "Paris-made" winding clocks in each guest room, multiple restaurants, and an entire floor devoted to banqueting facilities.[10] It was the sometime home of opera star Enrico Caruso, and it was the birthplace of the martini, a gin cocktail devised by the hotel's bartender, Martini di Arma di Taggia. In addition to its famous tipple, the bar at the Knickerbocker Hotel also had a secret that its mystery-loving namesake would have appreciated: a subterranean entrance via a platform of the newly created Times Square subway station. The brass sign over that unobtrusive, underground door read simply "Knickerbocker"—a winking welcome, for those who could find it, to the pre-Prohibition glamour that was just inside.[11] It was also a subtle reminder, for those who might remember Irving's work, that the hotel's literary name was as deeply embedded in New York's history as the new subway was in dense Manhattan schist.

A monument to Edwardian excess, the Knickerbocker Hotel would have made an ideal backdrop for Lily Bart, the decadent, doomed heroine of Edith Wharton's *The House of Mirth*, published the same year that Astor opened the hotel for business. Although the annual "Knickerbocker Dances" of the first decade of the twentieth century took place at another Astor property, the Waldorf-Astoria, erected on the site of Mrs. Astor's famous ballroom, Lily Bart could very well have celebrated New Year's Eve under the merry gaze of the Knickerbocker's Maxfield Parrish mural of Old King Cole, who presided over the revelry of thousands who dined, danced, and toasted their way to "Auld Lang Syne" at the hotel each year.[12] Like Wharton's fragile heroine, however, the hotel was ill equipped for modern life, and after the Eighteenth Amendment passed in 1920, banning the "manufacture, sale, or transportation of intoxicating liquors" in the United States, the Knickerbocker shut its doors with precipitous speed. Astor renovated the property into profit-making office space, and Old King Cole was dismantled and shipped first to the New York Athletic Club, where it remained until the repeal of Prohibition, and then to the St. Regis Hotel, another Astor property, where the mural remains to this day. "No hotel in the city which ever had anything approaching the popularity and patronage of the Knickerbocker was ever closed in so short a time," the *New York Times* declared, noting that the "many Times Square habitués who fondly recall the pleasing sociability of the famous cafe" will blame the hotel's closing on "the ultra-dry wave now legally experienced throughout the country." But the Knickerbocker's celebrated café with the subway entrance did survive the hotel, suggesting that New Yorkers had not abandoned Times Square, even if the out-of-towners had fled to more wholesome neighborhoods. After a reported $250,000 in Art Deco renovations the "famous" Knickerbocker Grill reopened, and it rode out the first years of Prohibition with Roaring Twenties panache. The Grill even brought musical fame to Irving's Dutch moniker, launching the Knickerbocker Grill Orchestra, a group of moonlighting Los Angeles Symphony Orchestra members led by classical violinist Eddie Elkins, who would record Jazz Age hits such as "Dapper Dan" and "I Want You, Morning, Noon, and Night" (both 1921) for Columbia Records. The restaurant's celebrity did not entirely protect it from Prohibition, however: in 1922, the Grill was raided by detectives who found "ten bottles of beer containing more than ½ of 1 percent alcohol"— the amount of alcohol needed to make a drink "intoxicating," and thus illegal, per the 1919 Volstead Act. Although they made several arrests, the inspectors were ultimately thwarted in their attempt to close the restaurant because they had been "unable to buy liquor, although they allege[d] they saw it served to others." Much like its namesake, the Knickerbocker Grill survived to thumb its nose at the new regime a little longer.[13]

If the beer seized at the Grill had been Knickerbocker Beer, no arrests would have been necessary. In 1919, anticipating the passing of the Eighteenth Amendment, the Ruppert Brewery of New York City had made application for a trademark on a formulation of "near beer," to be called Knickerbocker. By the time Knickerbocker Beer was christened, the Ruppert Brewery had long been considered one of Manhattan's foremost beer manufacturers and was an established presence in the metropolitan area. The brewery, which had been founded by Jacob Ruppert in Yorkville in 1867 and incorporated in 1910, was still a family business by Prohibition, led by Ruppert's son, "Colonel" Jacob Ruppert Jr., a former Democratic congressman and, since 1914, co-owner of the New York Yankees. With a Manhattan pedigree such as this, Colonel Ruppert's choice of names for his Prohibition-era beverage might not be considered remarkable, if it had not been for World War I and the passing of the War-Time Prohibition Act in

1918, which forbade the use of "grains, cereals, fruit, or other food product . . . in the manufacture or production of beer, wine, or other intoxicating malt or vinous liquor for beverage purposes" until the war and subsequent demobilization were over. During World War I, the government suspected many German immigrants to the United States of being "enemy nationals," and the War-Time Prohibition Act threw the same suspicion on German American beer manufacturers. Brands formerly considered wholesome and American were vilified as insidious foreign weapons, traitorous tools of military and moral corruption. "Pabst, Schlitz, Blatz, and Miller," one politician expounded, "are the worst Germans who ever inflicted themselves on a long-suffering [American] people." Like Ruppert, many of the targeted brewers had been in the United States for generations and were notable philanthropists in their adopted cities, but these considerations did not stop the U.S. Custodian of Alien Property from seizing some German brewers' assets. Colonel Ruppert himself was suspected of "financing and organizing enemy propaganda in a nation at war" and was investigated during a series of Senate hearings organized to look into the accusations that foreign national brewers were using their influence and wealth to spread wartime propaganda and fix local American elections.[14] It did not seem to matter that the Ruppert Brewery was one of the oldest in continuous operation on the island of Manhattan, or that the brewery represented a tradition of beer manufacturing in New York dating back to the seventeenth century.[15] He and his fellow immigrants were still targets of the era's anti-German blacklists, and no proof of their allegiance was proof enough.[16]

Against this xenophobic backdrop, Ruppert's decision to name his Prohibition-friendly beverage Knickerbocker demonstrates an intriguing understanding of marketing and a sophisticated political intuition.[17] By appropriating Irving's narrator as his mascot, the brewer asserts his own ties to New York City (and, by implication, to the United States over which the city now reigned as tastemaker supreme). He brings the old Dutch associations of the name back into the marketplace, reminding prospective buyers that beer was a favorite drink in New Amsterdam long before the first German immigrant arrived (and well before the founding of the Women's Christian Temperance

Union). Ruppert's literary borrowing also allows him to share in the genteel authenticity that was ascribed to the hundred-year-old original. Certainly, Knickerbocker was a more evocative and consumer-flattering choice than the names given to the "near beers" produced by his rivals, such as Bevo, Quizz, Hoppy, and Lux-o.[18] And finally, by giving the name to an essentially nonalcoholic "cereal beverage" that would not be outlawed by the inevitable passage of the Eighteenth Amendment, Ruppert ensured both the continuance of his own brewery after Prohibition had been decreed and the grudging goodwill of the Anti-Saloon League. It is also possible that the Knickerbocker name simply suggested itself to Colonel Ruppert after an incident, in 1914, when the driver of a Ruppert Brewery "electric truck" was taken to the aptly named Knickerbocker Hospital in Harlem with injuries sustained in a traffic accident. The *New York Times* had declared the deliveryman's crash to be an act of civic heroism: according to the paper, he had "[turned] sharply to avoid children playing in the street." Perhaps Ruppert meant to pay homage to the decency and compassion of everyday New Yorkers in his native city, or perhaps he was longing for the halcyon days of 1914, when his product could still contain 3 percent alcohol by volume and the German origins of his brewery were not cause for prejudice or attack. Regardless of the reason, the name, as we will see, was an immensely popular and lucrative choice, and it would grace Ruppert bottles and cans for more than half a century to come.[19]

Ruppert Brewery was not the only trafficker in Knickerbocker pedigrees in the 1920s. The same year that Colonel Ruppert applied for the trademark for Knickerbocker Beer, the society columnist Maury Paul adopted the nom de plume of Cholly Knickerbocker. Early in his career Paul had had numerous columns and numerous aliases, including Polly Stuyvesant, Billy Benedick, and Dolley Madison, names that demonstrate his deep understanding of the camp possibilities inherent in the Anglo-Dutch aspirations of his readership, flattering his own snobberies—he was a distant relative of the Biddles, one of the founding families of Philadelphia—at the same time. But it was as Cholly Knickerbocker that Paul would popularize the terms "café society," to describe America's new class of Gatsbys, and "the Old Guard," to characterize any living remnants of Mrs. Astor's antediluvian Four Hundred. And it was as Cholly Knickerbocker that Paul, writing for William Randolph Hearst's *New York Journal-American*, would come to be one of the most highly paid newspaper columnists of his era and a factory for syndicated columns that enlarged on *Town Topics*–style themes such as "First Families," "Ask Cholly," and "Tragedies of Society." Cholly Knickerbocker was aided and abetted in his scandalmongering by the very society ladies, or "turreted tiara set," as he dubbed them, who were his targets.[20] These *Social Register* debutantes and wives (or ex-wives) of robber barons were increasingly in demand as "celebrity" endorsers of commercial products. They included Mrs. Reginald Vanderbilt and the daughter of J. P. Morgan, both of whom endorsed Pond's Cold Cream; the interior decorator Elsie de Wolfe, who stumped for Willys-Overland automobiles; and Mrs. A. J. Drexel Biddle, who praised the "genius" construction of the Simmons mattress.[21] Knickerbocker names were recruited by Madison Avenue, too, and Mrs. Van Rensselaer's "goede vrouwen" would have been horrified to see one of their descendants, Mrs. Brookfield (Adele) Van Rensselaer, reclining with a Camel cigarette for an advertisement in the pages of *Good Housekeeping.*[22] In such a fluid, unflappable social marketplace, though, there were very few "patriarchs" left for Cholly Knickerbocker to shock.

The social scribe was already so well known by 1929 that Cole Porter included a mention of the tattle-sheet columnist in his song "Where Would You Get Your Coat?" in which a furrier exhorts his female customers to be "bourgeois in their habits" so that

> Cholly Knickerbocker might have nothing to write
> And *Town Topics* would cease to be read.[23]

Porter would also include references to Cholly Knickerbocker in songs from his musicals *Red, Hot, and Blue* (1932), *Let's Face it* (1941), and *High Society* (1956), in part because the column outlasted its creator. After Paul's death in 1942, the Ukranian émigré Igor Loiewski-Cassini would inherit both the name and the newspaper column, which he re-inaugurated with the deadly serious prediction of a new Gilded Age for America and the emphatic, desperate announcement "Society is here to stay!"[24]

Society's staying power may have been debatable, but the ownership of Knickerbocker was still being contested. In 1924, Mrs. John
King Van Rensselaer published *The Social Ladder*, a final attempt to
arrest the evolving portrait of her ancestors. Calling Irving a "moody
man, subject to fits of sullen depression," the author admits that his
History hit its target and "lacerated the sensibilities of . . . ancestor-
worshipping New Yorkers," although she declines, for obvious reasons, to critique the practice of ancestor worship herself. Instead,
the author once more asserts the unbridgeable distance between
the descendants of the Dutch settlers of "gentle blood [with] great
estates . . . princes in everything except name," and those who were
widely regarded as the "princes" of New York in the 1920s: "To members of the old regime, who valued names above notoriety, and lin-
eage above bank books, New York Society, as the average person uses
the term today, is not composed to any great extent of the socially
elect or of New Yorkers. . . . Readers come to regard those persons
most frequently featured by the press as belonging to 'old Knickerbocker families.' In nine cases out of ten their judgment is wrong."
But even the author cannot, finally, avoid employing Knickerbocker
as a descriptor: particularly for those who trafficked in sentimental
snobbery, as Mrs. Van Rensselaer did, Irving's icon was a juggernaut
that could not be ignored. Impossible, when Irving's own publisher,
G. P. Putnam and Sons, had spun off a press named for Knickerbocker
(as well as launching the Knickerbocker Series of Choice American Novels) and even published *The Knickerbocker Jingles*, written by
Maud Stoutenburgh Eliot under the name Judith Stuyvesant, to ex-
plain in rhyming couplets "Why the name Knickerbocker / Attendeth
[New Yorkers] like Fate."[25]

Others contested the pretentious associations that still clung to
Knickerbocker and suggested different arenas for the city's erstwhile
mascot. A menu from the January 17, 1918, "Knickerbocker Dinner in
Olde New York," hosted by the "Ye Olde Settlers Association of Ye West
Side," suggests that New Yorkers were perfectly capable of lampoon-
ing their own snobberies, or at least those of their neighbors across
Central Park. With a winking assertion that its membership must
be limited to men who have lived twenty years or more "between
Sixtieth and 120 Streets and west of the Park," the association at once

acknowledges and deflates the ambitions of their earnest and restrictive genealogical counterparts (such as the Daughters of Holland Dames). The Knickerbocker Dinner itself, subtitled the "Dinner of Our Daddies," lampoons the faux vintage feasts of the Saint Nicholas Society and other turn-of-the-century ancestor worship societies by offering not "coquilles à la Knickerbocker" or "East River Oysters" but instead "New Hampshire Bean Soup . . . Yankee Pumpkin Pie, [and] Gingerbread, 'Mayflower Brand.'"[26] This last, ostensibly store-bought item is a reminder that the icons of New England's founding families were already being exploited in the American supermarket, right alongside Knickerbocker (beer) and the aforementioned William Penn (oats). But the Knickerbocker brand, thus deflated, regains some of the mischief of the original, and the association's spoof returns Irving's work to its homespun, satirical roots. Rejected by Van Rensselaers and embraced by West Siders: what would the post-patriarchal Knickerbocker be?

The Settlers Association had it right: New Yorkers were patently less concerned with the demise of high society after World War I than they were with the vanishing of its "Old Guard" haunts and ancestral sites. Despite the early work of the Scenic and Historic Preservation Society and New York's genealogical crusaders, during the first decades of the twentieth century the city turned a blind eye to the demolition of several buildings of architectural and historical significance. These included Saint John's Chapel, a Varick Street church designed by architect John McComb Jr. and completed before McComb's most famous New York structure, City Hall, had marked the western frontier of Manhattan, a hundred years before. Anthony Wood notes that these losses to New York's built environment spurred photographic surveys of endangered structures (such as Gracie Mansion) by the city's Art Commission and also galvanized Park Commissioner Francis Gallatin to develop a prescient set of guidelines for landmarks legislation in order to "save any building of antiquarian or sentimental interest or of architectural beauty."[27] To New York's future detriment, Gallatin's guidelines were never adopted by the city, but they may have been the inspiration behind the early twentieth-century offerings of a genre we have already studied: the portrait of "Old New York." Some writers imposed their own pedigree on the landscape of New Amsterdam, praising the skyscrapers "soaring into the empyrean" and the "unpretentious, substantial, liveable" new homes lining Riverside Drive and Fifth Avenue, at the expense of Victorian artifacts such as the Castle Garden, which only "the folk with neither New York ancestry nor history" think are old enough to be worth preserving.[28]

The fate of New York itself was at stake in *Little Old New York*, a 1922 magazine that attempted to capture the city's increasingly famous zeitgeist by educating its residents with preservation-minded articles such as "How Old Is New York?" "Dutch New York," and "How New York Grew." *Little Old New York* was forward-thinking and populist, as well as nostalgic, and offered a forum for editorials about New York's "vehicular congestion" and innovative public transportation schemes (such as a shuttle subway loop around Central Park). This surprising combination of reminiscence and reform suggests that New Yorkers were beginning to wonder about the impact of sprawl on urban infrastructure and connecting that danger, as Gallatin did, to the loss of all that they considered "little" and "old" about their beloved city.[29] Another slim volume, entitled *Yesterdays in Little Old New York*, published in 1929, offered a refresher course in the Dutch contributions to New York, crediting the colonists with bringing "Commercial Enterprise, Cosmopolitan Spirit, Religious Toleration, Free Public Education, [and] Representative Municipal Government" to the present-day city. This work anticipates Edith Wharton's lament, in her memoir, for the city's "Atlantis-fate" by pointing out that the very expression "Little Old New York" is a "somewhat elastic phrase," since "not a building remains to link us to the time of Stuyvesant," except in the memories of those whose "fathers and grandfathers were born where the crooked little streets still twist and turn."[30]

Ironically, it was precisely this ancestral nexus of "crooked little streets," once the fashionable heart of colonial New York, which would be the site of New York's next monument to Knickerbocker: a large-scale, middle income development called Knickerbocker Village, erected by real estate mogul Fred F. French in 1933. At the time of French's planning, the area bounded by Catherine, Market, Monroe, and Cherry streets was considered to be squarely within the bounds of the Lower East Side, the commercial and cultural hub of working-class Eastern European emigration to New York. It was a parcel of Manhattan that was not without history, however, for the newly inaugurated President George Washington and his wife had first lived at No. 3 Cherry Street, before moving to a more centrally located home on Broadway, and No. 7 Cherry Street had been the first New York home to be lit by gaslight, in 1824.[31] French bought 14.5 acres of this neighborhood for the construction of a model development, with plans to house thirty thousand lower-middle- and middle-class tenants. Most of these tenants, it was anticipated, would be civil servants or small business owners, and thus able to walk to work in the neighborhood or in the municipal buildings, "downtown."[32] Although the Depression forced French to reduce his plans, a two-tower version of Knickerbocker Village was erected with historically significant help in the form of financing from New York state and the federal Public Works Administration—the first time the state had contributed to an urban housing development.[33] Knickerbocker Village can be understood as a "village" only in its city context: with its sophisticated and diverse amenities, it more closely resembled Manhattan's Greenwich Village or Gramercy Park neighborhoods than a suburban town. Like Gramercy Park, the complex had been designed with a private garden for its residents, as well as a robust network of social and athletic clubs (including photography and fencing), and the building management would later support a cooperatively run nursery school for Knickerbocker Village children and a number of children's sports teams, whose members were affectionately known as the Knicks. The development offered upwardly mobile residents a primer in city living, combining the streamlined conveniences of a modern apartment tower with the social and civic engagement of an established community. It was an innovative, even experimental project, and among its first tenants were the alleged Soviet agents Julius and Ethel Rosenberg, first-generation Americans and young parents who lived in a three-room apartment on the eleventh floor of Knickerbocker Village from 1942 until 1950, when they were arrested for espionage, a charge that would ultimately result in their double execution three years later.

In many ways, the Rosenbergs were quintessential Knickerbocker Villagers, and typical New Yorkers, too. As Joshua Freeman has shown,

the demography of New York changed dramatically during the first
half of the twentieth century, and by 1950, while first- and second-
generation whites were still the majority population in the city, nearly
half of all New Yorkers were Catholic and over a quarter were Jew-
ish. Freeman suggests that by midcentury there was a "widely shared
sense, among both New Yorkers and non–New Yorkers, that New
York was in the United States but not of it," and Knickerbocker Village, of necessity, would have reflected this shared sensibility that the
city offered an experience that was at once insular and international.
The complex also embodied the political transformation of the working and middle classes in New York, particularly the emphasis on
progressivism and reform that many new immigrants expected to
find in their democratic new homeland.[34] The Knickerbocker Village
Tenants Association was historically outspoken in support of residents' rights and rent control, undaunted by the fact of the government largesse that gave them their homes in the first place, and even
spearheaded the development of a City-Wide Tenants League in 1936.[35]
Knickerbocker Villagers were representative of a relatively new variety of New Yorker: the socially engaged, economically motivated immigrant, determined to better their own lot and to improve their
adopted city at the same time. They had more in common with the
Tammany-fighting Father Knickerbocker, or even the Knickerbocker
stagecoach driver, than they did with Cholly Knickerbocker's Anglo-
Saxon "First Families," But their proud affinity with Gotham and all
its idiosyncrasies bespeaks an equal—or possibly even greater—claim
to the evolving meaning of Knickerbocker.

It is unlikely that Fred F. French was predicting the progressive
politics and activism of his tenants when he chose a name for the
first federally subsidized housing project in New York City. However,
an informal survey of New York's contemporary public housing developments suggests that they are primarily named for the streets
on which they are found, or for the building or landmark that used
to occupy that site. Sometimes these names have storied associations
that Irving and his "Knickerbocker School" would have appreciated,
such as the Rutgers Houses, built on the site of Dutch settler Henry
Rutgers's family farm, also on the Lower East Side, or the Dyckman
Houses, which were built in upper Manhattan near the rescued Dutch

colonial farmhouse of that name. But there was no Knickerbocker Street adjoining the site of Knickerbocker Village in 1930s New York, nor did the neighborhood have any explicit connection to Washington Irving, who had grown up more than a mile downtown, on William Street. It is probable that French, like Colonel Jacob Ruppert, simply anticipated that the "old New York" echoes of the name would give his development an associative patina and offer homage to the original New Amsterdam cityscape, even as projects like his all but obliterated what little visible evidence of that colony remained.

Building on the example of Ruppert's Brewery, "Knickerbocker" was also a savvy marketing choice for French. The name advertised the project's status as a relatively high-end development in a low-rent neighborhood, and the builder could safely rely on the Knickerbocker name (now more than a hundred years old) to resonate with newer New Yorkers, as well as city dwellers of long standing.[36] It was a strategy that had been successful for French's more celebrated development, Tudor City, an immense brick and limestone complex in midtown decorated with half-timbered "Tudor" lobbies, which was designed to appeal to well-heeled midtown office workers. Like Knickerbocker Village, Tudor City had used the aristocratic implications of its name to mitigate some of the drawbacks of its geography; the development was perched on a bluff in midtown, with its back set resolutely against the unappetizing sights and smells of the First Avenue stockyards (the future site of the United Nations). It's possible that French also had a subtler gesture in mind with his second development, a pun made literal in concrete and steel: that of homage to a bona fide Knickerbocker, a Dutch-descended New York native and former governor of New York, whose interventionist policies enabled the project's completion—President Franklin Delano Roosevelt.

The election of a second President Roosevelt marked a turning point in Knickerbocker usage in New York City and gave it a national resonance as well. According to Roosevelt biographer Jean Edward Smith, Franklin Delano Roosevelt was sworn in as the thirty-second president of the United States in 1933 with his hand on the family Bible that his Dutch ancestor Claes van Rosenvelt had brought with him when he arrived in New Amsterdam in the seventeenth century—the same Bible he had twice used to be sworn in as governor of New York.[37] It is a small detail but a significant one, a reminder that the president, despite a progressive New Deal platform that dismayed wealthy Americans, was intimately connected to the "old New York" that his Democratic followers hoped to reform. FDR's New York pedigree was much like that of Edith Wharton: both descended from solid—if unglamorous—Dutch and Anglo New York families, with family trees reaching back to the colonial settlement. But although Franklin Roosevelt's older half brother, James, had married an Astor and had been a member of the original Four Hundred, and the Roosevelts were to be found in the *Social Register*, neither the president nor his wife, Eleanor (who was herself a Roosevelt cousin of her husband), was considered to be part of either "society" *or* "café society." As a result, FDR's patrician connections attracted considerably less media attention during his bids for the governorship and the presidency than might otherwise be expected.[38] Perhaps this was because the van Rosenvelt family farm had long since been parceled into city lots, just north of Stuyvesant's old Bouwerie and south of the site of the old Croton Reservoir, now the New York Public Library. But Roosevelt's ancestral homestead could not be entirely divorced from his ambitions for New York, for it included the site of the just-finished Empire State Building, then the tallest building in the world.[39]

In fact, the Knickerbocker associations of the Roosevelt presidency are inextricable from the New Deal platform with which he captured New Yorkers' imaginations—and their votes. Roosevelt supporters used the name of Irving's historian not only as a handle for the sterling integrity and crusading social policies of their leader but also for the doggedness and sheer nerve he showed throughout his four terms in office, as he countered the politics of his class with an agenda of liberalism and reform.[40] To this end, the Roosevelt Democrats in the five boroughs of New York banded together as "Knickerbocker Democrats," swearing to defeat the "reactionary" forces of Tammany Hall with the help of energetic New York mayor Fiorello La Guardia. Around the same time, a media mogul named Donald Flamm christened his fledgling New York–based radio empire the Knickerbocker Broadcasting Company, a gesture of support to both the city and the New Deal administration. Flamm's company proved to be even more of an agitator than its namesake: in addition to being the first to broadcast a young orchestra leader named Rudy Vallee, it also aired "advertorials" for the birth control product Birconjel, a marketing decision that would result in a reprimand from the Federal Communications Commission. A still more scandalous episode at the Knickerbocker Broadcasting Company made the front page of the *New York Times* several days running, when the company was charged with "intercepting and rebroadcasting secret coded messages sent out by the German and British Governments," activity that nearly cost the company its license and, executives suggested, may have been done as a wartime radio "promotional stunt."[41]

It may have been these renegade usages that led to a rise, in the 1920s and 1930s, in the use of the expression "Pa Knickerbocker" as a metonym for New York City as a whole. This was a less-than-respectful nickname, adopted primarily, the evidence suggests, by newspapers in other cities. "Pa Knickerbocker always takes his city elections very seriously," a 1937 *Los Angeles Times* editorial entitled "New York's Election" began, while the *Chicago Tribune* chuckled over a Prohibition-era seizure of smuggled whiskey, "Pa Knickerbocker's Blue Grass Medicine Seized."[42] This was decidedly not the aristocratic Manhattan paterfamilias of Andrew Haswell Green's 1898 consolidation efforts, nor the quiescent muse of the *Knickerbocker Magazine*. What did it mean to have a bona fide Knickerbocker in the White House? For New Yorkers, it meant that the native cosmopolitanism and the conviction of inherited civic responsibility that they ascribed to Irving's historian could be found at the highest level of government, assisting their own scrappy, pugnacious New York "Pa" in the battle to survive the Depression and World War II with dignity and style.

The Knickerbocker sensibility of Roosevelt's presidency was not without its significant critics. The president's New Amsterdam antecedents gave the composer Kurt Weill and librettist Maxwell Anderson the ideal screen for *Knickerbocker Holiday*, a scorching musical satire about the New Deal administration. First performed on Broadway in 1938, *Knickerbocker Holiday* disguised its dissection of Roosevelt's presidency as a fable about life in the Dutch colony under Peter Stuyvesant, complete with ironic musical numbers such as "All Hail the Political Honeymoon" and "There's Nowhere to Go but Up."

Anderson's overbearing, warmongering Stuyvesant character stood in for the president himself, and the play even pressed "Washington Irving" into service as narrator, ostensibly to drive the Knickerbocker point home.[43] The message of *Knickerbocker Holiday* was pacifist and libertarian: the playwright Maxwell Anderson was well known for his political commentary and had been awarded the Pulitzer Prize for Drama in 1933 for *Both Your Houses*, a satire on the behavior of the U.S. Congress. Roosevelt confronted his critics at a Washington, D.C., performance of the musical at the National Theater, where, as the press reported, "the actors had to compete with the Presidential box for audience" as the commander in chief's fellow theatergoers scanned his face for reactions to "anti-New Deal cracks . . . quips and thrusts" such as the remark, uttered by the character of Stuyvesant, that "democracy is government by amateurs." The Roosevelt genealogy was even represented on stage by "one Roosevelt, a Councilman, a small, corpulent Dutchman," but the president loudly applauded both his fictional ancestor and the entire play, thus publicly acknowledging and identifying with the Knickerbocker imagery that enveloped him and colored his political career, for good or for ill.[44]

Perhaps *Knickerbocker Holiday* gave Roosevelt some ideas, or perhaps he was already thinking, like the marketers of *Little Old New York*, about how to commemorate the contributions of his New Amsterdam ancestors before their colonial traces were entirely erased— a process that was, as demonstrated by Knickerbocker Village, sometimes being hastened by the mandate of his own New Deal programs. Whatever the reason, Dutch icons and motifs appear in a number of New York–area New Deal projects in whimsical and sometimes inexplicable ways. A 1943 official photo album displaying examples of the Works Progress Administration's Education and Recreation District Office activities for New York City children, young adults, and recent immigrants includes the image of a "sextette" of small girls learning "Dutch folk dances," complete with old-fashioned aprons, peaked white caps, and wooden clogs. It is the only image of ethnic identification in the album, which concentrates, for the most part, on more practical enrichment programs, such as citizenship workshops, "Household Training" for young women destined for the service sector, and woodworking classes for truant boys (tersely described as the "Adjustment Program for Problem Cases").[45] The singling out of Dutch folk culture in a diverse city with few recent immigrants from the Netherlands is not explained in the album, but it may stem from the same impulse that led New York's city planners to use windmills, vividly rendered in orange and blue tiles, as a recurring decorative motif on the sides of the sections of the East River Drive and Sanitation Department depots built during Roosevelt's presidency.[46] Along with the previously mentioned beaver, the windmill is an element of the seal of the City of New York (first adopted in 1796 and last ratified in 1915), itself laden with Dutch iconography.[47] But an American eagle presides over the seal: why not put eagles on the East River Drive instead of windmills? The gesture is not Quixotic but Knickerbockerian. At such a remove from their colonial purpose, the Dutch emblems of the historian and his ancestors served the city as a universal semaphore, signaling New York's particular heritage of tolerance, idiosyncrasy, and above all "authenticity" and linking together people from different cultures, religions, and economic strata in a common identity—that of a real New Yorker.[48]

Throughout Roosevelt's four terms, Knickerbocker was repeatedly invoked as New York's patron saint and continued to serve as the conduit between the city and the nation at large. "Dr. Knickerbocker Says" was the title of a free health education pamphlet distributed to New Yorkers in the 1930s; a 1940 broadside entitled "Father Knickerbocker Looks at the Roosevelt Record: A New Deal for New York City" trumpets the metropolitan New York–area improvements sponsored by the Works Progress Administration, including "La Guardia Field Airport," the Queens-Midtown Tunnel, the East River Drive, "18 new bridges," and "298 new park and school playgrounds." Furthermore, the Democrat-sponsored broadside asserted, "the magnificent record of the New Deal in New York City is an account of direct benefits to the people. Do not take them for granted. Study this record. Learn the facts. THE NEW DEAL IS A SQUARE DEAL FOR ALL. The Roosevelt record is a solid foundation on which Democrats stand in the 1940 campaign."[49] The New Deal did indeed offer "direct benefits" to New Yorkers, and to the nation as a whole: Roosevelt's comprehensive program employed more than three million Americans, created thousands of schools, hospitals, and parks around the country, and added over half a million miles of new or improved interstate roads. But in New York, the majority of the improvements cited in the broadside were actually made possible through the work of the powerful city planner and New York City park commissioner Robert Moses. Moses had used the funds provided by the New Deal to greatly enlarge the total acreage of New York City's parks, playgrounds, beaches, public pools, and other recreational facilities, as well as to build and improve highways and parkways around the metropolitan area (and even upstate). But Moses had also made a bitter enemy of President Roosevelt (and Eleanor) when he abandoned plans to build a tunnel under the East River in favor of a dramatic "Brooklyn-Battery" suspension bridge, which would have cut through the historic Battery Park and changed the ancient Castle Clinton, then in use as a popular aquarium, beyond recognition. In addition to Roosevelt, who ultimately approved the War Department's decision to veto the project on grounds of national security, the bridge was challenged by preservationists and ordinary New Yorkers alike, including a group of tunnel diggers, or "sandhogs," who dramatized the conflict by wearing colonial costume to march on the Battery in protest against Moses and the potential loss of work for them that his bridge represented.[50] The sandhogs (and their powerful allies) prevailed, but Moses still managed to tear the roof off Castle Clinton, and he closed the aquarium in preparation for the Brooklyn-Battery Tunnel. In the aftermath of this bitter fight, it is not surprising that the Democrats might prefer to credit a figurative Father Knickerbocker with Greater New York's many improvements, his high colonial knee-breeches made suddenly populist and politically significant again by the sandhogs' costumed protest, rather than have to acknowledge a planner who had so little regard for the most cherished historical structures that remained in the city.

Perhaps the enmity between Moses and Roosevelt accounts for the relative absence of Knickerbocker paraphernalia from the 1939–1940 World's Fair, an elaborate cross-cultural extravaganza that put Moses's public works on prominent display. Father Knickerbocker makes a brief appearance as the "portly" escort of "Miss Manhattan," presiding queen of the fair, but the near-total absence of local history from this celebration of Moses's public works is evident in the guidebooks that accompanied the fair itself.[51] Titles like *So You're Visiting New York City!* and *Here Is New York* and *Metropolis: A Study of New York* hint at what the ceaseless forward propulsion of the city, 130 years after Irving's book, may finally have left behind for good. "This Guide," one author wrote, "concerns itself primarily with the study of bigness. . . . Little remains of the past, for New York is forever tearing down to rebuild."[52] Even as they praise the efforts of Moses for "reviving interest in the history of the city" through the restoration of abandoned public spaces such as Bowling Green, these armchair guides wonder what place there will be in the new city for the old. "The early American homes that fringed St. Mark's-in-the-Bowery are rapidly disappearing," Helen Worden writes in *Here Is New York*. She notes that the "nuns of Madonna House" saved Alexander Hamilton's Cherry Street home (which was near Knickerbocker Village) from destruction and restored it for the public, "but tourists seldom stray in. Few have ever heard of the little red brick Colonial house on Cherry Street."[53] There was no room for preservationist charity or wistful nostalgia in Moses's relentless ambition for New York, and it would be nearly thirty years before the city had a landmarks law that could protect similar treasures from the city's past.

KNICKERBOCKER TAKES A HOLIDAY

"Give Colonel Jake Ruppert the right to make good beer again and
I'll have no trouble signing any contract with the Yankees for 1933."

—BABE RUTH[54]

Knickerbocker, unlike Alexander Hamilton's forlorn homestead, had not been made irrelevant by the passage of time. Instead, once again, he was repurposed by New Yorkers who were not ready to discard their nostalgic mascot for Robert Moses's futuristic vision and who had no desire to relinquish the pleasing feeling of ownership over the city that his name imparted to all they did. Instead, the onetime Cassandra of "olden" Gotham became the happy symbol of beer and basketball, twin obsessions of many New Yorkers to this day. After Roosevelt's repeal of Prohibition in 1933, brewer Jacob Ruppert had famously delivered a case of "good" (i.e., alcoholic) Knickerbocker beer to Governor Albert E. Smith—the first New York beer to be legally delivered to the governor's mansion after the repeal.[55] For the next four decades the names of Ruppert and of Knickerbocker Beer were inextricably linked to New York. This link was no accident: Ruppert spent millions each year to promote the Ruppert, Knickerbocker, and Ruppiner brands of beer (and, later, Jacob Ruppert Ale, advertised as "for men only"), and he made sure that each bid for market share was more extravagant than the last.[56] Knickerbocker Beer was best known to many as the official beer of the New York Giants (despite the fact that the Ruppert family owned the Yankees, not the Giants), and fans listening to live broadcasts from the Polo Grounds were regularly encouraged by game announcers to "Knock for a Knick" and to enter Knickerbocker's "Prize-a-day Give Away" during "Each Home Game the Giants Play." Ruppert also sponsored saltwater fishing contests and, later, television shows, in an effort to maintain brand visibility.[57] No advertising gesture (except a Knickerbocker dirigible, an idea that Ruppert reportedly rejected) was too outlandish for consideration. In 1952, Ruppert flipped the switch on a Knickerbocker Beer sign that hovered over Bruckner Boulevard, a major highway in the Bronx. At two hundred feet long and seventy-five feet tall, as the *New York Times* reported, the gargantuan advertisement was, at the time, the "largest single incandescent illumination in the country," easily visible "from Manhattan, Long Island City, Queens, and northwest Brooklyn." Knickerbocker's sign likely brought an unwelcome perpetual daylight to the neighborhood it dominated, something the Bronx borough president may not have considered when he assisted at its inauguration.[58]

Ruppert didn't just emblazon the city with "Knickerbocker." He resurrected the colonial mascot of Greater New York to be his advertising ambassador. Taking his cue from Miss Manhattan's escort at the World's Fair, Ruppert's Knickerbocker was dressed much the same as his consolidation-era predecessor, with a tricorn hat, knee-breeches, and those essential shoe buckles. By now, his face is clean-shaven, in keeping with twentieth-century fashion, and it is considerably more cheerful than that of the beleaguered parent of urban consolidation. Instead of hoisting a charter for the creation of five boroughs,

Ruppert's icon is shown thrusting a foaming glass toward the on-looker. He has been enlisted to woo beer drinkers, sports fans, and urban sophisticates, instead of an apple-cheeked Miss Brooklyn and her wary kinsmen, and unlike his predecessor, he has no Tammany tigers to contend with, only fierce competition from rival brews.[59] The Ruppert "Father Knickerbocker" image appears to have made his debut the year after the World's Fair, in a 1940 calendar campaign for "Old Knickerbocker" beer. The calendar featured a portly Knick-erbocker figure carrying a gilt-topped walking stick and presiding over a variety of scenes of Dickensian holiday cheer. In print adver-tisements this Knickerbocker exhorted consumers to try "Ruppert's Knickerbocker Beer (Old Style)," the "Extra Good Beer [at] No Extra Cost." "Important!" a 1940 ad insisted; "the Ruppert Beer *now* on sale everywhere is brewed according to the 'Old Knickerbocker' formula that made the name Ruppert famous. . . . Have *you* tried it recently?" What other American beer mascot could stump for an "old" recipe with such authority? It mattered little that the Ruppert Brewery was not actually older, in 1940, than many of its German American rivals, all of whom had pre-Prohibition brands to showcase in a similar manner, or that a number of them (like Schlitz and Anheuser-Busch) had more impressive national reputations and larger distribution areas than the "Colonel" of Yorkville. No other beermaker had the foremost narrator of "Little Old New York" on the payroll: this was Ruppert's bankable "formula" for success, and it worked, by adver-tising industry standards, for quite a long time.

New York City responded to Ruppert's popular new figurehead by putting its own "Father Knickerbocker" back on the payroll in 1949. This latest municipal iteration of New York's "patriarch" was not an actor but a professor emeritus of romance languages named Dr. James J. O'Brien, who was reported to have spoken with an Irish brogue. Even if his accent was Old World, he apparently possessed the right physique and temperament for a New World costume that in-cluded a "snuff-brown Colonial jacket . . . four-tiered jabot . . . gold-buckled slippers [and] tight knee-breeches," as well as "square-rimmed spectacles," a touch that hearkened back to the previously discussed Darley illustrations of Irving's *History*. But the City Knickerbocker proved to be a wasted opportunity, much like his predecessor at the

1939 World's Fair. Instead of reestablishing his reputation as a champion of New York interests in the context (and location) of New York itself, the freelance impersonator with the hokey gray periwig and "Knickerbocker clay pipes" was sent to Calcutta, Damascus, and Dublin as part of an "eighteen-day world tour to publicize New York's World Trade Week."[60] While Dr. O'Brien was called upon to cut the ribbon at the next Moses-orchestrated World's Fair, in 1964–1965, that fair also gave New Amsterdam short shrift. The designated "Little Old New York" area (which was sponsored by the Rheingold Brewery), was anodyne and hardly "old" at all: it featured a "gaslit street and park of about 1904" and a restaurant that served "oysters Rockefeller and Beef Stroganoff," with not a Dutch doughnut in sight.[61] Although Dr. O'Brien repudiated Ruppert's version as a "commercial Knickerbocker," something less than the "living symbol" that he was supposed to represent during his short (1949–1953) tenure, it was the brewer's historian who was the most faithful to Irving's original and who exalted his native city above all things.

The images used in print ads for Knickerbocker Beer play up New Yorkers' sense of superiority and difference. For Ruppert, this combination was the sales pitch of New York City itself: what other American metropolis could claim both a sophisticated, storied past and a gleaming future? Like Andrew Green's Father Knickerbocker, Ruppert's spokesman had an "imperial" authority like no other. And so, for the first time since Irving, Knickerbocker was given back his role as historian and storyteller, even if sometimes the only moral of his story was an exhortation to drink Ruppert products. The brewery posed Knickerbocker against the stylized but unmistakable backdrop of the New York skyline; he was added, *Zelig*-like, to a variety of contemporary and faux colonial New York street scenes; and his likeness (and sometimes his profile, looking rather more like Thomas Jefferson than the weary parent of consolidation) adorned a variety of collectible Ruppert trinkets, from church keys, drink coasters and beer foam scrapers to drink trays and electric bar clocks. In 1954, the brewery ran a series of full-color print advertisements that effectively repatriated the Dutch historian and made an explicit connection to Irving and the *History of New York*. The series was called "Famous New York Traditions of Father Knickerbocker," but the focus was really the text of Irving's burlesque, and excerpts from the *History* were presented in each ad. Paintings by the celebrated muralist Lumen Martin Winter accompanied each excerpt. Thus Irving's account of the "Dutch Landing at Communipaw," with its tale of how the guttural Low Dutch greetings of the arriving colonists put the "natives" to terrified flight, is illustrated by a comical but skillful rendering of the same—the martial prowess of befeathered native Americans confounded by a boatload of chubby Dutch folk in Old Master getups. "Hudson Sights Manhattan" is equally vivid and anachronistic: with a long Dutch pipe and a parrot on his shoulder, the Ruppert version of Henry Hudson is half Peter Stuyvesant, half Captain Kidd. Each of these scenes is framed with a cameo of Knickerbocker, reading over his own manuscript of the *History*, as well as the image of a frosty glass and bottle of beer and the slogan "Knickerbocker: New York's Famous Beer." As we have seen, by 1954 Knickerbocker was already both "famous" and "traditional," so it is intriguing to speculate why this series of ads was commissioned: was it to remind consumers of the beer mascot's literary pedigree, or was the fame of Irving's *History* sufficiently diminished, 145 years after publication, that its satire could be presented as a literary and advertising novelty? How many New Yorkers still knew the true origins of Knickerbocker, and how many cared to learn?

While this last question may not be answered with any assurance, what is certain is that Diedrich Knickerbocker's contract with Ruppert ran out. An attempted buyout by Anheuser-Busch in 1957 prompted the company to revamp its advertising yet again, and in 1960 Ruppert rolled out a sleekly modern campaign for the new decade, complete with new slogans: "Ruppert people have a thirst for living!" and "Live a little! Have a Ruppert Knickerbocker!" Instead of the historian Knickerbocker (who was relegated to a corner of the bottle label), this series featured images of "happy, young 'New York type' people in lively group settings," taken by the photographer Richard Avedon, who was then on the staff of *Harper's Bazaar*.[62] "Ruppert people," if these photographs are any guide, were white, suburban, and 75 percent male. The brewery insisted that the campaign, with its clean lines and bright colors, offered a "strong link to the past," but only the plaintive ad copy suggests history of any kind: "it took four generations of *family tradition* to produce the matchless Ruppert Knickerbocker flavor. One swallow and you'll know why it took so long. Fine beer, like a fine family name, gains character with each generation."[63] Whether "Ruppert" or "Knickerbocker" is the "fine family name" that readers and drinkers should remember is left purposefully unclear. The brewery may have retired the signature Dutchman, but the historical, faintly aristocratic associations of his famous surname would make cash registers ring a little longer.

Even after Ruppert Brewery and all its assets were purchased in 1963 by the real estate developer Marvin Kratter, the "fine family name" of Knickerbocker still held sway. The Bronx-born Kratter had demonstrated a fondness for New York landmarks; he had purchased Ebbets Field after the Dodgers' move to Los Angeles and built apartment complexes on the site of the beloved stadium. But in an effort to avoid becoming the Walter O'Malley of New York beer, Kratter had initially promised to keep Ruppert's Yorkville beermaking operations in business. Like generations of Knickerbocker appropriators before him, he moved quickly to assert the legitimacy of his claim to the dynastic brewery—and to the pedigree that "Knickerbocker" confers. "He doesn't smoke and drinks only a little," the *New York Times* noted in a profile of Kratter. "The night he bought control of Ruppert's, however, he was in the brewery, talking to the men on the production line. One offered him a glass of Knickerbocker beer that had not yet been pasteurized. He downed it with relish. A joke among his associates is that he now has beer in his blood and that the large letter "K' that adorns some of his structures really stands for Knickerbocker."[64] Kratter appears to be adopting the Knickerbocker name, much as Edith Wharton and Cholly Knickerbocker's social climbers cloaked their newness in borrowed family crests. More insidiously, Kratter's remark about "beer in his blood" hearkens back—unconsciously, no doubt—to the nativist possibilities inherent in Knickerbocker imagery and reminds us that twentieth-century New Yorkers still looked to totemic words like Irving's to certify their authenticity and belonging. But the developer's promise of an authentic "Knickerbocker" conversion finally proved hollow: just two years after his visit to the production line, Kratter sold the Ruppert name and beer recipes to the Brooklyn-based Rheingold, itself a storied German brewery, and the Yorkville plant was closed. Rheingold, at the time a subsidiary of PepsiCo, promised to brew Ruppert's signature beers "without interruption," but the New York had gone out of Knickerbocker Beer for good.[65]

The Knickerbockers, however, still remained in New York. In 1946, the New York Knickerbockers were among the earliest franchises in the Basketball Association of America, a group that merged in 1949 with the National Basketball League to form the present-day National Basketball Association (NBA). While many of the other founding teams in the early Basketball Association of America chose names that reflected the geography, primary industry, or particular ethnography of their city (the Pittsburgh Ironmen, the Saint Louis Bombers, the Washington Capitals, the Boston Celtics), New York's franchise chose Knickerbocker. The decision was not meant to suggest that beer (such as Ruppert's products, which were still using Father Knickerbocker in their advertising campaigns at that time) was Manhattan's chief export but rather, as the present-day NBA insists, that "the Dutch settler 'Knickerbocker' character" was already "synonymous with New York City," and "Father Knickerbocker," with his "buckled shoes and . . . knickered pants," was New York's "most popular symbol of the late 19th and early 20th centuries." It is possible, as the NBA suggests, that this team, named for Irving's creation, was capitalizing on the celebrity of their Knickerbocker baseball predecessors and celebrating (although the NBA never acknowledges this) the centennial of that league of "gentlemen amateurs."[66] Or perhaps the athletes and their supporters were remembering an image from the most glorious moment in New York's recent sports memory: the 1941 World Series between the New York Yankees and the Brooklyn Dodgers. That historic contest featured a souvenir program emblazoned with a giant Father Knickerbocker, beaming as he stands astride the East River and the Brooklyn Bridge. The colossal consolidator, one buckled shoe planted in midtown Manhattan and one in Brooklyn, holds aloft a set of scales with a Yankee player on one balance and a Dodger on the other. This gargantuan Knickerbocker looks like he would be right at home on a basketball court.

Whatever its original inspiration, the name and the first logo of the New York Knickerbockers certainly builds on the city's comfortable familiarity with Irving's icon by this time. Following Ruppert's lead, the NBA resurrected the Father Knickerbocker image for the Knickerbocker team logo, creating the most playful Knickerbocker to date. In a black-and-white caricature drawn by famed sports cartoonist Willard Mullin (an illustrator for the *New York World-Telegram* who had also created the infamous "Brooklyn Bum" image for the Dodgers), a few quick strokes deliver a Father Knickerbocker who is dribbling an enormous basketball with evident glee, colonial pigtail aloft and coattails flying. Compared to the painterly style of the Ruppert beer illustrations, it is a crude design, but still a charming one. Mullin does not forget to include the historian's sartorial elements: Knickerbocker is playing the game in buckled shoes, lace jabot, and tricorn hat. The team, thankfully, was not required to wear a similar uniform but instead has always donned orange, blue, and white, the official colors of New York City, and those of New Amsterdam, as well. The ballplaying Knickerbocker was the trademark of the Knicks from their inaugural 1946–1947 season through 1963–1964, when it was abandoned in favor of the "roundball" symbol (which was itself retired in the 1990s in favor of the "triangle" and "subway token" trademarks, which are still in use). While the Boston Celtics, who had adopted an Irish leprechaun as their logo in the 1950s, never dismissed their first mascot, the Knicks' kitschy inaugural symbol is now little more than a forgotten footnote in basketball history. But its significance to this history is manifest: the NBA's usage is the last time that a figural rendering of Knickerbocker has been used in New York advertising and culture.

Even though the Knicks replaced Irving's historian with an abstract symbol and truncated his famous name (perhaps also suggested by Ruppert, who had developed a "Little Knicks" line of petite beer bottles), the team's history gives evidence of a Knickerbocker sensibility, one that builds on the twentieth-century idea of a "New York way" of doing or being. This may not have been clear during the Knicks' early years: while they narrowly won the first game of the Basketball Association of America on November 1, 1946, against the Toronto Huskies, and made the NBA Finals three years running (1951–1953), they had few memorable players and none of the swagger of their contemporary New York baseball counterparts. They did, however, have the most rigorous program of any team in the NBA, including the league's first training camp and first athletic trainer. By the 1960s, the team's luck had changed, and between 1964 and 1968, they drafted a number of star players, including Bill Bradley, Dave DeBusschere, Walt "Clyde" Frazier, and Willis Reed. Suddenly, the Knicks were a championship team, and the Knickerbocker name was once again shorthand for world-class style and for success. But what kind of success? Several of the team's most memorable players during the first championship years were criticized for accepting record-breaking salaries, including the Princeton-educated Rhodes Scholar Bill Bradley, who was sometimes referred to as "Dollar Bill" and sometimes as "Mr. Knickerbocker." Bradley and Frazier were arguably the team's first celebrities, and both imparted a particular elegance and gravitas to a sport that was still making a national name. In addition to their courtside prowess, Frazier was famous for his sharp wardrobe and even sharper business acumen, and Bradley was advertised as the sport's first scholar-athlete—a product of Princeton and Oxford, as well as the Garden. The team's coach, Red Holzman, wrote of Bradley's first season: "No rookie in history was asked to do what he did. The Knicks were forced to arrange a press conference in every city on his first swing around the league. That was the kind of excitement he generated. That was the kind of burden he had to carry. That was the kind of demand there was for him."[67] Why was Bradley such a media darling? Why did Frazier's clothing warrant public commentary? Perhaps because these early celebrity Knicks had the kind of ineffable, cosmopolitan cool that New York had come to expect from its citizens, whether native or adopted. They were as fast, skilled, and ambitious as the city for which they played, and they dominated the court with a fierceness and grace that warranted the hero-worship they received. The New York Knickerbockers were, after all, the embodiment of the city's chief export: its own outsized idea of itself. Looking back on his time in the Knicks, Bill Bradley, who went on to represent New Jersey in the U.S. Senate from 1979 to 1996, remarked that while he didn't know where the word "Knickerbocker" came from when he was a New York Knick, he knew instinctively that it was "rooted in a sense of place" and could "only have meant New York."[68] These giant Knicks might technically have been smaller than the East River–straddling Father Knickerbocker from the 1941 World Series, but they loomed larger—and, so far, longer—in the New York imagination.

The Knicks are also representative of Knickerbockerian New York because, like their mascot, they have sustained the city during tumultuous and difficult times. The team was an emblem of interracial harmony at a time when American cities were once again wracked with race riots and assassinations and fearful of the impact of "white flight." The Knicks brought glamour and championships back to New York sports during a dry spell for the Yankees (and while the Mets were still too new to be a brand name). And in the 1970s, with the addition of Earl "the Pearl" Monroe and others, they boosted the morale of a city fending off increasing street violence and impending fiscal collapse. The rest of the country came to rely on Madison Square Garden's "patriarchs" to bring maximum dazzle and delight to the sport, just as the Yankees and the Dodgers had done for baseball. Each season held out the promise that there might still be new ways for New York City to surprise and astonish the continent that lay beyond its narrow contours, even as it reveled in the myopia that Saul Steinberg had depicted with such tender accuracy in his 1976 drawing "A View of the World from Ninth Avenue," one of the most recognized, reproduced, and redrawn New Yorker covers ever.

The filmmaker, native New Yorker, and Knicks fan Woody Allen has speculated, with his typical partisanship, about the effect of the team on the larger world as well and confessed, in an article about the Knicks, that "when Frazier was shipped to Cleveland, [I wondered], what was a guy like Clyde going to do to keep amused late nights in Ohio?" Allen updates the nineteenth-century Knickerbocker lexicon by suggesting that what fans loved about star players like Frazier and, later, Patrick Ewing was that they were "homegrown." But neither athlete was, in fact, a native New Yorker: Allen's definition of "homegrown" was "a Knick drafted right out of college and not acquired in a deal." It is this distinction, the fact that they "began their professional lives here," meaning Manhattan, that sets them apart from other New York players and puts, as Allen remarks, "something extra into their pedigrees."[69] Allen's echo of Irving's language of class and rank may be unintended, but it is suggestive of how the twentieth-century city, the famous crucible of cultures and races, finally made Knickerbocker over in its image. At long last, the Dutch historian's peculiar "pedigree" belongs to all those whom New York claims, and all those who claim New York.

The events of the twentieth century flung Knickerbocker's name up to the Bronx skies, over the airwaves and down into the labyrinth of the subway system. Somewhere between the shuttering of the Knickerbocker Hotel and the first game of the NBA, the mythic historian became a symbol available to all New Yorkers—from the oldest family in the Saint Nicholas Society to the newest tenant in Knickerbocker Village—and the name, once shorthand for "patrician," came to stand for all that was cosmopolitan about Irving's hometown. "New York is not a completed city," Le Corbusier wrote in 1947. "It is a city in the process of becoming. Today it belongs to the world."[70] As New York's adoptive "Father," Knickerbocker had overseen that process for two centuries and, through his protean image, helped to harmonize the city's diverse, often dissonant voices and offer a common platform from which it could observe its own "becoming" and narrate its "authentic" history as a phenomenon unlike any other, anywhere.

CONCLUSION

Father Knickerbocker stands on the Brooklyn side of the East River. Just behind him the diminutive outlines of the Statue of Liberty, Governors Island, and the skyline of lower Manhattan are visible, but whether they are dwarfed by his size or a trick of perspective, it is impossible to say. His walking stick is tucked under his arm, and his lace cuffs have been pushed back, freeing his hands to grasp a giant fisherman's net that has been cast across the river and in which the daguerreotype portraits of some half-dozen prominent New Yorkers, including Cass Gilbert, the architect of the Woolworth Building, appear to have been caught. Emblazoned over his head is the question: "What Constitutes a New Yorker?"[1]

What did constitute a New Yorker in 1907, the year the *New York Times* article featuring this illustration was published? Nearly a century after Irving published his spoofing *History of New York*, readers of the *Times* were told that a "strange mixture of nationalities makes up New York City," of which the largest groups were (in descending order) German, Irish, Russian, Italian, Austrian and English. The article also informed them that a typical New Yorker is one who is no New Yorker at all, but a person who came to the city from someplace else. Some of these newcomers hoped to make their fortune in Manhattan (following the examples, the *Times* notes, of John Jacob Astor or August Belmont); to spend it (like John D. Rockefeller or Henry Clay Frick); to gain political capital (as Alexander Hamilton did) or to achieve "artistic or intellectual" fame (the article cites William Dean Howells and the previously mentioned Gilbert). "One of the most distinguishing traits of the New Yorker," one commentator told the

Times, "is his independence of every one and everything outside of his city. . . . [H]e feels he is at headquarters, where the big things are done."

Without question, New Yorkers feel they are "at headquarters" today. Thus far into the twenty-first century, New York City remains "The City," as Jan Morris declared in the 1970s: "That title, so long the prerogative of Constantinople, must now go to New York, a world epitome." Morris agrees with the verdict of 1907; from her more contemporary vantage, New Yorkers still *do* consider themselves to be independent of the rest of the world, sometimes taking this insularity to the far edge of reason, as when their "intensely clever, cynical, introspective, [and] feverishly tireless . . . febrile brightness" crosses over into "the utter self-absorption of the schizophrenic." It is a contagious narcissism, she warns: "few residents of Manhattan really much care what happens anywhere else."[2] Perhaps, like the citizens of the medieval village for which Irving named them, those who live in latter-day Gotham are as mad as they are wise. But the question remains as fresh now as it did in 1907, or in 1809, when Irving first wrote. What does constitute a New Yorker? Are New Yorkers truly myopic, self-made, brilliant, insane? Has the contemporary city's "strange mixture" of ethnicities and origins, as the *Times* suggested, finally made such generalizations impossible? And if this is indeed the case, is there even such a thing as a "New Yorker" anymore? Some observers of the city make apocalyptic predictions about their beloved metropolis: Cynthia Ozick despairs of Manhattan's "metamorphoses between disappearances," so that "every seventy-five years or so another city bursts out . . . new shapes, new pursuits, new immigrants with their unfamiliar tongues and worried, uneasy bustle." New York, she adds, "means to impress the here-and-now, which it autographs with an insouciant wrecking ball."[3] Thomas Bender argues eloquently for the essential "unfinished"-ness of New York, suggesting that New York is a "paradoxical modern metropolis," which is endlessly engaged in the absorbing task of "finding itself and explaining itself to itself."[4] Rem Koolhaas dubs this ceaseless transformation "Manhattanism," the social and spatial creation of a "Culture of Congestion," a culture in which all New Yorkers, by their very existence, necessarily take part.[5] But if the city cannot stand still long enough to gather and protect its landmarks, its languages, and its memories before they are destroyed, built over, or remade beyond recognition, how can its citizens claim to have any history? Can they have any collective identity at all? One answer may be found by returning to the man holding the giant net—to Knickerbocker. New York is still imbued with Knickerbocker, and his name hovers at the edges of everyday life, all over New York City. Contemporary New Yorkers still cross avenues, visit dry cleaners, frequent restaurants, and belong to clubs that bear the name of Knickerbocker. They can be found on Knickerbocker Avenue in Bushwick, Brooklyn, in Knickerbocker Village downtown, and in the Knickerbocker, a luxury condominium on a fashionable stretch of the Upper East Side. When notable native-born New Yorkers die, they are often remembered as "Knickerbockers," or, as in the case of George Plimpton, "the last Knickerbocker" (with no credit given to the 1904 novel of that name).[6] The Knickerbocker name still speaks to those looking to market Manhattan cachet to non-New Yorkers, from the high-end Knickerbocker condos in Miami's South Beach to the recently reopened Knickerbocker Hotel in Times Square, which carries the tagline "A legendary New York landmark reborn" and cannily suggests that "posh authenticity" is among its unique amenities. And yet most citizens of the five boroughs have little to no understanding of what the "Knickerbocker" designation means, or why they use it. Thus divorced from its context, Irving's borrowed name has become little more than a comical handle, a Dutch-inflected sound—or a heartbreaking season at Madison Square Garden.

But Knickerbocker has more to offer twenty-first-century readers than just the promise of a genial mascot in a colonial costume. The chief message of Irving's historian is at the heart of the idea of New York itself. Diedrich Knickerbocker was a snob to the snobbish; he was the champion of a vanquished cause; and he bequeathed a knowing swagger to the city that admits no rival to itself *but* itself. His name has served New Yorkers as a crucial signpost in the midst of unceasing change, and the city's age-old struggle between insularity and inclusion, between the "arts of gain" and the art of creating a beautiful and a noble metropolis, between conservation and progress, may be mapped across the many and competing incarnations of Knickerbocker that this book has discussed. His persistence over two centuries of wrenching urban transformation, from the post-colonial to the postmodern, suggests that Irving's protean "patriarch" was indeed the right spokesman for New York's first two hundred years of independence. Whether you called it blood, style, attitude, or moxie, the little Dutchman could and did deliver.

Irving's *History* also ushered in an era that has not yet passed, and indeed shows no signs of waning: the era of the New York Story. Readers the world over take it for granted that New York warrants all the encomiums, epithets, nicknames, and slogans that have been showered on it, and they demand to be told more: what other city could at once be Walt Whitman's "Mighty Manhattan," Kander and Ebb's "city that never sleeps," and J. J. Hunsecker's "dirty town"? How else could Walter Winchell's assertion that the Stork Club was "the New Yorkiest place in New York" pass without comment on its redundancy? The appealing combination of enthusiasm, self-aggrandizement, and irony that marked the *History* has become the hallmark of the city's promotional culture: regardless of the medium, all of its chroniclers share a belief in the singularity of the New York experience, as well as a confidence that the audience clamoring for fresh takes on the New York Story will never be sated. They have not been proven wrong. New York remains a hub for the production of books, movies, television shows, and popular music, much of it about—what else?—life in New York. Irving, as we have seen, was not just the first writer to identify and exploit this market: his narrator became a market in and of itself. At the crucial nineteenth-century intersection of tradition and progress, monarchy and democracy, the *History* asked, whose structures, rituals, catchphrases, and prejudices should New Yorkers preserve, and how? More than forty-five years before Walt Whitman asserted that the islands of New York would captivate ferry passengers "a hundred years hence, or every so many hundred years hence," Knickerbocker wondered aloud exactly what Manhattan those millennial passengers would see, and why it would enchant them.[7] New Yorkers and all those who love the city and demand a place in it still wrestle with these questions today.

The questions of urban history, preservation, and New York identity that preoccupied Irving's historian are just as lively and pertinent on his two hundredth anniversary as they were at his creation. Few dispute that New York still serves as tastemaker to the rest of the country—and arguably to the rest of the world. The city is still canonized in every medium, from "great American novels" to video games. But the uncomfortable question remains: how can New York keep its distinctive identity from being diluted? As a Gotham sensibility is exported globally, how can city dwellers retain their authenticity at home? Instead of patriotism or nationalism, New Yorkers could not do better than to return to their first brand—to Knickerbockerism. Taking Irving's creation as their inspiration, they should seek out and celebrate their city's patchwork, ambivalent, multiethnic heritage, with all the risk and freedom for the future that it implies. Happily, some city groups have already embraced this very challenge. Institutions such as the Municipal Art Society work to ensure that the demolition of landmarks such as Penn Station is never repeated and advocate for new historic designations that represent the quicksilver diversity of the five boroughs, not just the patriotic homesteads of other people's colonial ancestors. Urban planners and arts groups have begun to update Robert Moses's futuristic fantasies with their own utopian designs and to adaptively reuse the city that they have inherited.[8] And grassroots preservation and collection movements have begun to offer New York's past as an accessible, neighborhood curiosity shop, a place crammed with the artifacts of everyday urban living.[9] Every New Yorker, these developments suggest, can be a Knickerbocker for the particular Gotham in which he or she lives and works and can contribute his or her own "curious sort of a written book" to the city's communal history—no Dutch heirlooms required.

What other icon unites New York in sympathy for the underdog, the dreamer, the memory-keeper, or, most important, the "authentic New Yorker"? The image of Knickerbocker—shabby and superior, ironic and intellectual, a purveyor of satirical "fake history" nearly two centuries before Jon Stewart—is at once a poignant reminder of the priceless value of the city's character and the most fitting standard to carry into the battle for its preservation.

NOTES

INTRODUCTION

1. For more on the advertisements leading up to the *History*'s publication, see Andrew Burstein, *The Original Knickerbocker: The Life of Washington Irving* (New York: Basic Books, 2007). Burstein, one of Irving's most recent biographers, relates how some New Yorkers were taken in by the hoax advertisements, to the point where they suggested posting a reward for Knickerbocker's safe recovery. He also notes that Irving's identity was kept secret by his publishers, Inskeep and Bradford, until the actual day of publication.

2. "From the *Boston Palladium*," *Federal Republican and Commercial Gazette*, 24 Jan. 1810, 2.

3. *The Diary of Elihu Hubbard Smith*, ed. James E. Cronin (Philadelphia: American Philosophical Society, 1973), 126.

4. According to I. N. Phelps Stokes, the play was first performed in the United States at the Park Theater on May 25, 1804. The dromedaries were exhibited in 1806. I. N. Phelps Stokes, *The Iconography of Manhattan Island*, vol. 5 (New York: Robert H. Dodd, 1924), 1419, 1446.

5. Quoted in Mark Kurlansky, *The Big Oyster* (New York: Ballantine Books, 2006), 88.

6. Bayrd Still, *Mirror for Gotham: New York as Seen by Contemporaries from Dutch Days to the Present* (New York: NYU Press, 1956), 52. Still takes this quotation from Ray W. Pettengill's *Letters from America, 1776–1779*, 165–166.

7. *Letters of Mrs. Adams: The Wife of John Adams*, vol. 2 (Boston: C. C. Little and J. Brown, 1840), 209.

8. Theodore Dwight, quoted in Ric Burns and James Sanders, *New York: An Illustrated History* (New York: Alfred A. Knopf, 1999), 51.

9. It is no accident that Philip Lopate begins his excellent anthology *Writing New York* with an excerpt from Irving's *History*. Lopate credits Irving with creating the "ironic, disenchanted voice" that would "set the tone for much New York literature to come," although, in considering Knickerbocker himself "one of history's 'losers,'" he misses the joyful, celebratory aspect of Irving's text and

Knickerbocker's narration—an aspect that is as crucial to the Knickerbocker identity as irony. *Writing New York* (New York: Washington Square Press, 1998), 1.

10. Edith Wharton, *A Backward Glance* (New York: Macmillan, 1933), 55.

1. THE PICTURE OF KNICKERBOCKER

1. *New-York Evening Post,* 6 Sept. 1809. All subsequent quotations describing this event are from this account.

2. Dr. Samuel Miller, "Discourse, designed to commemorate the Discovery of New-York, delivered before the New-York Historical Society, September 4th, 1809, Being the Completion of the Second Century Since That Event," in *Collections of the New-York Historical Society for the Year 1809* (New York: I. Riley, 1811), 20, 39.

3. John Pintard, "To the Public, New-York Historical Society," *New-York Herald,* 12 Feb. 1805.

4. I. N. Phelps Stokes, *The Iconography of Manhattan Island,* vol. 5 (New York: Robert H. Dodd, 1924), 1419, 1446, 1470, 1446.

5. John Lambert, *Travels Through Canada, and the United States of America, in the years 1806, 1807, & 1808: to which are added biographical notices and anecdotes of some of the leading characters in the United States* (London: C. Cradock and W. Joy, 1814), 55.

6. According to Stokes, the Plymouth anniversary celebration took place on December 21, 1805. *Iconography,* 1434.

7. Bayrd Still, *Mirror for Gotham: New York as Seen by Contemporaries from Dutch Days to the Present* (New York: NYU Press, 1956), 52.

8. Stokes, *Iconography,* 1478.

9. Ibid., 1510. The Common Council also heard a remonstrance from a private citizen who called for a halt to the common practice of "turning cows on the Battery [and] dusting carpets and drying clothes" on that popular promenade. Ibid., 1492.

10. Elizabeth Blackmar, *Manhattan for Rent: 1785–1850* (Ithaca, NY: Cornell University Press, 1989), 99. Blackmar notes, "Between 1800 and 1812, when New Yorkers still defined convenience in relation to the lower wharf district, a particularly fine town house on Broadway rented for more than $1,000 a year, while a substantial brick house on a less prominent but still centrally situated street went for about $700 a year" (87).

11. The most famous of these creeks was the Minetta, which the Dutch had also dubbed Bestaver's Killetje, after the farmer who owned the surrounding property. The narrow Minetta Lane in Greenwich Village is on the site of that former waterway. The streets of the Five Points are now Mulberry, Worth, Park, and Baxter: Little Water Street no longer exists.

12. Saint Patrick's on Mott Street would be the cathedral of Roman Catholic New Yorkers for the next seventy years, despite a fire that destroyed the church in 1867 (it was rebuilt and reconsecrated the following year). While Saint Patrick's

Cathedral moved to its present location, the city block between Fifth and Madison Avenues and Fiftieth and Fifty-first streets, in 1879, "Old Saint Patrick's," as it is now known, continues to be an active parish in the neighborhood alternately known as "Little Italy" or "Nolita."

13. Stokes, *Iconography*, 1458. This cost analysis comes from Eric Homberger's *Historical Atlas of New York City* (New York: Henry Holt, 2005), 59.

14. Stokes, *Iconography*, 1438.

15. Blackmar, *Manhattan for Rent*, 85.

16. Stokes, *Iconography*, 1417. In *Gotham*, Edwin G. Burroughs and Mike Wallace point out that "after a decade of yellow fever epidemics, the Assembly had charged the [Streets Commission] with laying out 'streets, roads, and public squares' in such a manner as to 'promote the health of the city . . . [and] allow for free and abundant circulation of air.'" As late as 1822, city government "declared everything below City Hall an 'infected district' and established a picket-fence barricade along Chambers Street. Thousands of residents fled north." *Gotham: A History of New York to 1898* (New York: Oxford University Press, 1999), 419–420, 448.

17. Lambert, *Travels*, 55.

18. Stokes, *Iconography*, 1495.

19. The patriotic name changes took place gradually: Little George Street, Thames Street, and Duke Street may still be found on the 1807 Kirkham Map of New York City.

20. Stokes, *Iconography*, 1490.

21. See Henry Moscow, *The Street Book: An Encyclopedia of Manhattan Street Names and Their Origins* (New York: Hagstrom, 1979), 40; and Sanna Feirstein, *Naming New York: Manhattan Places and How They Got Their Names* (New York: NYU Press, 2001), 26.

22. In addition to draining the pond, the council had to obtain from the heirs of its original owner, Anthony Lispenard, the deed to the marshy land around it, a plot that was sometimes referred to as the Lispenard Swamp. Feirstein, *Naming New York*, 45.

23. *Collections of the New-York Historical Society for the Year 1809* (New York: I. Riley, 1811), 13.

24. Ibid., 9, 7.

25. Ibid., 28.

26. Ibid., 23. Emphasis in original.

27. Samuel L. Mitchill, *The Picture of New York, Or, The Traveller's Guide Through the Commercial Metropolis of the United States, By a Gentleman Residing in This City* (New York: I. Riley, 1807), iii.

28. Patrick M'Robert, *A Tour Through Part of the North Provinces of America* (Edinburgh: printed for the author, 1776; rpt. New York: Arno Press, 1979), 5.

29. Henry Wansey, *The Journal of an Excursion to the United States of North America in the Summer of 1794* (New York: Johnson Reprint, 1969), 226, 229.

30. Mitchill, *Picture*, 1, 12, 105.

31. Ibid., 96.

32. Ibid., 28.

33. Ibid., 160.

34. The presentation copy of Irving's *History* is recorded in the first catalog of the society's library, indicating that the author was as good as his narrator's word. See R.W.G. Vaill, *Knickerbocker Birthday: A Sesqui-Centennial History of the New-York Historical Society, 1804–1954* (New York: New-York Historical Society, 1954), 42.

35. James Kirke Paulding eventually published a second series of *Salmagundi*. In fact, Paulding continued on in the *Salmagundi* vein for the rest of his literary career, with treatises on Anglo-American relations such as *The Diverting History of John Bull and Brother Jonathan* (1812) and *Old England: By a New England Man* (1822), and a spoof of Sir Walter Scott, *The Lay of the Scottish Fiddle: A Tale of Havre de Grace* (1813). Paulding is credited with significantly popularizing the history of another regional legend, Davy Crockett, in his play *The Liar of the West*. "Fifth Avenoodledom": Walt Whitman, *New York Dissected* (1855–1856; New York: R. R. Wilson, 1936), 96.

36. Clifton Hood, David Waldstreicher, and Sean Wilentz have all looked at the ways in which early American festivals exposed the dialectic between national and regional interests and, particularly in New York City, how seemingly republican celebrations could become outlets for class sentiment and social segregation. See Hood, "An Unusable Past: Urban Elites, New York City's Evacuation Day, and the Transformation of Memory Culture," *Journal of Social History* 37, no. 4 (2004): 883–913; Waldstreicher, *In the Midst of Perpetual Fetes* (Chapel Hill: University of North Carolina Press, 1997); and Wilentz, *Chants Democratic* (1984; Twentieth Anniversary Edition, New York: Oxford University Press, 2004).

37. See *The Encyclopedia of New York City*, ed. Kenneth T. Jackson (New Haven: Yale University Press, 1995), 475.

38. *HNY* 476. Interestingly, the twentieth- and twenty-first-century descendants of Herman Jansen Knickerbocker agree that Knickerbocker is not a last name that exists in Holland. In *Allied Sketches of the Family Knickerbacker-Viele* (Quintin Publications, 1916), Katherine Knickerbacker Viele suggests instead that the name is a corruption of "Hermen Jansen van Wyekycback(e)," thus upending Knickerbocker's own confident etymology and substituting his strange moniker for one that is even more delightfully comical.

39. Irving biographer Andrew Burstein asserts that Irving and Herman Knickerbocker did not meet until after the publication of the *History* and that Irving, at the time of its writing, "simply borrowed the euphonic name." *The Original Knickerbocker: The Life of Washington Irving* (New York: Basic Books, 2007), 72. I would add that it is likely that Irving, at work on the *History* and alert to the kind of "New York news" that the Historical Society might overlook or snub, would have noted the spring 1809 election and taken the name from that report.

40. Saint Nicholas of Myra, the patron saint of sailors and of children, among others, was also the patron saint of numerous cities and countries, including the Netherlands. The fact that Irving has Knickerbocker invoke him with such

effusive liberality may be interpreted as a criticism of the New-York Historical Society, which had named "Sancte Claus" the patron saint of the city in 1809.

41. New York's Common Council passed a resolution in 1807 to celebrate Christmas on December 25, as a "day of solemn thanksgiving and prayer." See Stokes, *Iconography*, 1480. Subsequently, the January 25, 1808, issue of *Salmagundi* reproved the municipal decision to pass over December 6, Saint Nicholas Day, for New York's official holiday, noting that the saint some "called Santaclaus" was the one "most venerated by true hollanders, and their unsophisticated descendants" (*S* 346). Despite Irving's original usage, the modern apotheosis of Santa Claus is generally credited to Clement Clarke Moore. How Christmas was subsequently appropriated into the Knickerbocker New York culture will be discussed in chapter 2.

42. For a careful analysis of Dutch culinary traditions in New Amsterdam, see Peter Rose's delightful guide, *The Sensible Cook: Dutch Foodways in the Old and the New World* (Syracuse: Syracuse University Press, 1989). Rose gives several recipes for "Krullen," "Oly-Koecks," and "Oly-Bollen," as well as one for "Suppaen," or cornmeal mush, which supports Irving's claim on Barlow's poetic dish.

43. The first American cookbook was Amelia Simmons's *American Cookery*, published in 1796. It included specifically "American" recipes such as "Indian Slapjack." Irving might have registered the competitive market created by the subsequent publication of *New England Cookery*, in 1808, or, as John T. Edge's wonderful *Doughnuts: An American Passion* (New York: G. P. Putnam, 2006) suggests, Irving may have known about a piece of New Amsterdam "folklore," in which "a lady named Joralemon . . . a 'genuine *vrouw*' . . . opened Manhattan's first donut shop in 1796, selling *olykoeks* and coffee in the financial district between Broadway and Maiden Lane" (14, 16). Regardless of whether or not Mrs. Joralemon is apocryphal, Edge concurs that while the doughnut "is not endemic to America," the Dutch claim to have popularized it, as demonstrated in Irving's Knickerbocker works and supported by Peter Rose, is highly probable.

44. See Hilde Gabriel Lee's *Taste of the States: A Food History of America* (Charlottesville: Howell Press, 1992), 55. Lee notes that Samuel Fraunces also shipped particular delicacies, such as "pickled oysters and lobsters," out of the city, a comment that suggests that the renown of "New York foods" began well in advance of the bagel, the knish, and the founding of Zabar's.

45. As Kenneth Cmiel has shown, American literature was the site of ongoing negotiations over the role and limitations of plain speech and all that it entailed politically in the decades that followed the Revolutionary War, and "the republican distaste for aristocratic usage made Americans wary about showy language. At the same time that the broad diffusion of genteel speech became a political goal, the opportunity for the elite to set itself off via the grand style was foreclosed. The combined pressures, increasing participation and education below, and the distrust of overrefinement above, threatened to strip from the gentry their cultural distinctiveness. A republican discourse had to find the right pitch, refined but not *too* refined, a gentleman's language but not an aristocrat's. Negotiating these boundaries became an issue that nagged well into the nineteenth

century." *Democratic Eloquence: The Fight over Popular Speech in Nineteenth-Century America* (Los Angeles: UCLA Press, 1990), 39. Cmiel's discussion of early American self-consciousness about republican speech is particularly interesting in light of Irving's trajectory, as an American man of letters in England.

46. In *Everyday Nature*, Sara S. Gronim takes note of a poem by Jacob Steendam entitled "The Praise of New Netherland," in which he lists at least twenty-four species of fish to be found in the colony. *Everyday Nature: Knowledge of he Natural World in Colonial New York* (New Brunswick, NJ: Rutgers University Press, 2007), 21. A closer inspection of the poem shows that these include "shad . . . not scarce, but quite innumerable," and also, interestingly, salmon. Knickerbocker never cites Steendam, thus missing the opportunity to add yet another layer of historiography—and mischief—to his account. "The Praise of New Netherland," in John Gilman Shea and Henry Reed Stiles, *The Historical Magazine and Notes and Queries Concerning the Antiquities, History and Biography of America* (New York: Henry B. Dawson, 1861), 191.

47. Appendix to Miller's "Discourse," *Collections*, 41–43.

48. *New-York Commercial Advertiser*, 12 Jan. 1810. This advertisement also riffed on Irving's own make-believe "Distressing" notices by declaring, "Those who wish to purchase this valuable little work are informed that the sole object of the publisher is *money*; and that the whole amount goes to his own pocket, and not to pay off any of Mr. Knickerbocker's *Grog Bills*." Such a lighthearted pitch would likely have galled the serious and scholarly Mitchill.

49. It was also not the last time that Dr. Mitchill would find himself in the middle of a public debate over a fish: after publishing a monograph entitled *The Fishes of New-York* in 1815, he became the "star witness" in *Maurice v. Judd*, an 1818 court case that sought to determine, for the purposes of taxation on fish oil, whether a whale was a fish or a mammal. In his fascinating account of that case, D. Graham Burnett suggests that the trial "became a showdown between . . . buyers and sellers, leathermen and chandlers, Knickerbockers and Yankees," noting that the participation of sophisticated scholars such as Mitchill threw the class and regional differences between the merchant elite and their seagoing contractors into high relief. *Trying Leviathan* (Princeton: Princeton University Press, 2007), 193. However, in 1818, the year of *Maurice v. Judd*, Irving's *History* had only been in print for nine years, and New Yorkers were just beginning to awaken to the idea of a "Knickerbocker" identity. While Irving certainly exploits the Yankee stereotypes in his Knickerbocker works, as we shall see, the chief enemy of the incipient Knickerbocker persona is not a New Englander, per se, but *anyone* who dares to suggest that the City of New York is not second to none.

50. Wansey, *Journal*, 234.

51. The New York accent has been in the news in recent years, as linguistics alternately predict its demise or speculate on changes to its characteristic profile, brought about by immigrant New Yorkers in the outer boroughs. But Knickerbocker's jingoism remains: in one recent article, New Yorkers and language specialists alike agreed that regardless of how the accent evolves, it will always remain "distinctive" and "unique." *amNewYork*, 20 Feb. 2008.

52. Charles William Janson, *The Stranger in America* (London: Albion Press, 1807), 92.

53. The 1848 edition of Irving's *History* expands on these ideas, replacing "local nobility" with "legitimate nobility" and championing the "well authenticated claims of our genuine Dutch families . . . that have been somewhat elbowed aside in latter days by foreign intruders" (*RHNY* 302). As I noted in the introduction, Irving's revisions are his response to the popularity of his creation and his acknowledgment of the market for "legitimate" social authority that it inspired.

54. Lambert, *Travels*, 99.

55. While Knickerbocker is spoofing the New England custom of giving children tongue-twisting Old Testament or Puritan first names (which, when combined with English last names, could have unintentionally humorous results), he has slightly missed his Yankee target here. Preserved Fish was indeed the given name of an actual shipping magnate (1766–1846), but the Fish family had been prominent in New York since before the Revolutionary War (and would later include New York governor Hamilton Fish) and was related by marriage to Elizabeth Stuyvesant, a great-great-granddaughter of Peter Stuyvesant.

56. "The rolls of soldiers reads like a who's who of Dutch and English names in the valley: two Broncks and five Ingersolls, twenty-four van Rensselaers and twenty-six Livingstons, twenty-three Schuylers and nineteen Hudsons. About 450 citizens with names like Livingston, Schuyler, Hardenbrook, and Van Cortlandt stripped the lead from their windows to make bullets for the soldiers." Tom Lewis, *The Hudson: A History* (New Haven: Yale University Press, 2005), 149.

2. INHERITING KNICKERBOCKER

1. In his memorial tribute to Irving, Evert Duyckinck notes that the "highest honor ever paid to the authentic history of Knickerbocker was the quotation from it—in good Latin phrase—by Goeller, German annotator of Thucydides, in illustration of a passage of the Greek author: 'Addo locum Washingtonis Irvingii Hut. JiotiEboraci' lib. vii., cap. 6. (*Classical Museum*, October, 1849)." *Irvingiana: A Memorial of Washington Irving* (New York: Charles B. Richardson, 1860), vii.

2. *National Intelligencer and Washington Advertiser*, 25 Dec. 1810.

3. *New-York Commercial Advertiser*, 12 Jan. 1810; *Columbian*, 5 April 1810.

4. See James Grant Wilson, *Bryant and His Friends: Some Reminiscences of the Knickerbocker Writers* (New York: Fords, Howard and Hulbert, 1886), which erroneously considers James Fenimore Cooper and Edgar Allan Poe to be "Knickerbocker Writers." See also Kendall B. Taft, *Minor Knickerbockers* (New York: American Book, 1974).

5. *New-York Gazette & General Advertiser*, 21 Nov. 1818; *New-York Daily Advertiser*, 8 Sept. 1818; *National Advocate*, 6 Jan. 1816.

6. *New-York Gazette*, 9 Oct. 1817.

7. Advertisement, *National Advocate*, 3 July 1813; advertisement, *New-York Commercial Advertiser*, 24 April 1811; advertisement, *Columbian*, 4 June 1812.

8. *New-York Evening Post*, 24 Dec. 1818.

9. Although he did begin revising the *History*: Inskeep and Bradford published the first revised edition in 1812.

10. See James W. Tuttleton's chronology in the Library of America editions of Irving's works. Tuttleton's terse, episodic descriptions of events in Irving's life provide an immensely satisfying overview. For example: "1813–1814: Writes a regular column, biographical sketches, and literary criticism, but dislikes editing and is relieved when firm publishing *Select Reviews* (renamed *Analectic Magazine*) fails. Swears never to edit again." *Washington Irving: History, Tales, and Sketches*, ed. James W. Tuttleton (New York: Library of America, 1983), 1096.

11. Republished in the *New-York Spectator*, 17 Oct. 1820.

12. "To a New England Poet," *The Norton Anthology of American Literature*, 3rd ed., vol. 1 (New York: W. W. Norton, 1989), 740.

13. Elizabeth Blackmar, *Manhattan for Rent: 1785–1850* (Ithaca, NY: Cornell University Press, 1989), 173.

14. "The houses of the higher class were generally constructed of wood, excepting the gable end, which was of small black and yellow Dutch bricks, and always faced the street, as our ancestors, like their descendants, were very much given to outward show. . . . The house was always furnished with an abundance of large doors and small windows on every floor, the date of its erection was curiously designated by iron figures on the front, and on the top of the roof was perched a fierce little weathercock, to let the family into the important secret, which way the wind blew" (*HNY* 477).

15. Thomas Wermuth, *Rip Van Winkle's Neighbors: The Transformation of Rural Life in the Hudson River Valley, 1720–1850* (New York: SUNY Press, 2001), 26. Wermuth also notes that eighteenth-century "Hudson Valley towns regulated newcomers for social reasons" as well, in keeping with "the desire to maintain the form and spirit of the corporate community," which suggests that the Dutch clannishness that Rip's Tarry-town neighbors manifest *after* the Revolution is an indication that they, like he, have largely slept through the national transformation (27).

16. Irving biographers dispute whether the author named his hero for the publisher or the choice was coincidental.

17. I. N. Phelps Stokes, *The Iconography of Manhattan Island*, vol. 5 (New York: Robert H. Dodd, 1924), 1511.

18. The Dutch language was still common around New York City well into the nineteenth century, so much so that "during legislative debates about a new state constitution in 1846 it was suggested that literacy in both English and Dutch be a requirement to vote." *The Encyclopedia of New York City*, ed. Kenneth T. Jackson (New Haven: Yale University Press, 1995), 352.

19. Theodore Roosevelt, *Historic Towns: New York* (New York: Longmans, Green, 1891), 17.

20. See Tuttleton, *History, Tales, and Sketches*, 1055.

21. Wermuth notes that some "back-river valley communities . . . were dramatically transformed in size, scope, and economic development" as a result of the canals. *Rip Van Winkle*, 116.

22. S. Woodsworth, ed., *The Ladies' Literary Cabinet* (New York: Samuel Huestis, 1820), 156.

23. *Saratoga Sentinel*, 3 June 1823 (racehorse); *National Advocate*, 29 Nov. 1820 (yacht club); *Evening Post*, 24 April 1820 (council); *Nantucket Enquirer*, 28 Jan. 1823.

24. In a recent *New York Times* article entitled "Gluttonous Rite Survives Without Silverware" (30 Jan. 2008), writer Paul Lukas notes that "beefsteaks—boisterous mass feeds featuring unlimited servings of steak, lamb chops, bacon-wrapped lamb kidneys, crabmeat, shrimp and beer, all consumed without such niceties as silverware, napkins or women—held sway in New York for the better part of a century." Irving's reference suggests that they have been in existence (although not, perhaps, in the same culinary combination Lukas offers) for much longer: nearly two hundred years.

25. Irving is prescient in yet another way: both local oysters and canvasback ducks, mainstays of nineteenth-century gustatory excess, would see their local habitats destroyed and would fall off *haute* New York menus by the end of the Gilded Age.

26. Stokes, *Iconography*, 1447; Sanna Feirstein, *Naming New York: Manhattan Places and How They Got Their Names* (New York: NYU Press, 2001), 78. A 1915 *Standard Cyclopedia of Horticulture* (New York: Macmillan) notes that Stuyvesant had "forty or fifty negro slaves" working as gardeners on his property, which at one point stretched down to the East River. It's interesting to note that the author, one Liberty Hyde Bailey, borrows heavily from Knickerbocker's mournful, nostalgic vocabulary to describe the gardens, concluding: "The Bowery of these degenerate days has lost the Eden-like features that distinguished its illustrious progenitor" (1506).

27. Edgar Allan Poe, *Doings of Gotham*, ed. Jacob E. Spannuth and Thomas Ollive Mabbot (Pottsville: Jacob E. Spannuth, 1929), 26.

28. Ibid., 31, 43, 65.

29. Frederick Phillip Stieff, *Eat, Drink, and Be Merry in Maryland* (New York: G. P. Putnam's Sons, 1932), 296.

30. Poe, *Doings*, 25.

31. Ira Rosenwaike, *Population History of New York City* (Syracuse: Syracuse University Press, 1972), 42. The census data for 1850 included country of origin for the first time. The change in the population of Brooklyn (Kings County) was much more dramatic: from 5,700 inhabitants in 1800 to 138,000 by 1850, suggesting that many new immigrants found their way across the East River in search of real estate (and perhaps some New Yorkers did, too).

32. Ibid.

33. Hasia R. Diner notes that "between 1847 and 1851, a total of 1.8 million immigrants disembarked in New York, of whom 848,000 were Irish men and women and the rest mainly German." She adds that not all émigrés to New York remained there: some went upstate or west to work on "railroad or canal-building

projects." "'The Most Irish City in the Union': The Era of the Great Migration, 1844–1877," in *The New York Irish*, ed. Ronald H. Bayor (Baltimore: Johns Hopkins University Press, 1987), 91.

34. Elizabeth Blackmar notes that the "Five Points' tenant houses, brothels and saloons had become, to many citizens' dismay, a major tourist attraction as the center of the city's lowlife." She points out that in his *Notes on America* Charles Dickens "likened the Points to London's own notorious East End." *Manhattan for Rent*, 179–180.

35. It is no coincidence that New York City's parochial school system was founded at this time, a formal self-segregation by Catholic New Yorkers that many took as an outright criticism of the populist, Protestant institutions such as the Free School, with which DeWitt Clinton had hoped to ensure Manhattan's eternal primacy.

36. Burroughs and Wallace suggest that this study of the Dutch colony, which included interviews with "old Dutch families in Flatbush and Gravesend," the very communities singled out by Samuel Mitchill, "came as a revelation to those who had incautiously assumed Irving's satirical 'history' was the real thing." *Gotham*, 696.

37. Edward Widmer, *Young America: The Flowering of Democracy in America* (New York: Oxford University Press, 1999), 130.

38. *Baltimore Sun*, 19 Oct. 1852; advertisement, *Macon Weekly Telegraph*, 11 April 1848. In his recent cocktail history *Imbibe!* David Wonderich notes that the Knickerbocker, later called a "Knickerbocker Punch," was first recorded in Boston in 1852 or 1853 and contained lime juice, raspberry syrup, "one wine-glass of Santa Cruz rum," and a dash of curaçao. A later "Knickerbocker Punch" from an 1867 guide entitled *American Bartender* is very different: "half brandy and half port, with pieces of orange and pineapple in the glass," which Wonderich calls "delicious, but no Knickerbocker." (New York: Perigee, 2007), 105–106. Another nineteenth-century guide, *Cooling Cups and Dainty Drinks*, dubs the rum drink a "Knickerbocker a la Monsieur," to distinguish it from a "Knickerbocker a la Madame," which is a frozen drink with lemon and Madeira flavoring. (New York: George Routledge, 1869), 207. And the *Trader Vic's Bartender's Guide* suggests that it is merely gin with sweet and dry vermouth—a variation on the contemporary martini. For more on the connection between the martini and Knickerbocker, see chapter 3.

39. Lydia Maria Child, *Letters from New York* (New York: C. S. Francis and Co., 1845), 108.

40. *Knickerbacker Magazine*, Jan. 1833, 6–7.

41. Ibid., 9, 11.

42. Knickerbocker is again conjured to give the blessing for this change, and, in fact, to insist upon it. "I have repented of the permission given to thy esteemed predecessor . . . as to altering my name," he is quoted, "and wish thee to restore it to its original spelling, as it stands in my celebrated History. It is but ill repaying Fame, for extending my celebrity to the utmost corners of the earth, thus to find fault with her scholarship." *Knickerbocker*, July 1833, 5

43. "Home Literature" was the title of an article Whitman wrote for the *Brooklyn Eagle* on July 11, 1846.

44. *Knickerbocker Magazine*, Dec. 1845; Lewis Gaylord Clark, *Knick-Knacks from an Editor's Table* (New York: D. Appleton, 1853), 82–83. In all fairness, while Irving was the first American literary celebrity to see his work baldly copied, he was not the only one at this time. Fitz-Greene Halleck's epic poem "Fanny" was the jumping-off point for a B-grade story of the same name, published in the *Knickerbocker* in 1833, and the magazine also printed a poem entitled "Recipe for Making Sweet-Potato Pudding" that was doubtless inspired by (if hardly on the level of) Barlow's "Hasty-Pudding." *Knickerbocker*, Feb. 1833, 120.

45. Clark, *Knick-Knacks*, 82–83.

46. Thomas Bender has suggested that the "Knickerbocker School" were "gentlemen who wrote, not writers," a distinction that more accurately describes the younger acolytes of what Bender calls the "triptych" of Irving, Cooper, and Bryant—writers such as Giulian Verplanck and Joseph Rodman Drake. *New York Intellect* (Baltimore: Johns Hopkins University Press, 1987), 131. The idea of a "Knickerbocker School" of literature was perpetuated in the nineteenth century by, along with Lewis Gaylord Clark himself, historians such as James Grant Wilson, who published *Bryant and His Friends: Some Reminiscences of the Knickerbocker Writers* in 1886 (New York: Fords, Howard and Hulbert), and in the twentieth century to most lasting effect by the critic Van Wyck Brooks, whose literary biography of nineteenth-century America began with a volume suggestively titled *The World of Washington Irving* (New York: H. Wolff, 1944). Brooks situates Cooper, Bryant, and Poe in Irving's extended orbit—a cosmogony those authors would certainly have rejected—particularly Poe, who famously mocked the *Knickerbocker* and its contributors in a series of essays for *Godey's Lady's Book*, "The Literati of New York City," and Cooper, who was never a fan of Irving. Perry Miller and Kendall Taft reiterate this arrangement of early American literary superstars in *The Raven and the Whale* (New York: Harcourt, Brace, and World, 1956) and *Minor Knickerbockers* (New York: American Book, 1947), respectively.

47. Jackson, *Encyclopedia*, 219; *Knickerbocker*, July 1833, 29.

48. Michael Warner, "Irving's Posterity," *ELH* 67, no. 3 (2000): 789.

49. "That Irving should have permitted his nephew to insert revisions in his manuscript is not surprising. He was impatient of his 'monthly recurring task' as a contributor to the *Knickerbocker Magazine*, and he devoted no more pains to preparing copy than was absolutely necessary. He may indeed have employed Pierre M. Irving on a fairly regular basis as his unofficial editor and liaison with Lewis Gaylord Clark." Wayne R. Kime, ed., *Miscellaneous Writings, 1803–1859: The Complete Works of Washington Irving* (Boston: Twayne, 1981), 411.

50. "Conspiracy of the Cocked Hats," *Knickerbocker Magazine*, Oct. 1839, 305, 307–308.

51. See Brian Jay Jones, *Washington Irving: An American Original* (New York: Arcade, 2008), 386.

52. There is considerable disagreement over whether or not Clement Clarke Moore wrote *A Visit from Saint Nicholas*, but several critics have pointed out that

Moore's poem riffs on the meter and syntax of Puritan poet Michael Wigglesworth's "Day of Doom," a dire warning from the seventeenth century of the coming apocalypse that, I would agree, only a former seminarian and the son of an Episcopal bishop would be likely to know. Irving's influence over the contemporary depiction of Santa Claus even extended to artistic representations, as Lauretta Dimmick has shown: the famous Robert Weir portrait of Saint Nicholas evolved in tandem with Irving's revisions, with both the saint and the sleeping household he is visiting becoming increasingly "Dutch" in dress and decor over time. "Robert Weir's *Saint Nicholas*: A Knickerbocker Icon," *Art Bulletin*, Sept. 1984, 465–483. For more on the evolution of Santa Claus, see Karal Ann Marling's *Merry Christmas! Celebrating America's Greatest Holiday* (Cambridge: Harvard University Press, 2000), and Steven Nissenbaum's *The Battle for Christmas* (New York: Knopf, 1996).

53. Interestingly, 1835 was the same year that Irving purchased the Tarrytown cottage that would become his retreat, Sunnyside. This coincidence suggests that Irving was, as readers of his biography might suspect, eager to leave New York City and certainly not as engaged in this city-based genealogical society as his (mostly) Dutch-descended peers.

54. Menu, Saint Nicholas Society Anniversary Dinner, 6 Dec. 1851.

55. See Leonard L. Richards, Marla R. Miller, and Erik Gilg, *A Return to His Native Town: Martin Van Buren at Lindenwald, 1839–1862* (National Parks Service, 2006), 23–24.

56. Emphasis Ogle's. Quoted in Edward Boykin, *Congress and the Civil War* (McBride, 1955), 157.

57. Jones, *Washington Irving*, 331.

58. Washington Irving, *Wolfert's Roost* (New York: G. P. Putnam, 1861), 29.

59. *Letters of Washington Irving*, vol. 4, ed. Ralph M. Aderman, Herbert L. Kleinfield, and Jenifer S. Banks (Boston: Twayne, 1982), 184.

60. "In the Churchyard at Tarrytown," *The Poetical Works of Henry Wadsworth Longfellow* (Boston: Houghton Mifflin, 1890), 208.

61. In his excellent compendium of Irving scholarship, Andrew B. Myers describes mourners and visitors' vandalizing homage to Irving. *The Knickerbocker Tradition: Washington Irving's New York* (Tarrytown: Sleepy Hollow Restorations, 1974).

3. Fashioning a Knickerbocracy

1. John W. Francis, *Old New York: or, Reminiscences of the Past Sixty Years* (New York: Charles Roe, 1858), 376.

2. Thomas H. Johnson, *The Oxford Companion to American History* (New York: Oxford University Press 1966), 67. In *National Pastime: How Americans Play Baseball and the Rest of the World Plays Soccer* (Washington, DC: Brookings Institution Press, 2006), Stephen Szymanski and Andrew Zimbalist point out that the Knickerbocker team did not give baseball the "knickerbocker" style of uniform

trousers: "the famous knickers . . . were first introduced by the Cincinnati Red Stockings team in 1869" (16).

The origins of baseball are the subject of much passionate debate. The Mills Commission of 1905–1907 came to the conclusion that Doubleday was responsible for devising the game that we recognize as baseball today, but latter-day enthusiasts and even Baseball Hall of Fame staff have questioned the supremacy of Doubleday and Cooperstown. No baseball authority asserts that Cartwright made up the game himself, but there appears to be unanimous agreement that the Knickerbocker team was the first to codify the rules. For more on the Knickerbocker origins of American baseball, see Elmer Berry, *Baseball Notes for Coaches and Players* (Brattleboro, VT: Hildreth, 1916), 84; and Richard L. Sartore, *Seasons of Change: Baseball in America* (Hauppauge, NY: Nova Science Publishers, 1999), 2.

3. Benjamin A. Baker, *A Glance at New York* (1848; Brooklin, ME: Feedback Theatrebooks, 1996), 11; George G. Foster, *New York by Gaslight and Other Urban Sketches*, ed. Stuart Blumin (Berkeley: University of California Press, 1990), 105, 134, 164.

4. Moses Yale Beach (New York: *Sun*, 1842), n.p. It is interesting to note that while Cornelius Vanderbilt has already made it onto this list, his estimated net worth is only $200,000 in 1842.

5. George G. Foster, *New York in Slices* (New York: W. F. Burgess, 1849), 61; Foster, *New York by Gas-Light*, 163.

6. Foster, *New York by Gas-Light*, 127

7. This figure comes from Tyler Anbinder's *Nativism and Slavery: The Northern Know-Nothings and the Politics of the 1860s* (New York: Oxford, 1992), 50.

8. Published in 1844 by the American Republican Party.

9. "Historical Notes of New-York Family," *New York Times*, 30 June 1866.

10. From "Democratic Vistas," *Whitman: Complete Poetry and Collected Prose* (New York: Library of America, 1982), 946; "July 4 Oration" in Alan Trachtenberg, *Democratic Vistas* (New York: G. Brazilier, 1970), 69–70. Despite his (often self-righteous) emphasis on racial and ethnic commingling, Whitman was not above the occasional genealogical inquiry himself. In "Specimen Days" he gives in to what he calls "old pedigree-reminiscences" and outlines his mother's Dutch ancestry (her maiden name was Van Velsor) and his father's English colonial family, landed gentry who are, he notes, recorded in "Savage's 'Genealogical Dictionary'" as having arrived in America "before 1664." Whitman, *Complete*, 691–692.

11. Charles Astor Bristed, *The Upper Ten Thousand: Sketches of American Society* (New York: Stringer and Townsend, 1852), 11, 58–59.

12. Irving noted the 1847 wedding in a letter to his friend Gouverneur Kemble: "Brevoort . . . is marrying his children to all the fortunes in the Country." *Letters of Washington Irving*, ed. Ralph M. Aderman, Herbert L. Kleinfield, and Jenifer S. Banks (Boston: Twayne, 1978–1982), 139.

13. Bristed, *Upper Ten Thousand*, 47–48.

14. "The Kip's Bay House," *Pittsfield Sun*, 27 Apr. 1848, 1.

15. Bristed, *Upper Ten Thousand*, 48.

16. John Vose, *Fresh Leaves from the Diary of a Broadway Dandy* (New York: Bunnell and Price, 1852), 117–118, 122–123; Bristed, *Upper Ten Thousand*, 48.

17. James Unsworth, "The Stage Driver (On the Knickerbocker Line)" (New York: H. De Marsan, n.d.). I am grateful to Norman Cazden, Herbert Haufrecht, and Norman Studer's *Folk Songs of the Catskills* (New York: SUNY Press, 1982) for background information on this song, which I originally discovered through the Smithsonian *American Songs and Ballads* finding aid; they note that "The Stage Driver" predates another song with a Knickerbocker title, "The Knickerbocker Polka," by two years (47).

18. It bears mentioning that Irving, who had touched on matters of race in the *History*, when he chided the Dutch for claiming New York from the Indians by the "Right by Extermination, or, in other words, the Right by Gunpowder" does introduce an African American character into the Knickerbocker pantheon, albeit a minor one. One of the stories in the Knickerbocker-narrated "Money Diggers" section of *Tales of a Traveller* is "Adventure of the Black Fisherman," the account of "Black Sam," a former slave on a Dutch farm who takes Wolfert Webber on a hunt for pirate treasure he had seen buried on the shoreline of Long Island Sound.

19. Irving's health was failing at the time, and his illnesses were widely reported as matters of national concern. He would die in November of 1859, eight months after the *Dictionary* was published.

20. John Russell Bartlett, *Dictionary of Americanisms*, 2nd ed. (Boston: Little, Brown, 1859), 231, viii.

21. Ibid., 312, 412, 302, 430, 452. By 1859, "oly-koeks" and "sour krout" were well known to American cooks from the pages of recipe books such as the aforementioned *American Cookery* and, as Peter Rose suggests, from Anne Grant's *Memoirs of an American Lady*, published in 1846 with a lavish description of a Dutch family's tea table, in Albany. However, Bartlett also does not acknowledge the "Knickerbocker Pickle" in his culinary definitions. The "Pickle" was a method for "preserving beef, pork, and hams" that was "strongly recommended for family use." The recipe, first published in the *New York Advocate* in 1823, called for nine pounds of salt, three pounds of brown sugar, a quart of molasses, saltpeter, and pearl ash to be boiled together and poured over the meats in question. It is worth noting that despite the fact that cured meats of this specific description do not feature in Irving's texts, by the early 1820s the recipe, because of its Albany origin, was already being claimed for "Knickerbocker."

22. Edwin Burroughs and Mike Wallace, *Gotham: A History of New York to 1898* (New York: Oxford University Press, 1999), 903; "Letter from New York," *San Francisco Bulletin*, 18 March 1864; "On This Day in History: February 20," *Brooklyn Daily Eagle*, 25 Feb. 2008 (online). The Sanitary Fair in Brooklyn was also known as the Brooklyn and Long Island Fair, since what is now called the Borough of Brooklyn, or Kings County, was then commonly considered to be part of Long Island, since it is on the same land mass.

23. Descriptions of the Knickerbocker Kitchen come from *A Record of the Metropolitan Fair, in Aid of the United States Sanitary Commission Held at New*

York, in April 1864 (New York: Hurd and Houghton, 1867), 183, 185–186; and Elizabeth Fries Elliet, *The Queens of American Society* (Philadelphia: Henry T. Coates, 1867), 292. In his book *The Americans* (New York: Putnam, 1969), Joseph Chamberlain Furnas notes the presence of the "Beekman Cradle"; the commission's report does not mention it. The Coinage Act of April 1864 created two-cent coins that rendered the Knickerbocker tokens obsolete, but the privately minted coins were not deemed illegal by the federal government until June of that year.

24. A "Programme of Tableaux" from the Fitchburg Town Hall in 1854 lists "Grandfather Knickerbocker" among the scenes to be performed. Other tableaux on the roster include "Uncle Tom and Eva," "The Washington Family," and "Oliver, Asking for More." It is difficult to say what "Grandfather Knickerbocker" is meant to represent, but he may have been a forerunner of the Rip Van Winkle play. At any rate, Irving's inclusion in this list of stock scenes familiar to an American audience is instructive.

25. *The Diary of George Templeton Strong* (New York: Macmillan, 1952), cited in Neil Harris, *The Artist in American Society: The Formative Years, 1790–1860* (Chicago: University of Chicago Press, 1982), 85.

26. "National Nomenclature," *Knickerbocker Magazine*, Aug. 1839, 161.

27. Burroughs and Wallace, *Gotham*, 877.

28. Nathaniel Parker Willis, *Out-doors at Idlewild* (New York: Scribner, 1855), 376; Wesley R. Andrews, *The American Code of Manners: A Study of the Usages, Laws and Observances Which Govern Intercourse in the Best Social Circles* (New York: Andrews, 1880), 289.

29. Norval White and Eliot Willensky, *AIA Guide to New York City* (New York: Three Rivers Press, 2000), 421. The agreement for the New York Public Library, Astor, Lenox and Tilden Foundations was signed in 1895, but the Carrère and Hastings building on Fifth Avenue at Forty-second Street was not completed until 1911.

30. Henry James, "The Absent Occasions," in *The American Scene*, ed. Richard Howard (New York: Library of America, 1993), 491.

31. Sven Beckert, *The Monied Metropolis: New York City and the Consolidation of the American Bourgeoisie, 1850–1896* (Cambridge: Cambridge University Press, 2001) 247, 268; James, "The Absent Occasions," 491. Beckert argues that this savvy cross-pollination demonstrated that "the Metropolitan Museum integrated the old mercantile elite with new segments of the city's upper class into a class-wide institution" (268). In contrast, Mary Cable notes (but cites no primary source evidence) that "when it was suggested that the [New-York Historical Society] should amalgamate with the Metropolitan Museum . . . the members refused on the grounds that certain founders of the Museum were unacceptable socially." *Top Drawer: American High Society from the Gilded Age to the Roaring Twenties* (New York: Atheneum, 1984), 52.

32. Francis Gerry Fairfield, *The Clubs of New York* (New York: Henry L. Hinton, 1873), 60; Walt Whitman, *New York Dissected* (1855–1856; New York: R. R. Wilson, 1936), 96; Eric Homberger, *Mrs. Astor's New York: Money and Social Power in a Gilded Age* (New Haven: Yale University Press, 2002), 183. Homberger

suggests that the founders of the Knickerbocker had found the Union Club to be stuffy, a verdict that is borne out, in part, by Fairfield's critique in *Clubs of New York* of the "aristocratic monotony of that Knickerbockerism" that is manifest in the Union Club and the "grand fetish of pedigree" that characterized the "Bourbons of New York," whom he calls "Van Dunderheads," while their arriviste rivals are given such names as "Mr. Petroleum Parvenu" (60).

33. "The Knickerbocker Apartment Company have purchased the Knickerbocker Club House, and propose to erect upon its site an apartment house of the first class at a cost of about $1,000,000." *Manufacturer Builder*, July 1882, 152.

34. At the first annual dinner of the Holland Society of New York, held in 1886, one member justified the creation of this new genealogical group thus: "Why this along with the St Nicholas Society? Why, then, should we form another? It is because you and I have felt our blood on fire when we were present at those dinners and have heard it said: 'This is not a Dutch Society. The pipes are Dutch; the menu is in alleged Dutch; but this is merely a society of old New-York, and includes men of all nationalities and of no nationality.' That is why the Holland Society was founded." Clipping, Collection of the New-York Historical Society, 1886, n.p.

35. William J. Murtagh notes that these groups were primarily interested in exploring local demographic concerns and providing genealogical and archival research support for their members. *Keeping Time: The History and Theory of Preservation in America* (New York: John Wiley and Sons, 1997), 25–26. T. Jackson Lears links the fad for pedigrees and coats of arms—"premodern emblems of authority"—to the heightening racism and class clashes that had become a feature of increasingly heterogeneous urban life. *No Place of Grace: Antimodernism and the Transformation of American Culture, 1880–1920* (Chicago: University of Chicago Press, 1994), 188. Beckert is more specific, distinguishing between "class identity" and identities "based on religious beliefs and heritages," which served as the impulse behind clubs such as the Harmonie Gesellschaft, the Saint Nicholas Society (discussed in chapter 2), and the New England Society, as well as the founding of the New York Genealogical Society (1869), the Sons of the American Revolution (1889), and the Daughters of the American Revolution (1890). Interestingly, Beckert includes the founding of the American Museum of Natural History (1871), in this roster, thus demonstrating the popularity of the ethnographic connection which Edith Wharton, Thorstein Veblen, and others made between social and biological destiny. "Social Darwinism," Beckert comments, "became a convenient tool for understanding and legitimizing the world of Gilded Age New York." *Metropolis*, 265, 212. In rebuttal, at least one genealogical society suggests that the "national pride and optimism" engendered by the "White City" of the Chicago Columbian Exposition of 1893 was the impetus behind the founding of "a society of ladies of colonial ancestry," the Colonial Dames of America. See P. Gordon B. Stillman, *One Hundred Years in New York: The Story of the First Century of the National Society of Colonial Dames in the State of New York* (New York: NSCDA, 1996), 5.

36. Rosenwaike, *Population*, 67; *North American Review*, Oct. 1853, 301. See Clifton Hood, "An Unusable Past: Urban Elites, New York's Evacuation Day, and the Transformation of Memory Culture," *Journal of Social History* 37, no. 4 (2004): 883–913, for a discussion of the revival of the patriotic Evacuation Day celebration that took place in 1883 on the centennial of the evacuation of the British from New York. Hood connects the celebration to the rampant interest by the city's elite in the cultural genre of "Old New York" and suggests that the anniversary was part of a "larger elite project to idealize the historical memory of colonial New York," a project that manifested itself, during the Gilded Age, in expressions of Anglophilia (900). I would propose that the "Old New York" "project" significantly predated the revitalization of Evacuation Day and that the colonial city that New Yorkers longed for itself predated the English: "Old New York" is imbued with the spirit and the trappings of Irving's New Amsterdam.

37. *Harper's*, Jan. 1884, 299; "Veteran Corps to Dance," *New York Times*, 21 Dec. 1923; Bayrd Still, *Mirror for Gotham: New York as Seen by Contemporaries from Dutch Days to the Present* (New York: NYU Press, 1956), 63; *Knickerbocker Greys, 1881–1949* (self-published pamphlet, 1949), 1, 5.

38. In the case of the previously mentioned Van Alen house in Kinderhook, New York, life would imitate art: as a result of Irving's homage to its rustic charms, a nearby one-room schoolhouse (c. 1850) was christened the Ichabod Crane Schoolhouse, and as of this writing the Van Alen House itself is a museum of Dutch domestic culture, one of the most treasured restorations in the Hudson River Valley.

39. David T. Valentine, *History of the City of New York* (New York: G. P. Putnam, 1853); Thomas A. Janvier, *In Old New York: A Classic History of New York City* (New York: Harper and Brothers, 1894; rpt. New York: St. Martin's Press, 2000), 155, 250.

For the pear tree, see William Leete Stone, *History of New York from the Discovery to the Present Day* (New York: Virtue and Yorston, 1872), 565, 597. It had been planted in Governor Stuyvesant's time and was removed from its place at what is now Third Avenue and Thirteenth Street in 1867. A plaque marks the spot where it stood.

40. Stone, *History*, 656.

41. John Van Dyke, *The New New York: A Commentary on the Place and the People* (New York : Macmillan, 1909), 264. He also suggests that New York "ignore" its émigré applicants, and compel those who have arrived to support themselves. "There has been perhaps too much charity, too much help" (267).

42. Janvier, *In Old New York*, 148.

43. Thomas J. Rush, "Race in Genealogy and the Chinese Emigration: An Address on the Twelfth Anniversary of the New York Genealogical and Biographical Society," *Record*, Feb. 1881, 1. Emphasis in original.

44. "'In the April number of the RECORD, on p. 97, I notice your inquiry for the oldest New York Family now represented in the city. You tentatively suggest Stuyvesant, in the city from 1647. Let me speak for my own line. There may be older families, but none can be much older. We go back to 1633, and it is

interesting to know that we have never ceased to be represented in the city since that year.' David Cole, pastor of Reformed Church, Yonkers." *Record*, July 1882, 143–144.

45. Abram C. Dayton, *Last Days of Knickerbocker Life in New York* (New York: George W. Harlan, 1880, 7, 6, 27.

46. Edith Wharton, *A Backward Glance* (New York: Macmillan, 1933), 55; Mrs. John King Van Rensselaer, *New Yorkers of the XIX Century* (New York: F. T. Neely, 1897), foreword.

47. Mrs. John King Van Rensselaer, *The Goede Vrouw of Mana-ha-ta: At Home and in Society, 1609–1760* (New York, Charles Scribner's Sons, 1898), 392, 397.

48. Agnes Carr Sage, *A Little Colonial Dame: A Story of Old Manhattan Island* (New York: Stokes, 1898), 119. It is interesting to speculate why Sage did not dedicate *A Little Colonial Dame* to the Society of Daughters of Holland Dames, a genealogical organization founded in 1895, three years before her work was published. That group, rather than the Colonial Dames of America (whose membership could have ancestors from any country, provided they served in leadership positions—broadly defined—in the thirteen colonies), would seem to be the most appropriate honoree for the story of Rychie Van Couwenhoven. Perhaps Sage herself had the genealogical prerequisites for one group but not the other.

49. "New York as a Field for Fiction," *The Century: A Popular Quarterly*, Sept. 1883, 785–788.

50. Herman Knickerbocker Vielé, *The Last of the Knickerbockers* (Chicago: Herbert Stone, 1901), 14, 13, 18, 121.

51. Ibid., 48, 5, 159–160, 98, 123, 29. It may be speculated that "Oro City" inspired Wharton's fictional "Apex City," birthplace of the socially ambitious Undine Spragg, heroine of *The Custom of the Country*, published in 1913.

52. Amy Kaplan, *The Social Construction of American Realism* (Chicago: University of Chicago Press, 1988), 84–85; Wharton, *A Backward Glance*, 9. Kaplan credits R.W.B. Lewis's biography of Wharton for the information about Wharton's reaction to Scribner's original book jacket for *The House of Mirth*. "Throughout her career," Kaplan notes, "Wharton was sensitive to the charge that she practiced class tourism in the upper ranks of society."

53. Edith Wharton, *The Age of Innocence* (1920; New York: Scribner, 1996), 68.

54. Wharton, *A Backward Glance*, 10–11.

55. "Forms of Disembodiment," *The Cambridge Companion to Edith Wharton*, ed. Millicent Bell (New York: Cambridge University Press, 1995), 21.

56. Wharton, *The Age of Innocence*, 29.

57. Wharton, *The House of Mirth* (Boston: Bedford Books of St. Martin's Press, 1994), 222.

58. Clare Preston, *Edith Wharton's Social Register* (New York: St. Martin's Press, 2000), 10, 11. Preston notes that Wharton's system "obey[s] the high-caste habit, still extant in America, of using surnames as male first names: hence Newland, Thorley, Sillerton, Dallas, Van der Luyden, Lovell, Manson, and Lefferts all appear as first *and* last names in [the] novels"; Wharton, *The Age of Innocence*, 344.

59. Wharton, *The Age of Innocence*, 120.

60. Edith Wharton, *Old New York* (1924; New York: Scribner, 1951), 238, 86; Knickerbocker Vielé, *The Last of the Knickerbockers*, 160.

61. The mention of social and civic responsibility in the novellas of *Old New York* is glancing, at best, and will be echoed by Wharton's memoir, *A Backward Glance*. "According to their creed," Wharton writes in "The Spark," "gentlemen subscribed as handsomely as their means allowed to the Charity Organization Society, the Patriarchs' Balls, the Children's Aid, and their own parochial charities. Everything beyond savored of 'politics,' revivalist meetings, or the attempt of vulgar persons to buy their way into the circle of the elect." *Old New York*, 210.

62. Henry James, "The Jolly Corner," in *The New York Stories of Henry James* (New York: New York Review Books, 2006), 467, 481; Wharton, *The Age of Innocence*, 362.

63. Beckert, *Metropolis*, 154. See also Jerry E. Patterson, *The First Four Hundred: Mrs. Astor's New York in the Gilded Age* (New York: Rizzoli, 2000), 120. A firsthand account of the Delmonico's dinners can be found in Ward McAllister's *Society as I Have Found It* (New York: Cassell, 1890), 166–170. Schlesinger writes: "While members of the middle class could not emulate Mrs. Vanderbilt's ball or afford to give a $10,000 dinner party at Delmonico's, they enviously followed the activities of the Four Hundred in the society columns. . . . New York, as America's commercial capital, inevitably became America's social capital, elbowing aside Washington, which had served as the court of last appeal for the preceding generation." *Learning How to Behave: A Historical Study of American Etiquette Books* (New York: Macmillan, 1947), 30.

64. Quotations from *Town Topics* are variously drawn from 24 July 1886, 6 Jan., 27 Jan., 24 Feb., 17 May 1887; Edith Wharton, *The Custom of the Country* (1913; London: Penguin, 1987), 19.

65. McAllister, *Society as I Have Found It*, 224. Hearkening back to Lambert's comments on the early City Assembly–Junior Assembly rivalry, it is amusing to note that, according to the reports in *Town Topics*, the ultra-exclusive "Patriarchs' Ball" was quickly followed by a "Matriarchs'" reception, presided over by women with surnames of equal vintage, and by a "Junior Patriarchs' Ball."

66. Interestingly, the "Four Hundred" was in fact just 319 people strong, with a total of 162 different surnames. See Patterson, *First Four Hundred*, 8.

67. Beckert, *Metropolis*, 265.

68. Charles Wilberforce DeLyons Nicholls, *The Ultra-Fashionable Peerage in America* (New York: G. Harjes, 1904), 82, 7, preface (n.p.), 76, 32.

69. For "record of Society," see *Social Register 1887: Facsimile Edition* (New York: Social Register Association, 1986), 2.

4. Knickerbocker in a New Century

1. Andrew Haswell Green, *Municipal Consolidation Inquiry Communication of Andrew H. Green, to the Legislature of the State of New York, Copy of Act*

Creating Commission of Inquiry, and Addresses of the President to the Commissioners (New York: Stettiner, Lambert and Co., 1893), 57.

2. That company's mascot, alternately said to resemble Benjamin Franklin or William Penn, was trademarked in 1877.

3. It is intriguing to note that neither the Consolidation-era cartoonists of Knickerbocker nor the ones that followed ever borrowed or caricatured the features of Washington Irving for their purposes. Perhaps they exempted him from this kind of posthumous roasting out of respect for his early work as a satirist, or perhaps his face just wasn't serious enough to look silly on the page.

4. Greater New York Government: 1902–1903: Father Knickerbocker Adrift (New York: Fusion Record Publishing, 1903), 1, 3; Rupert Hughes, *The Real New York* (New York and London: Smart Set Publishing, 1904), 222. *J'y suis, j'y reste* translates as "Here I am, here I'll stay."

5. For an astute and concise description of the panic that began with the Knickerbocker Trust, see Jean Strouse, *Morgan: American Financier* (New York: Random House, 1999).

6. "200,000 in Children's Fete: That Many May Take Part in Hudson-Fulton October Festival," *New York Times*, 17 July 1909.

7. New York Staff Association, *Wake Up! Father Knickerbocker: Your Library Needs You*, 1924, from the New-York Historical Society's Broadsides Collection; no publisher or author referenced. Noting that there were "45,612 fewer books . . . [in library branches] in 1924 than in 1920," the association requested a six-figure book budget appropriation from the city and a uniform salary increase for its members. These concerns are still paramount for New York City librarians today, whose funding is a complicated blend of private and public monies.

8. Henry James, *The American Scene*, in *Collected Travel Writings: Great Britain and America* (New York: Library of America, 1993), 420.

9. J. M. Vandergrift, *Father Knickerbocker; or, Bag-dad on the Subway* (New York: J. Montanye Vandergrift, 1920), 3.

10. Christopher Gray, "Streetscapes: The Knickerbocker Hotel," *New York Times*, 16 Feb. 1997. This does not appear to have been the only Knickerbocker Hotel in New York: there is an advertisement for a Knickerbocker Hotel on West Street in the collection of the New York Public Library, with an acquisition stamp of 1900–1901; and there are extant mid-twentieth-century signs for a Knickerbocker Hotel on West Forty-third Street, just one block from Astor's palatial flagship, by that time a complex of business offices.

11. The sign is still visible from the Times Square subway shuttle platform.

12. Parrish was an apt choice of artist for the walls of the Knickerbocker Hotel: he had illustrated a deluxe edition of *The History of New York* in 1900.

13. "Big Rent Increase in Times Square," *New York Times*, 16 May 1920; "Many Big Loans in Uptown Centre," *New York Times*, 4 Dec. 1920; "Knickerbocker Grill Opens," *New York Times*, 30 Sept. 1921; "Raid Knickerbocker Grill," *New York Times*, 26 May 1922.

14. Maureen Ogle, *Ambitious Brew: The Story of American Beer* (New York: Harcourt, 2006), 172–173, 179; Stanley Nadel, *Little Germany: Ethnicity, Religion,*

and Class in New York City, 1845–80 (Chicago: University of Illinois Press, 1990). In New York City's German-dominated Yorkville neighborhood, local brewers funded the hospital that would become Lenox Hill Hospital, as well as supporting the area's cultural and educational associations. Nadel notes that the hospital's original name was German Hospital, which undoubtedly only contributed to xenophobic fears of a Teutonic takeover.

15. "Most historians date the ascendancy of beer in New York to the arrival of the first German immigrant in the early nineteenth century, but New York was a big beer town long before that. The oldest maps of New Amsterdam show the Red Lion brewery in business well before 1680. The Dutch settlers were beer drinkers and old records show that many small taverns and other New Amsterdam businesses made and sold beer commercially. The first of the German breweries in this area were built in Brooklyn because the old braumeisters did not like the water in Manhattan and the Bronx. Not until the Croton Aqueduct began to bring in fresh water between 1840 and 1850 did George Gilig build a brewery on Manhattan." Frank J. Trial, "A Look at Why City Brewery Industry Went Flat," *New York Times*, 9 Feb. 1974, 31. Coincidentally, during Prohibition workmen discovered the underground remnants of "huge catacombs for the cooling and aging of beer . . . under the present plant of the Knickerbocker Ice Company" on East Fifty-first Street. They had been used by the Schaefer brewing company in the nineteenth century. "Find Beer Vaults at Beekman Place," *New York Times*, 12 April 1925.

16. In fact, in 1917, the *New York Herald* published a newspaper insert with the headline "Complete and Alphabetical List of Names and Addresses of German Alien Enemies Registered in New York City in the State Military Census" that includes one "Joerge Ruppert" of 2204 Mermaid Avenue, in Brooklyn, among the names in its roster. It is unclear whether this is a relative of the Jacob Ruppert family, but the presence of the name suggests that despite fifty years of New York residence, the Ruppert name was still not considered an "American" one during World War I.

17. Of course, Ruppert can hardly have helped his cause with his attempt to fight the Eighteenth Amendment before it was enacted: he sued the U.S. Attorney's Office in an effort to bring attention to the undue powers given to Congress by the War-Time Prohibition Act and to dispute the definition of "intoxicating," as laid out in the Volstead Act. Although his appeal reached the Supreme Court, a decision against Ruppert was ultimately handed down by Justice Louis Brandeis. It is a verdict Knickerbocker clearly anticipated when he made application for "Knickerbocker" near beer the year before.

18. Ogle, *Ambitious Brew*, 185.

19. It is possible, if a little macabre, that Ruppert may also have wished to reclaim the Knickerbocker name from its negative associations for the German community: The *General Slocum* steamship, whose 1904 wreck in the East River drowned more than a thousand mostly German day-trippers from the Kleindeutschland neighborhood of New York (and was the largest loss of life in New York City until September 11, 2001), was found to be the fault of the Knickerbocker

Steamship Company, which owned the *General Slocum*, although only one of its employees was given a criminal sentence.

20. "Cholly" is "Charlie," pronounced with a vaguely upper-crust, quasi-English drawl that the writer Tom Wolfe would later refer to as "the New York Honk" ("A City Built of Clay," *New York Magazine*, 6 July 2008). On the columns, see Sam G. Riley, *Biographical Dictionary of Newspaper Columnists* (Westport, CT: Greenwood Press, 1995), 242; and Eve Brown, *Champagne Cholly: The Life and Times of Maury Paul* (New York: E. P. Dutton, 1947), which suggests that Knickerbocker's "First Families" column had to be discontinued after six years because "there were no more First Families with coats of arms" (159). For "turreted tiara set," see ibid., 62.

21. Roland Marchand, *Advertising the American Dream: Making Way for Modernity, 1920–1940* (Berkeley: UCLA Press, 1985), 196, 128; Mary Cable, *Top Drawer: American High Society from the Gilded Age to the Roaring Twenties* (New York: Atheneum, 1984), 204. Marchand shows how these advertisements enabled potential consumers to vicariously take part in "displays of class standing" even when the "social tableaux" on view—much like the inherited authority of the "old New Yorker" shown in the ad—were so obviously out of their economic reach.

22. "Don't I Know You from the Party Pages?" *New York Times*, 25 June 2006. At the time that Adele Van Rensselaer posed for Camel (with a caption that read "'I can't bear a strong cigarette—this is why I smoke Camels'"), the article notes, "she was divorced with two children, and Camel probably paid well."

23. From the play *Fifty Million Frenchmen* (1929); *The Complete Lyrics of Cole Porter*, ed. Robert Kimball (New York: Da Capo, 1992), 120.

24. "Eager Igor," *Time*, 5 Nov. 1945.

25. Mrs. John King Van Rensselaer and Franklyn Van de Water, *The Social Ladder* (New York: Ayer, 1975), 121, 32, 139; *The Knickerbocker Jingles* (New York: Knickerbocker Press, 1927), 3.

26. "Ye Olde Settlers of West Side Dine," *New York Times*, 24 March 1911; "Ye Olde Settlers Association" menu, 17 Jan. 1918, from the Miss Frank E. Buttolph Menu Collection, The New York Public Library, Astor, Lenox and Tilden Foundations.

27. "A City Beautiful Is Gallatin's Hope," *New York Times*, 7 Jan. 1923. Cited in Anthony C. Wood, *Preserving New York: Winning the Right to Protect a City's Landmarks* (New York: Routledge, 2007), 36. Wood notes that "all we know about the meeting at which Gallatin was to present his idea to Mayor Hylan is that nothing came out of it."

28. John Van Dyke, *The New New York : A Commentary on the Place and the People* (New York: Macmillan, 1909), 296, 143.

29. At the same time, *Little Old New York* encouraged tourism, larding its pages with ads as nostalgic as its articles, such as one for the "Tally-Ho Restaurant . . . New York's Unique Dining Place" in Murray Hill, where guests were invited to "dine in the Stalls of the one time Famous Astor Stable"—giving a very different meaning to Cholly Knickerbocker's "Café Society."

30. James H. Callendar, *Yesterdays in Little Old New York* (New York: Dorland Press, 1929), 106; Edith Wharton, *A Backward Glance* (New York: Macmillan, 1933), 55.

31. Even when Washington lived there, Cherry Street was no longer the apogee of fashionable neighborhoods: in 1790, shortly before the federal government moved to Philadelphia, the Washington household left Cherry Street for a more capacious house closer to the center of New York society, at No. 39 Broadway. When Washington's house was demolished in 1856, some of its materials were apparently used to make a ceremonial chair for the president of the New-York Historical Society. I. N. Phelps Stokes, *The Iconography of Manhattan Island*, vol. 5 (New York: Robert H. Dodd, 1924), 1237.

32. According to Joshua B. Freeman, the municipal government was the city's largest single employer by 1950. *Working Class New York: Life and Labor Since World War II* (New York: Free Press, 2001), 21.

33. Christopher Mele notes that "Knickerbocker's significance had less to do with its success as a middle-class project than its inclusion of the state as a player in a development project. The 'rescue' of Knickerbocker Village elevated the state as a major stakeholder in the redevelopment of the Lower East Side." *Selling the Lower East Side: Culture, Real Estate, and Resistance in New York City* (Minneapolis: University of Minnesota Press, 2000), 97.

34. Freeman, *Working Class*, 25, 26, 36.

35. *Knickerbocker Village Tenants Association Bulletin*, 1948: "Supreme Court Justice Edward R. Koch yesterday vacated the injunction on the Landlord. . . . [H]e did not direct the tenants to pay the increase. . . . Your Tenants Association urges you to withhold the rent increase; whether you paid before or not. If you were on thirty day notice pay only the old rental from May 1st. FIGHT RENT INCREASE AND RISING COST OF LIVING WITH UNITED ACTION."

36. As Philip Lopate points out, the Knickerbocker Village development occupies the site of the "Lung Block," a series of decrepit, slumlord-owned tenements whose residents collectively had the "highest tuberculosis incident of any street in the city." An inspiring, proudly New York name like Knickerbocker could be calculated to help erase the memory of the street's unhappy and unhealthy history. *Waterfront* (New York: Crown, 2003), 275.

37. Jean Edward Smith, *FDR* (New York: Random House, 2007).

38. The eight-generation Dutch pedigree of FDR's famous cousin Teddy was taken for granted in newspaper reports on his presidency, where he was described as the scion of an "old Knickerbocker family" that was known for its patriotism and philanthropy. Perhaps because of his reputation as the de facto commandant of the Rough Riders, he was not often identified with his New York roots during his presidency (this despite having penned his *History of New York City*). "Mr. Theodore Roosevelt: Varied Career of the Next President of the United States," *New York Times*, 14 Sept. 1901.

39. There is some dispute about whether the Van Rosenvelt farm included this site, perhaps because it was a combination of "common land" and a farm owned by an English colonist, John Thomson, by the time of the Revolutionary

War. It subsequently became the site of Mrs. Astor's famous ballroom and, later, the first Waldorf-Astoria Hotel. See Jonathan Goldman, *The Empire State Building Book* (New York: St. Martin's Press, 1980).

40. I am grateful to Sean Abbott for pointing out to me that FDR was not the only "Knickerbocker" demanding change in the 1930s and 1940s. At the same time, the investigative journalist and native Texan Hubert Renfro Knickerbocker (known by his byline, H. R. Knickerbocker), was busy covering the rise of Hitler (beginning with the Beer Hall Putsch of 1923) and the Soviet Union (for which he won a Pulitzer Prize). He was vociferously critical of Hitler and of the United States' reluctance to enter World War II. While coverage of H. R. Knickerbocker never connected him to his fictional antecedent, he was by all accounts a worthy (and appropriately obstreperous) namesake.

41. Herbert Rosenberg, "Program Content: A Criterion of Public Interest in FCC Licensing," *Western Political Quarterly*, Sept. 1949, 375–401; "FCC Summons Station WMCA on War News," *New York Times*, 13 Sept. 1939;

42. *Los Angeles Times*, 1 Nov. 1937; *Chicago Tribune*, 5 Feb. 1920.

43. It was not the first time that Irving's material had been transformed beyond recognition for a stage production: Joseph Jefferson's enormously popular 1859 (revised in 1861) adaptation of "Rip Van Winkle" turned Rip's enchanted sleep into a drunken stupor, giving Irving's tale a vigorous temperance message that appealed to the play's Victorian audience.

44. *Los Angeles Times*, 16 Oct. 1938; *New York Times*, 16 Oct. 1938.

45. Works Progress Administration Photo Album; Collection of the New-York Historical Society, n.p.

46. The East River Drive was later renamed the Franklin Delano Roosevelt Drive in honor of the president's Works Progress Administration.

47. According to Manhattan Borough Historian Michael Miscione, the date of the founding of New Amsterdam was added to the city flag in 1974 by then City Council president Paul O'Dwyer. O'Dwyer wished to replace the British founding date on the flag (1664) with the Dutch one, but the date he chose, 1625, is not a date with significance for the colony of New Amsterdam. The Dutch West India Company was formed in 1621, the first Protestant Walloon settlers arrived in the New Netherlands in 1624, and the Dutch acquired Manhattan Island from the Lenape Indian tribe in 1626. That same year the tip of the island was named New Amsterdam.

48. After all, it had been Roosevelt who declared Columbus Day a national holiday in 1937, thus tacitly acknowledging a holiday that had long been commemorated by the Italian American communities in the United States, particularly those in New York and San Francisco.

49. *Ways to Community Health Education* (New York: H. Milford, Oxford University Press, 1939), 24; 1940 New York Democratic Party broadside, n.p., Collection of the New-York Historical Society.

50. My thanks to Anthony Wood for including the fascinating *New York Times* photograph of this protest rally in *Preserving New York*.

51. According to the *New York Times*, "Father Knickerbocker" was represented

"for the week" only, by one "Harry P. Snyder . . . [a] 52-year old printer and publisher of 30 Ferry Street." "Theme Girl Chosen; Folk-Dancing Set for Today," *New York Times*, 9 May 1939.

52. Mary Field Parton, *Metropolis: A Study of New York* (New York: Longmans, Green, 1939), vi.

53. Helen Worden, *Here Is New York* (Garden City, NY: Country Life Press, 1939), 292, 374, 376. Moses had also been chairman of the Emergency Public Works State Commission that helped to fund Fred French's Knickerbocker Village.

54. Ogle, *Ambitious Brew*, 194.

55. However, Ruppert's beer was not the first to arrive at Governor Smith's door, as Ogle notes: "Jacob Ruppert, USBA president, had insisted that the city's brewers refrain from making midnight deliveries in order to avoid a 'carnival' atmosphere. As a result, the city that never sleeps drowsed through the celebration that brightened the night elsewhere." Ibid., 201.

56. "Advertising: Jacob Ruppert Is Coming Back," *New York Times*, 5 Nov. 1958.

57. The $10,000 Knickerbocker prize for the fishing contest was taken by a sixty-five-pound striped bass caught by "Louis Catine of New York"—an affirmation of the beer's essentially hometown appeal. "65-Pound Striped Bass Taken at Atlantic Beach," *New York Times*, 6 Nov. 1958.

58. "Bronx Sky Gets 'Lit,'" *New York Times*, 21 Aug 1952.

59. Ruppert's Knickerbocker did, however, have rival historical icons: the name and image of First Lady Dolley Madison (1768–1849), just to take one example, had been trademarked by a baked goods manufacturer and an ice cream company since 1912 and 1937, respectively.

60. Meyer Berger, "About New York: Father Knickerbocker Puffing in Rented Rig," *New York Times*, 29 May 1953.

61. *Official Guide to the World's Fair, 1964/1965* (New York: Time, 1964), 62, 39. A 1939 article in *The New York Times* entitled "Pride in New York as 'Offspring' Brought Netherlands to the Fair" (29 Aug.) notes that the Netherlands Pavilion at the 1939 fair sought to tell the tale Americans didn't know, that of the East Indies, better known to New Yorkers as the place Henry Hudson didn't find when he happened upon Manhattan Island. "Father Knickerbocker's Exposition Would Not Be Complete if 'Daddy' Were Not Represented," the article subhead ran.

62. "Advertising: Ruppert Is Shifting Emphasis," *New York Times*, 27 Jan. 1960.

63. *Tech* (Massachusetts Institute of Technology), 26 Feb. 1960.

64. "Personality: Real Estate Mogul Now Brewer," *New York Times*, 25 Aug. 1963.

65. "Despite the closing of the brewery, Ruppert's Knickerbocker beer will continue to be brewed without interruption by Rheingold Breweries, inc., which paid $12 million for the trademark, formula, and equipment." "Ruppert Brewery Is Closed Here," *New York Times*, 1 Jan. 1966.

66. "Why Knickerbockers?" at www.nba.com/knicks/history/why_knicker bockers.html. The Web page (which also quotes one early coach as saying the name "Knickerbocker" came out of a hat) has this curious note: "The baseball link may have prompted Casey Stengel to joyously exclaim, 'It's great to be back

as the manager of the Knickerbockers!' when he was named pilot of the new-born Mets in 1961."

67. Bradley is no relation to the author of this book. Red Holzman, *The Knicks* (New York: Dodd, Mead, 1971), 28, 30; Tom Peterson, *New York Knicks* (Mankato, MN: Creative Education, 1989), n.p.

68. From an interview conducted by the author with Senator William Bradley on May 1, 2008. Reproduced with Bradley's consent.

69. Woody Allen, "There's at Least One Fan Down Front Who Will Miss the Big Fella," *New York Times*, 8 Oct. 2000.

70. *When the Cathedrals Were White: A Journey to the Country of Timid People*, trans. Francis Edwin Hyslop (New York: Routledge, 1948), 25.

Conclusion

1. "Question: What Constitutes a New Yorker: Remarkable Study of America's Metropolis," *New York Times*, 17 Nov. 1907.

2. Jan Morris, *The World: Life and Travel, 1950–2000* (New York: W. W. Norton, 2005), 223, 240.

3. Cynthia Ozick, "The Synthetic Sublime," in *Quarrel and Quandary*, excerpted in *Empire City: New York Throughout the Centuries*, ed. Kenneth Jackson and David Dunbar (New York: Columbia University Press, 2002), 947, 949. Interestingly, Billy Joel's "Miami 2017," a protest song about the 1977 blackout (that would later be reinterpreted as a post–September 11 anthem) makes much the same prediction of urban decay and collective forgetting.

4. Thomas Bender, *The Unfinished City: New York and the Metropolitan Idea* (New York: New Press, 2002), xi, xiii.

5. Rem Koolhaas, *Delirious New York* (New York: Monacelli Press, 1994), 10, 293.

6. Alexandra Wolfe, "The Last Gentleman," *New York Observer*, 5 Oct. 2003. Brooke Russell Astor's recent death prompted a flood of (mostly flattering) remembrances, many of which noted that she lunched regularly at the Knickerbocker Club, where she was a member, but none referred to her as a Knickerbocker—because the "Last Mrs. Astor," as her biographer Frances Kiernan dubbed her, was born in Portsmouth, New Hampshire. See *The Last Mrs. Astor: A New York Story* (New York: W. W. Norton, 2007).

7. Whitman, "Crossing Brooklyn Ferry," *Leaves of Grass*, in *Walt Whitman: Complete Poetry and Collected Prose*, ed. Justin Kaplan (New York: Library of America, 1982), 308.

8. Including a new musical ensemble that has dubbed itself the Knickerbocker Chamber Orchestra, with plans to perform an orchestral repertoire in historically significant locations in Lower Manhattan.

9. These include everything from the African Burial Ground to the City Reliquary, as well as Web sites such as those of Place Matters and Forgotten New York.

INDEX

ABOUT THE AUTHOR

Elizabeth L. Bradley is the author of *New York*, a history of New York City, and the editor of Washington Irving's *A History of New York* and *The Legend of Sleepy Hollow and Other Stories*. She serves as a consultant to Historic Hudson Valley and writes widely about New York history, preservation, and culture.

Printed and bound by CPI Group (UK) Ltd, Croydon, CR0 4YY

13/04/2025

14656547-0002